THE

VISIBLE AND INVISIBLE IN PIANOFORTE TECHNIQUE

being a

DIGEST

of the author's technical teachings

up to date

BY

TOBIAS MATTHAY

British Library Cataloguing-in-Publication Data
A catalogue record for this book is available from the
British Library

A History of the Piano

The piano (an abbreviation of pianoforte) is a musical instrument played using a keyboard. It is widely used in classical and jazz music for solo performances, ensemble use, chamber music, accompaniment and for composing and rehearsal. Although the piano is not portable and often very expensive, its versatility and ubiquity have made it one of the world's most familiar musical instruments. A piano usually has a protective wooden case surrounding the soundboard and metal strings, and a row of black and white keys (52 white keys and 36 black keys). The strings are sounded when the keys are pressed down, and are silenced when the keys are released. The note can be sustained even when the keys are released, by the use of pedals at the bottom of the piano.

During the Middle Ages there were several attempts at creating stringed keyboard instruments with struck strings, and by the seventeenth century, the mechanisms of keyboard instruments such as the clavichord and the harpsichord were well known. The invention of the modern piano however, is credited to Bartolomeo Cristofori (1655-1731) of Padua, Italy. He was employed by Ferdinando de' Medici, Grand Prince of Tuscany as the Keeper of the Instruments. Cristofori was already an expert harpsichord maker and was well acquainted with the existing body of knowledge on stringed keyboard instruments. In an inventory made by his employers, a piano is listed in the year 1700 – but the three Cristofori pianos that survive today date from the 1720s.

Cristofori's great success was solving, with no prior example, the fundamental mechanical problem of piano design: the hammer must strike the string, but not remain in contact with it (because this would dampen the sound, as with a clavichord). Moreover, the hammer must return to its rest position without bouncing violently, and it must be possible to repeat a note rapidly. This new instrument remained relatively unknown until an Italian writer; Scipione Maffei wrote an enthusiastic article about it in 1711, including a diagram of the mechanism. After this the piano took off! Piano-making flourished in the late eighteenth century Viennese school, which included Johann Andreas Stein (who worked in Augsburg, Germany) and the Viennese makers Nannette Streicher (daughter of Stein) and Anton Walter. Viennese-style pianos were built with wood frames, two strings per note, and had leather-covered hammers. It was for instruments such as these that Wolfgang Amadeus Mozart composed his concertos and sonatas; the pianos of his day had a much softer, more ethereal tone than today's instruments, with less sustaining power.

By the 1820s, the centre of innovation had shifted to Paris, where the Pleyel firm manufactured pianos used by Frédéric Chopin and the Érard firm manufactured those used by Franz Liszt. In 1821, Sébastien Érard invented the double escapement action, which incorporated a *repetition lever* (also called the *balancier*) that permitted repeating a note even if the key had not yet risen to its maximum vertical position. This facilitated rapid playing of repeated notes, a musical device exploited by Liszt. When the invention became public, as revised by Henri Herz, the double escapement action gradually became standard in grand pianos, and is still incorporated into all grand pianos currently produced.

Mass production in factories made pianos more affordable for a larger number of people. They appeared in music halls and pubs during the nineteenth century, providing entertainment through a piano soloist, or in combination with a small band. Pianists began accompanying singers or dancers performing on stage, or patrons dancing on a dance floor.

During the nineteenth century, American musicians playing for working-class audiences in small pubs and bars, particularly African-American composers, developed new musical genres based on the modern piano. Ragtime music, popularized by composers such as Scott Joplin, reached a broader audience by 1900. The popularity of ragtime music was quickly succeeded by

Jazz piano. New techniques and rhythms were invented for the piano, including ostinato for 'boogie-woogie', and Shearing voicing. George Gershwin's Rhapsody in Blue broke new musical ground by combining American jazz piano with symphonic sounds. Honky-tonk music, featuring yet another style of piano rhythm, became popular during the same era, as did Rock and Roll music subsequently. In the late twentieth century, Bill Evans composed pieces combining classical techniques with his jazz experimentation.

As is evident from this brief introduction to the history of the piano, it is an incredibly versatile instrument, with a long and intriguing history. We hope the reader enjoys this book and is encouraged to find out more.

To

MY WIFE

WITHOUT WHOSE CONSTANT ENCOURAGEMENT
NO BOOK OF MINE PROBABLY WOULD EVER HAVE SEEN THE LIGHT

"For teaching is only of whither and how to go, the vision itself is the work of him who hath willed to see."

Plautinus

The Visible and Invisible in Piano Technique

PREFACE

It is now over a quarter of a century since my "Act of Touch" appeared — in 1903 — my first essay on Pianoforte Technique.

Necessarily it was cumbrous, since there was then little, if any, common-sense knowledge of the subject; and as the great majority of the ideas I had put forward were new, these were of necessity protected and fenced round with defensive arguments. But now all this has changed, the basic principles of my teachings are generally accepted, and indeed have become axiomatic as pianistic knowledge.[1]

True, some things which then seemed of the gravest importance have since passed into better perspective, while others, which then seemed almost subsidiary, have since loomed up into greater prominence. I have endeavoured both to clarify and simplify, enlarge and modify, my ideas in subsequent books and lectures, which have become more and more concise in utterance as the facts have become more widely accepted,—indeed my last booklet "The Nine Steps towards Finger Individualization" covers only four pages!

However, I feel the time has now come when all this material should be gathered together, for the convenience of teacher and learner, and also to prevent misunderstanding as to what my

[1] In fact they have become so much "Common Knowledge" that they are no longer attributed to me! Already in *1913* the "Musical Times" wrote: "And now? The one man's fad (as it had been supposed to be) has within ten "short years altered radically the whole system of modern pianoforte teaching. . . . "Probably never before in art has an almost world-wide revolution been accom- "plished in so short a space of time."

teachings *really are today*. In fact, there have been issued lately a number of *piratical works and writings* founded on my ideas, sometimes avowedly so, which, while showing much felicity in expression, are nevertheless inadequate, and most inaccurate upon very important matters, thereby forming actual *perversions* of my teachings. To mention only one instance, these writers have almost entirely overlooked the important changes of state of exertion and relaxation of the playing limb which form THE REAL BASIS OF GOOD TECHNIQUE, but which, *being invisible*, have escaped their attention. Hence I feel that it is most urgent that the present AUTHORITATIVE work be issued by me, and trust that it will serve as a corrective to so much spurious "Matthay teaching" which is to be met with today.

It will be seen that I do not here more minutely stress the locality of muscles or anatomical details at greater length than I thought fit in my first work, "The Act of Touch." There is good reason for this. The fact remains, that beyond certain quite simple generalizations, the attempted realization of the precise locality of the muscles concerned is not only futile, but is bound to impede the learner's progress, since it must take his attention away from the points where it is most directly needed. Anyway, it is futile, since it is practically *impossible*, both physiologically and psychologically, for us to influence or provoke any particular muscle *directly* into action, however hard we may try. No muscle responds that way! Moreover, were such attempt possible, it would indeed be hopeless to essay *so* to impart or acquire the correct playing actions, considering that even the most simple actions of our limbs (both the visible and the invisible ones) require a complexity of muscular interplay that would at once render such problem unthinkable.

Moreover, the precise action of the deeper-seated muscles in playing is still largely a matter of conjecture.

What we *can* learn and *should* teach is what may be termed the general *Muscular Mechanics* of the limbs we use. We can learn which section of the playing limb should be exerted and which should be left lax; and by thus willing the desirable LIMB-stresses into action and by inhibiting the undesirable ones, the concerned complex muscular co-ordinations will indirectly but surely be called into responsive operation. This basic principle which underlies all my technical teachings is also carried out in the present work.

Our business as teachers is to make clear to the learner which are the *limb*-stresses (both visible and invisible) needed in playing, and which are the ones to be avoided. It is the only way by which the learner can be directly helped.

The physiological aspect of Touch and Technique is usually found to be the most difficult problem to grasp by the learner. Necessarily it is complex. It is here that the most fantastic notions have arisen in the past, and are indeed still lamentably evident even in the work of some writers of today, who ought to know better.

To ensure that consideration of the necessary details does not jeopardize the true apprehension of the subject as a whole, I have planned my work on the same lines as in actual teaching; although in teaching one is able to bring the *details* to the notice of the pupil as required at the particular moment.

The main physiological facts are therefore first stated broadly in Chapter IV, "*The Physiology of Touch.*" This is followed by an exposition of the details implicated in Chapter V, "*The Physiological Details.*" These are further elaborated in the succeeding Chapters. "Additional Notes" are added in further elucidation of these matters. All is then clinched in a *Recapitulatory* Section of the work — a close-up Summary, under the title of "*Epitome.*"

This *Epitome*, however, is sufficiently complete in itself to form an independent booklet, and is issued separately *for School use*, etc.,—an important mission. It is followed by fifty-five "Daily Maxims" and a page of "Final Precepts" — concise axiomatic outlines intended as constant "close-up" reminders of the main technical essentials to be kept in view alike by Student, Teacher, and Artist.

Obviously this plan entails much repetition and reiteration. But unless the various facts are thus brought into close juxtaposition in their presentation, their bearing upon each other might easily be overlooked and lead to serious misunderstandings.

While such reiteration may be resented by the casual reader, it is imperative for the *true student.* It is only by repetition of the same point under various aspects that facts are eventually brought home and grasped; and vision of the whole not lost sight of while in pursuit of the details of structure.

A genius may not need such treatment; he may see things in a flash of intelligence. Geniuses in the past have thus subconsciously realized the true processes of technique, else there never would have been any great players before the appearance of the "Act of Touch"! A work of the present nature, however, is designed as an endeavour to help the ordinary worker and Seeker after Truth; the genius, himself, may also save years of time and feel surer of his ground by taking the trouble to master the facts thus *intellectually*, as well as by "intuition."

NOTE. — Where more detailed information is desired, my older works should be referred to, preferably in the inverse order of their publication. Thus: —

"*The Nine Steps towards Finger Individualization*" along with "*The Child's First Steps*" (Joseph Williams), and its complement for Children, "*The Pianist's First Music-Making*" (Oxford University Press), "*First Solo Book*" and "*Play-things for Little Players*" (O. U. Press), "*First Principles*" and its complement "*Some Commentaries on Piano Technique*" (Longmans); "*Relaxation Studies*" (Bosworth), and finally, "*The Act of Touch*" (Longmans). Along with these should be studied (not merely read through) my most important work of all, "MUSICAL INTERPRETATION, its laws and principles" (Williams); and the recently issued supplement to this "*The Slur or Couplet of Notes*" (O. U. Press); also when needed: "*On Method in Teaching,*" "*On Memorizing*" (O. U. Press), "*Forearm Rotation*" (Williams), etc., etc.

I wish to acknowledge the great help I have had with my proofs from my devoted disciple Alvin Goodman.

NOTE. — Also I must thank Miss Helen Marchant for her patiently devoted work as stenographer and typist.

TOBIAS MATTHAY.

HASLEMERE. SURREY, ENGLAND.
April, 1931.

CONTENTS

CONTENTS OF DIGEST

ADDITIONAL NOTES

CONTENTS OF EPITOME

DIGEST:

The Visible and Invisible in Piano Technique by

TOBIAS MATTHAY

ERRATA

Page 53 — 13th line (fifth line of third paragraph)
correct "*humerus*" into "*ulna.*"

Page 160 — 7th line
correct Hugo into *Otto.*

Page 106 — Correct *diagram* and *note* underneath:—
the *blade* of the penknife should be between the fingers and thumb, not the *handle* as shown! and the words *handle* and *blade* in the note underneath should be reversed. Thus:

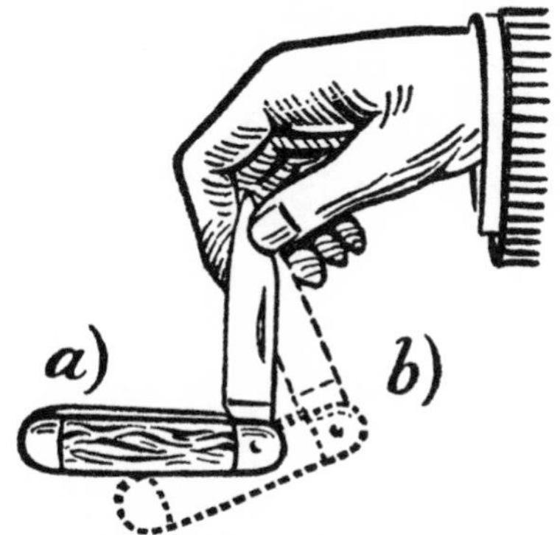

That is: the weight of the blade (upper-arm, *a*) is here pushed back by the weight of the hand and forearm, the handle, at *b*.

Chapter I

PREAMBLE

The meaning and purpose of Technique

Definitions:

1. TECHNIQUE means the power of expressing oneself musically. It embraces all the physico-mechanical *means* through which one's musical perceptions are expressed.

2. It is therefore absurd and hopeless to try to acquire Technique dissociated from its purpose to express Music.

3. Typewriter-like strumming or note-rattling does not constitute Music.

Technique is rather a matter of the Mind than of the "fingers."

4. To acquire the necessary muscular discrimination for playing, implies the acquisition mentally of the power muscularly, so to direct your limbs in their work, that your musical purpose shall accurately be fulfilled.

Technique and Music inseparable:

5. To acquire Technique therefore implies that you must induce and enforce a particular mental-muscular association and co-operation for every possible musical effect.

6. The folly in the past has been to suppose that one could acquire a musical technique *dissociated* from the practice of actual, real Music.

7. On the contrary, be sure to realize from the very beginning, that what you have to do, is to make a *strong bond* between Musical Intention and the means of its practical Fulfilment. From the very first, you must try to make strict association between the spiritual and physical in playing.

8. Never sound a single note without a distinct *musical purpose.* This implies a definite rhythmical Intention for each note, and also applies to your very first experiments at the keyboard.

The Act of Timing:

Realize that you cannot play any note with musical purpose without such accurate Timing.

9. Pianoforte technique is therefore essentially an act of "*aiming*" or *timing* the right activities of the limb at the musically right moment during key-descent — an accurate *timing* of the beginning, culmination, and cessation of the needed limb-exertions for each note. Solely by such Act of Timing, can you bind Technique and Music together.

Relaxation:

10. RELAXATION implies (*a*) the Elimination of all unnecessary exertions, (*b*) the Cessation of the needed impulses at the right moment, and (*c*) Weight-release — the cessation of limb-support, and hence Weight-manifestation where and when needed.

The connection between Music and Technique:[1]

11. *To summarize this:* no successful technique can ever be acquired without this element of *timing*. Mastery of Technique and mastery of Interpretation alike rest on the same basis — a basis of *rhythmic* impulse and control.

12. You now realize why the study of Technique should never be separated from the study of Music; how they are connected-up, and why they must be associated from the very beginning.

You must acquire a strict *mental* Association between every musical effect and its technical reproduction. Hence it is harmful to try to acquire a Technical effect without making such association.

13. *In short:* every note must be sounded with definite

[1] This is enlarged upon in Chapter III.

musical purpose — rhythmical purpose and tonal purpose, and this from the very beginning.

The four forms of Rhythmical Movement:

14. There are four main divisions of rhythmical purpose or attention in playing: —

(*a*) Key-movement — the swing of the key downwards, *towards* Tone-emission.

(*b*) The group-sensing of notes in a quick passage, as *groups* of notes always leading *towards* each next pulse or beat.

(*c*) The growth or progression of the Phrase-unit *towards* its rhythmical climax — near the end of the phrase, and

(*d*) The movement or progression of the piece as a Whole towards its climax.

15. The ever-present problem during Practice and Performance is never to let your attention flag or waver, either musically or pianistically, no matter whether you are a beginner or an experienced artist.

Remember, only through the *rhythmical sense* can you bring your mind on the *needs* of the Music and the Keyboard for every note. "Time-spot" is the ground upon which Mind and Matter here meet. This also fully describes *every other act* of Concentration.

16. While musical attention and technical attention thus *coalesce* (or are linked together) in the *rhythmical act*, we must remember that besides the laws of Physical technique there are also just as inexorable laws of Interpretation. These laws we must equally learn to obey, if the emotional effect of the music is to be achieved in good taste and effectively.[1]

[1] These laws of Interpretation are dealt with in my "*Musical Interpretation*" (Joseph Williams, London, and Boston Music Co., U. S. A.) and in its Supplement: "*The Slur or Couplet of Notes in all its Variety*" (Oxford University Press).

Chapter II

THE PHYSICAL OR KEY-ASPECT OF TECHNIQUE

Tone-production:

1. The more speed in the string, the louder the resultant sound. Only by making the *Key* (and the String therefore) *move quickly* can you produce loudness. There is no other way.[1]

2. The Piano Key is a leverage system, a machine, to enable you to get speed with the string, and to ensure dynamic control — of the exact speed (or tone) desired.

3. Open your Piano lid, so that you can watch the Hammer-heads. Now put a finger upon a key, and notice, when you depress the key its $\frac{3}{8}$ of an inch, that the hammer-head moves about *five times* that distance, and therefore *exaggerates by five times, the speed* with which you depress the key.

4. Also notice that it falls back the instant it has reached the string and has set the same into vibration (or movement) — although you may be keeping the key depressed afterwards. This is owing to the *hopper* device, which allows the hammer to rebound from the string. Without such a device the hammer would be jammed against the string, and all tone destroyed.

5. Note also, that as you put the key down you are lifting the *damper* away from its strings, thus leaving them free to continue sounding; and that the damper returns to the strings when you allow the Key to come up again, thus arresting (or "damping") the sound.

[1] Do not confuse *speed* with *vibration* of the string, they are two different things; the first implies *loudness*, the second implies *pitch*. You cannot alter the vibration-number of a string, it is constant; but you can alter the *amplitude* of those vibrations, — whether the vibrations are of small or large extent, — and that implies variation in the degree of speed, and the consequent degree of loudness. *See* p. 73, "The Act of Touch" (Longmans, Green & Co.).

6. The "Grand" action also includes a device (the "repetition lever") which enables you to re-sound the note, without having to allow the Key *to rise fully;* about an eighth of an inch should suffice.

The Action is also provided with a "check," which brings the hammer to rest after it has fallen back from the string, so as to prevent its rebounding and re-striking the string on its own, and thus spoiling the tone.

NOTE. — *See The Act of Touch* (Longmans, Green & Co.) where these things are described at length, and where a *Diagram* of the Pianoforte action is given on page 62.

Good and bad tone:

7. Realize, then, that you can only make tone by making the Key *move* and thus convey speed to the String.

8. The greater the *motion* attained during key-descent, the louder the sound.

NOTE. — Speed of the Key, during descent, must not be confused with speed in the *succession* of the notes! It seems unnecessary to point out that the quickest passages can quite well be played *softly* — but I have had letters on this question!

9. Bad tone, and lack of control over tone, arises when the Key is jerked down by a too suddenly applied impulse.[1]

10. We see then that Tone-amount depends purely on Key-speed, but Control of tone and Quality depends on *how* you produce that speed.

Key acceleration:

11. Good tone, ease in production, and control of tone, can only be obtained by *gradually* pressing the Key into motion. Only in this way can you obtain perfect control over tone, good "singing" tone, and good *quality* of tone.

12. Moreover, this necessary *acceleration* of the Key (for every note) is *not* a Plain Acceleration, but should be an accel-

[1] In this case the harsh upper-partials of the string are brought into prominence.

eration in acceleratingly *progressive* proportion during that short $\frac{3}{8}$ inch of descent.

You cannot control tone, and cannot play *musically* unless you succeed in acquiring this way of managing Key-descent.

Increase at increasing ratio, applies everywhere

13. This law of *increase* at *increasing ratio* applies in our use of all "Speed-Tools."

NOTE. — The racket, the bat, the golf-club, the hammer, the hatchet, even the gun, are illustrations of such "Speed-tools" — working at mounting-up increase!

***Cresc.* and *dim.* and *accel.* and *rit.* also come under same law**

It is exemplified, also, in effectively played *crescendos*, and *diminuendos*, *ritardos*, and *accelerandos* — all must be played as an increase at increasing rate.

The *notation* of *cresc.* or *dim.* is quite inaccurate. They should never be played as at A, but as at B:

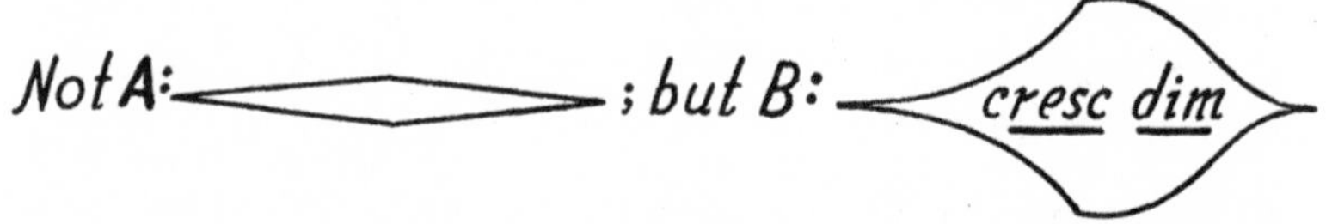

14. While this curve of acceleration is the "law of the Key" for all singing or good tone, it applies equally in the production

It applies also in *pianissimo*

of the softest *pp*. Thus, for real *pp*, you must slowly feel your way to that point in key-descent where you can feel the hopper beginning to slide from underneath the hammer "button"; you can feel this as a slight impediment, and from there only may you add the true tone-producing impulse; *ppp*-playing, in fact, is exaggerated singing-tone — so far as method of production is concerned.[1]

NOTE. — This slight impediment is caused by the lower end of the L-shaped hopper coming into contact with its set-off screw, and you then feel you are compressing the hopper-spring.

Unless you master this knack, you can never command a true *ppp*; and unless you can command that, your whole *range of tone* is much narrowed. Moreover, realize that your *fortes* are

[1] *See* Additional Note XVIII, An alternative form of *ppp*.

truly *fortes* only in proportion that your *pianos* are truly *pianos;* and that you can therefore only produce the effect of a true *forte* by being able to produce the *softest* sound.

How to play *ppp*:

15. To gain this trick of real *ppp* playing: Take a chord of three or four notes, and with fingers tolerably firmly fixed against the key-surfaces, move those keys down only so far as the hopper-impediment, and let them rise again. Repeat this a number of times, until you feel confident with it, then follow this movement *to* the hopper by the very slight additional one that will swing the hammer *to the string*, and will thus sound the notes really at their very softest. It is an excellent way of realizing what is meant by "Key-attention"!

The repetition of soft notes, and the "Bebung":

16. Notice also, that on a Grand Piano, properly adjusted, you can repeat the note softly *without* allowing the key to rise more than $\frac{1}{16}$th of an inch or so. This you are enabled to do, because the *repetition lever* of your Grand enables the hopper again to slip under the "button" of the hammer. Also, when you do this, the note can be repeated perfectly *legato;* because when you allow the key to rise so little, the damper *does not reach* the strings. Thus you can play the repeated chords of the opening of the "*Waldstein*" Sonata perfectly legato — and *pp* — quite a different effect from that produced when you allow the keys fully to rise. Try it!

As other examples, take the accompanying chords of the slow movement of Schumann's Sonata in G minor; also those softest "reverberated" chords (the second of each couplet) of the opening of Chopin's G minor Ballade. The reverberated effect here ("Bebung") is the same as required at various points in the slow movement of Beethoven's Op. 110, etc.

NOTE. — *See* "The Slur or Couplet of Notes." (Oxford University Press.)

Tone-production, momentary:

The short duration of the Tone-producing impulse:

17. Next realize, that NO tone, whether in *staccato* or *legato*, ever takes longer to *produce* than for *Staccatissimo* — the hammer instantly rebounds from the string, whatever you do, and thus leaves the tone after that quite unalterable.

18. Hence you have to live your "touch-life" during that short moment of Key-descent! You must *intend* the musically-needed sound, and you must accomplish the production of any desired tone-inflection during that flash of descent with the Key. Nothing, after that, avails as to tone-production.

Tenuto and Legato, and Tone-cessation:

19. To make a tone continue (as in *tenuto* or *legato*) you must hold the key down after the initial short sound-producing impulse has been completed; thus you hold the dampers off the strings, which continue sounding for a while, or until you *allow* the key to rise, when the dampers silence them.

Production of Tone and Duration always distinct:

20. The action of *holding* a note down should always be quite distinct from the action of *sounding* it.

NOTE. — Muscularly, it should also be quite distinct and different — a most important matter, as we shall see presently. *See* Chapter XIII, "On the Holding of Notes."

The key may be depressed quite violently for a *forte*, yet the holding down needs but a gentle action.

Staccato:

21. *Staccatissimo* is obtained by allowing the key to spring up the instant that its journey downwards is completed; the damper being thus allowed to reach the strings, the sound is instantly checked.

22. Clearly, you cannot *make* or compel a key to rise. You can only *allow* the key instantly to rise upon tone-production, thus permitting the damper instantly to reach the string.

Most *Staccati* are incomplete *Tenuti*

NOTE. — To obtain *Staccatissimo* the *effort* of tone-production and its subsequent immediate cessation must be so accurately timed that the key may rebound instantly. Anything *less short* than *staccatissimo* is therefore always in the nature of a *Tenuto*. This *tenuto* may last any degree up to the full extent of the written note. You may even allow the tone to last *longer* than its written value, and may thus overlap it into the next sound, when desirable; thus creating a *legatissimo* or *super-legato*. *See* Chapter XI, "How to play Staccato and Legato."

23. If you mis-apply (mis-*time*) the force with which you intend to produce a tone, and thus, instead of producing key-motion (and string-speed) allow the force to be wasted on the beds or pads under the keys, then your tone cannot correspond with your musically-*intended* wish, and the effect will be *unmusical* in proportion to your misjudgment of the exact requirements of the key.

On "Key-bedding" and Key-holding

NOTE. — I have termed this *mis-timing* of the TONE-PRODUCING FORCE "Key-bedding." If, however, you apply some slight force purposely upon the key-beds so that you may feel sure you are holding those keys depressed, that does NOT constitute key-bedding "within the meaning of the Act"! Whereas, to misfire one's intended *tone*-producing impulse upon the key-beds is bound to be tragically unmusical. *See* Additional Note XII, "On Key-bedding."

Agility and Accuracy of Tone-making:

24. Agility, to be attained with ease, also implies accuracy in TONE-AIMING in this sense. Each Key-moving impulse must be delivered accurately *before it is too late* to produce the intended key-motion (and tone), else your fingers, hand and arm, will become mechanically locked against the key-beds, and will thus not only ruin all musicality, but will also inevitably hamper all ease in your progression across the key-board — or so-called "Agility." Agility, therefore, depends upon rhythmical accuracy in this respect. In short, Agility is a rhythmical act!

NOTE. — Hence the benefit derived from practising Agility-passages *staccatissimo* at a *slow tempo* — provided your staccato is properly produced! — with hand lying loosely on Key-surface, between each note-sounding.

Chapter III

THE *LINK* OR *BOND* BETWEEN MUSIC AND TECHNIQUE

1. Clearly, you cannot make real music unless you can, at will, produce the precise degree and kind of intended tone — at the precise moment it is musically due.

2. Successfully to obtain the requisite tone, thus musically demanded for each note, you must accurately apply *the right degree of force* required for each key-descent.

3. The only way to achieve certainty in this respect is by actually *sensing* the varying *resistance* the key itself offers during descent.

The Work-sense:

4. This gauging of key-resistance is attained by the application of your Muscular-sense, or Work-sense.

Same degree of Energy required for loud and soft notes, but *feels* different

NOTE. — This is not merely a touch or contact-sense, but a sensation mainly derived from *work being done* by our muscles; wherefore, the American psychologists call this the "Kinæsthetic" sense, and include in this not only true *muscular*-sensation, but also the sensations caused by tension of the tendons, and the pressure or tension within the joints themselves. *See* Edward Bradford Tichener: *A Beginner's Psychology* (Macmillan), page 45, etc.[1]

[1] Note also, that it always takes precisely *the same amount of force* whether you move the key slowly or quickly, just as it takes the same amount of force whether you walk or run upstairs, etc. But to move the key quickly the total amount of work has to be concentrated during a *shorter space of time,* hence our muscles feel the strain more severely the quicker the work is done, and it is this difference in the resulting muscular-sensation of which we can become aware, *if we attend to the key* as we should, through our muscular-sense, Key-resistance-sense, or in short "Key-sense."

The phlegmatic servant, in cleaning a room, spends the *same* total amount of energy as the more energetic one; but the latter does the work in double-quick Time! He spends less Time, but he has to concentrate more vitality for the shorter period!

Always "feel the Key":

5. Unless you thus insist on *judging* what you are doing during each key-descent, you cannot make Music except by lucky accident. Therefore be sure always to "feel the key."

NOTE. — Moreover, this necessity quite puts out of court any system of Teaching founded on such flagrant misconceptions as Key-striking or hitting; since this would preclude judging the key's needs.

The swing-down *to* the key is always a comparatively slow process, but the movement *with* the key may on the contrary be a very swift one. This is a distinction not realizable through the eye, to which the correct action may *seem* like a blow. Hence arose, in days gone by, all that fallacious teaching of "key-striking."

Key-attention is Dual:

6. You will now realize, that Key-attention (or Technical-attention) is a *dual* form of attention: —

(*a*) You must *feel* the key, so as to supply the requisite force to move it with properly graduated acceleration; and

(*b*) You must *listen* for the beginning of each sound, so that you may successfully time and apply the force before it is *too late* in key-descent — a rhythmical act.

Key-sense and Music-sense inseparable:

7. Now you cannot choose this requisite force, nor time it, unless you have each note in your mind *as a purposed musical wish.* It is therefore only through *this* form of attention — ATTENTION TO MUSIC THROUGH THE PIANO-KEY for every note — that you can successfully forge the Bond or connection between each spiritually-conceived musical effect, and its material realization through the Piano-key.

"SENSING THE KEY" is the main factor towards expressing what you musically feel. There never has been any musical playing without its conscious or subconscious intervention.[1]

[1] This principle applies in all performance, whatever the instrument, and also in any pursuit needing muscular nicety of action; and the *giving* of such attention must of course become habit or "second nature" — subconscious — before we can freely translate our feelings through any instrument.

Chapter IV

THE PHYSIOLOGICAL PROBLEMS

— and how to use finger, hand and arm.

1. **Preamble:** (*a*) Technically to play well, necessarily implies the power to provide the correct limb-actions and inactions muscularly, and their being accurately timed with the Key.

(*b*) The problem is, *how* to bring such knowledge of correct doing within the learner's ken. Here, at the very outset, we are faced with formidable difficulties, for we must successfully analyse correct Doing muscularly, and discover its true principles.

(*c*) In the past, it was sought to accomplish such Diagnosis of Touch (or Technique) by carefully observing the MOVEMENTS exhibited by successful players.[1] Unfortunately, this method is not only very precarious, but is often quite misleading, since the *movements* which accompany touch give but little (or even illusionary and misleading) indication of those *hidden* and invisible stresses — exertions and relaxations of limb, which are the real CAUSE of the desirable and undesirable effects. Correct movements are therefore no guarantee whatever that the correct *actions* are being provided. Moreover, quite unusual movements may accompany quite correct *actions!*

Eye, the deceiver

NOTE. — For instance, in playing a note or chord with singing tone, you may *approach* the keyboard quite wrongly — with a visible forward movement of arm and elbow, and may yet *reverse all this* during the subsequent moment of key-depression; to the *eye* this will seem wrong, and yet to the ear it will sound acceptable! Or, *vice versa*, you may allow arm and wrist *apparently* to lapse quite nicely, sympathetically, *towards* the key, and you may yet, while actually moving the key, invisibly deliver a nasty, tone-destroying dig! The *ear* will be shocked, but to the *eye* it will seem quite in order!

In short: Touch cannot be analysed *by the eye.*

---

[1] Even some recent writers have tried to perpetuate this fallacy!

Limb-Knowledge is required, not Muscle-Knowledge:

(*d*) Of late it has been essayed to help the student totally from the opposite side, by trying to instruct him as to the precise *locality* and *nomenclature* of the muscles employed. This is even a more precarious and misleading method than the last, and is in fact not only futile, but likely to prove seriously harmful to the learner.[1] The anatomical road, moreover, is impracticable, and useless (so far as learning and teaching are concerned) for the two following cogent and quite insuperable reasons: —

I. It is physiologically and psychologically *impossible* for us *directly* to provoke or prompt any particular muscle into activity by any act of thinking of it, or wishing or willing it, no matter how concentrated our effort. Muscles can only be provoked into action INDIRECTLY, by our willing a particular *limb-exertion* or *movement.*

II. The muscular processes needed for many quite simple actions are so complex as to be practically unthinkable, even if we could separately prompt the required muscles into action — which we cannot do.[2]

Correct *limb*-stresses *can* be learnt:

(*e*) What we must know, *and can know*, is what particular stresses and relaxations are required of the *various portions* of our *playing-limb* — which parts of the limb to exert and which to leave passive. This knowledge *is* attainable, and is immediately and directly helpful. Such knowledge, however, cannot be got at *from without*, neither from eye-evidence nor from

[1] *See* PREFACE on this point, also Additional Note XI, "Useful and Useless Anatomy-teaching."

[2] A somewhat urgent warning is here desirable. With the excellent intention of being "thorough" or "gründlich" the folly has recently been committed, deliberately to urge (and misinstruct) the unfortunate student to try to think hard *of his own muscles;* this is advocated under the delusion that he could thereby learn to apply them accurately in playing! As I have just shown, this is bound to lead to disaster.

A Warning

See Additional Note XI on this point: "Useful and Useless Anatomy-teaching."

anatomical conjecture. It can only be obtained through analysis from within — by analysis of the *sensations* experienced while actually producing the right effects, and in no other way. Only by the *sensations* thus experienced can we realize what are the limb-*conditions* that obtain both in good and in bad playing, and by calling-up or recalling such *sensations* we can then reproduce the effects and can acquire right habits, and can teach others to acquire them. Here, however, we are again faced with a difficulty. Those few gifted ones, who instinctively stumble upon Right Doing, physically, are usually precisely the ones least fitted to help us by self-analysis. The greater their temperamental, emotional and musically-imaginative gifts, the more likely are they to be disinclined, opposed and even resentful towards any exercise of self-analysis, mechanically and physically. Hence we find that these usually prove to be quite bad teachers, technically, in spite of their own well-doing. Nevertheless, it is only a successfully musical player, who has really achieved technical mastery, and is *at the same time* gifted with powers of analytical and mechanical reasoning (a rare combination) who can possibly supply *the needed information;* that is, HOW IT FEELS, *physically, to play rightly*, and also how it feels to play *wrongly!*

It was by this method of self-analysis and synthesis that *The Act of Touch* was produced in 1903; and Time has proved that its general principles of technical teaching were founded on the right lines. Now to come to details: —

Technique is mental:

2. As already noted, you cannot teach your limbs or your muscles to act. All you can do is teach your *mind* to direct the required *limb*-conditions of activity and inactivity.

NOTE. — There is no such thing as "muscular habit" ! It is always *mental* habit — located either in the brain itself or in its subsidiary automatic centres.

3. The first important thing to learn physically (i.e. mentally) is to supply solely the required exertions, without interference from any undesirable ones.

The meaning of Stiffness:

4. If we allow the *opposite* exertions to be provoked into action along with the *required* ones, then we experience "stiffness" — a tug-of-war — within the limb, or portion of it.

NOTE. — If the two antagonistic exertions are precisely equal, then nothing happens *visibly*, but you can *feel* the tense struggle if you are observant, and your audience will certainly *hear* it — if they are musical. If the two exertions, however, are not quite of equal intensity, then *some* action or movement may result, but it will be constrained. And any such "stiffness" will preclude our attaining any *accuracy in tone*, or ease in performance; therefore it must be carefully guarded against.

5. Now remember, as already pointed out under ¶ 1 (d – I), you cannot *directly* will, prompt or think any muscle into action; you can only induce the exertion of a muscle *by willing the required exertion of a limb* or portion of it.

6. If you try directly to actuate a muscle, you will only petrify yourself and lose all control, for you *are taking your mind* AWAY from the only road open to you, and that is to concentrate upon the limb-action itself — in strict association with the *musical effect needed* from that particular Piano-key at that *particular moment.*

NOTE. — In short, as already indicated, you must be able to recall the *sensation* accompanying the correct exertion or movement *of the limb*. And to acquire such sensations of Right Doing, you must *experiment*, guided by information such as here given you.

Never *hit* a Key down:

7. The muscular process of sounding a note at the Piano is, however, by no means the simple thing it seems to the eye.

8. To begin with, it should never be in the nature of a *blow* upon the key, however much it may look like that. It never is in good playing, although the player himself may imagine that he is hitting the notes down.

9. Always realize, that the action of moving *to* a key and the action of subsequently moving *with* that key during its descent, should always be *two quite distinct things.*

Make tone *with* the Key:

10. You may reach the key either by a *movement* of the Arm, Hand or Finger, but whichever you employ, and however swift the movement may seem to the eye, the true tone-producing action is not applied until *after* you reach the key — if you play rightly.

11. Tone-production is always in the nature of a "follow-on" *pressure* upon the key *after* it is reached, and during key-depression. This tone-producing pressure must *increase in intensity* during key-descent. Yet it becomes useless (so far as tone-production is concerned) the moment the key is down, and it should therefore be ceased forthwith.

12. So-called "Finger-touch" may appear to the eye as if the fingers were used "like little hammers" (the "hammerette" action of the old German Schools), but in reality, with a good player, there never is any such real knocking action.

13. To the eye, the finger of a good player may seem to descend upon the key fairly swiftly, but its exertion upon the key (and *with* it during its descent) is always a thing *added* after contact.

To strike a Key down precludes sense of its needs:

14. Clearly, if you really knock a key down, this will inevitably prevent your playing musically, since it precludes your judging how much force is required for the colouring of each note, and precludes your giving that due acceleration of the key during descent necessary for good Touch.

NOTE. — Even a good typist does not really knock the keys down, although it may seem like that to her, and there is no actual tone to spoil in this case!

Exertion required of the Finger:

15. Obviously, it is by means of the Finger-tip that you must depress the Key into sound. Also it is obvious that your finger must therefore be *exerted* during the moment of key-depression.

Note. — Unless you play with your closed fist, as I recommend should be your first step at the Piano.[1]

16. Moreover, there is practically no such thing as tone-production solely by exertion of the finger. It must always be Finger-exertion PLUS hand and arm, in some form or other.

Note. — Theoretically, finger-exertion, alone, is a possibility, as I showed in *The Act of Touch;* and Finger-exertion, with loose-lying hand, may suffice to hold a note down once it is sounded; but in actual practice it does not suffice to sound notes *with certainty* (even in the softest passage) on our modern Pianoforte, whatever may have been the case in the old Clavichord days. But we are here learning to play the Pianoforte, not the Clavichord.

The distinction between Exertion and Movement:

17. Now, do not confuse Exertion and Movement of a limb as meaning the *same* thing. They are two quite distinct facts. It is possible to obtain a movement *without exertion*, as you do when you let the hand or arm fall of their own weight; but, on the other hand, you may make an exertion without showing any corresponding outward movement, as you do when you firmly hold something in your hand — maybe quite a considerable exertion — and yet nothing is revealed *visibly*.

Movement *v.* muscular condition

Note. — As already pointed out, most of the exertions and relaxations required in playing are *not* revealed by corresponding movements — they are invisible. Hence have arisen so many false theories on Touch. For instance, the old fallacy of "Pure Finger Touch" arose from the foolish attempt to diagnose the process of playing by observation of the finger-*movements* exhibited during performance. Whereas, as we have seen, movement gives hardly any indication whatever of what really does happen — no indication whatsoever of those constant *changes* in muscular exertion and relaxation of a limb (unaccompanied and undisclosed by movement), which conditions or states of limb form the true Cause of all Technique, whether of the past, present or future. It is essential to master this fact at the very beginning. *See* Additional Note, No. X: "The Pure Finger-work *Myth.*"

As an example: when you play a *forte* chord with what looks like (but is not) a fall of your whole arm, the fingers *seem to be passive,* whereas, as a matter of fact, when your finger-tips touch the keys the fingers must be *exerted* (maybe quite

[1] *See* "Child's First Steps" (Joseph Williams); "Pianist's First Music-making"; "Nine Steps towards Finger-individualization"; and "First Solo Book." (Oxford University Press.)

violently) during the moment of key-depression, — and the hand also! Unless they are thus exerted there will be no chord! Yet nothing is *seen* of this necessary exertion of the finger (and hand) during the moment of key-depression, therefore, it is often overlooked and not supplied; and then the chord playing, or singing-passage, sounds "flabby." Hence, also, have arisen those stupid criticisms from some quarters, that "RELAXATION and Weight-touch, etc., *lead to flabby playing!*" Indeed, if you attempt to use your fingers in playing *without* due help from the arm (as other obtuse ones would recommend) then, indeed, your tone will certainly be "flabby," more flabby in fact than when you *spoil your "Weight-touch"* by *not* giving correspondingly adequate finger-and-hand exertions! It is therefore of extreme importance that you understand this radical distinction between Condition and Movement — the *condition* of your finger, hand and arm during the action of Touch, and the *movements* that *may* optionally accompany such changes of Condition muscularly — and most of these last are quite *invisible.*

Until this distinction is clearly grasped, you cannot hope to form any rational idea whatever, of the processes (or *rationale*) of Touch or Technique.

Action and Reaction:

18. It is now necessary to realize that Action and Reaction are *always equal.* Thus, when you exert your finger-tip against the key *downwards,* there is an equal *reaction* (or recoil) at the other end of that finger-lever, *upwards* therefore at the knuckle. This *invisible* reaction or recoil upwards at the knuckle must again be *countered* at the knuckle by supplying a sufficiently stable *Basis* (or foundation) there for the desired action of the finger. In short, the exerted finger needs a Basis at the knuckle-joint, equal to the force to be exerted against the Key.

NOTE. — This necessity of a firm basis for every action was instinctively felt even by some of the older pedagogues; unfortunately they were quite vague and unclear as to what it meant physiologically; hence arose their mistaken idea of "FIXATION" — fixation of the *joints* during the moment of touch! A terrible mistake, leading to a paralyzing stiffening of the whole limb, unhappily copied by some recent authors. True, such Basis or Foundation must certainly be rendered stable and immobile during the moment of Touch, but it failed to occur to these writers that this stable condition can only be achieved by supplying *an invisible stress* from the *next-door* portion of the limb behind the joint or hinge in question!

Hand-exertion the Basis for the Finger:

19. This Basis for the Finger should be provided at the right moment by a *downward exertion* of the *Hand* — at the knuckle-

joint. This exertion of the hand must be precisely timed along with the exertion of the finger itself, during the moment of key-depression. Realize again, that no *movement* of the hand need be visible — however marked the exertion of it "behind" the finger.

20. Again in turn, the Hand also needs its own proper Basis during the moment of tone-production, else the wrist-joint will be driven-up by reaction or recoil, and Power and accuracy of tonal-result again lost.

Arm as Basis for Hand-exertion:

21. Now, at last, the Basis for this *hand*-exertion, must be provided by the Arm itself, in one of the *six* forms to be described in the next Chapter.

22. Thus we see that the Playing Apparatus roughly consists of Four Components — of four Living Levers: [1] —

1. Finger
2. Hand
3. Forearm, and
4. Upper-arm

We must now consider all these four *Components* or *Elements* of Touch in further detail.

[1] Some little while ago an absurd controversy was raised on this point. The writer contended that "The Act of Touch" was inaccurate in thus speaking of these four "living levers." He contended that they could not be levers! That a lever must have a "fixed fulcrum," whereas my "supposed" levers could not be "levers" because the fulcrums were *movable!* For my reply to this quibble on words *see* Additional Note XIV. Wonderful, how some people only seem to think in words, instead of the facts the words stand for!

Chapter V

THE PHYSIOLOGICAL DETAILS

A. The FINGER and how to use it:

1. The finger-tip is *exerted* downwards with the key during its moment of descent. The finger must not hit the key down; it must reach the key quite gently, but must then be exerted more or less forcibly, as needed by the tone.

The two distinct modes of Finger-use:

2. One can bring the finger *to* the key and exert it *with* the key during descent, in two quite distinct ways or directions: —

(*a*) One can use it in a *folding-in* direction, as in everyday life, when grasping anything. It is the best and should be the most usual action at the Piano; or

(*b*) One can use it in the opposite direction, as an *unfolding* or *opening-out* of the finger. One sometimes uses the middle finger like that, for instance when playing at marbles!

The condition of the upper-arm differs in sympathy with these two quite distinct finger-activities, as we shall see later.[1]

This difference in the direction or mode of the finger-action and exertion (which may be invisible) becomes *visible* when you play with ample preliminary movements *to* the key — that is, with a considerable preliminary *raising* of the fingers.

In this case you will see that with *a*) (the "clinging" finger-action) the finger when raised, is in a somewhat flattened-out position, and that it *folds in* when descending towards and with the key. Whereas with *b*) (the "thrusting" finger-action) the finger when raised, is considerably bent, or even fully *bent*

[1] *See* Chapter IX, "Flat *v.* Bent Finger-actions." *See* also Chapters XIII and XIV, "On Position and Nomenclature." *See* also "The Act of Touch," Chapters XVI and XVII, etc.

into an arch, and in this case the finger *opens out* when descending towards and with the key. This last has also been termed "bent finger" action, while the other has been called "flat finger." Nevertheless, this "flat" finger may be *quite curved* when it is *down* with the key — in fact, may then be as much curved as in "bent finger" technique. *See* photos of these two finger-actions, given in the EPITOME, facing page 35.

The two ways of Finger-use, muscularly:

3. Most important of all is the fact that both these movements or exertions of the finger ("bent" or "flat") can be provided in *two quite distinct ways* MUSCULARLY. That is, you can produce the action of the finger either by: —

1. Exertion of its "small" (or weak) muscles only; or,
2. Exertion also of its "strong" (or large) muscles.

Now the "small" flexing muscles of the finger (the lumbricales) are situated on the inside of the hand, whereas its "strong" flexing muscles are situated on the forearm. To make this clear to you as *sensation*, try the following experiment: —

(*a*) Rest very *lightly* on a table with all five fingers and a loose-lying hand. Now repeatedly tap the table quite lightly with one finger only — and you will find, (provided you do this lightly enough) that you are now using only the "small" muscles of the finger — you feel no action beyond the Knuckle.

(*b*) Now, instead, press considerably upon the table with the same finger, and notice the marked reaction at the Wrist-joint, and at the Knuckle also, which is almost driven up by it; you are now using the "strong" muscles of the finger, and you can feel a momentary tension on the under side of the wrist.

It is this *second* way of exerting the finger which you must employ in *sounding* the notes; whereas the *first* way suffices to hold notes down once they are sounded. *See* ¶ 40 of this Chapter, on the discoveries of the late *John Hunter* on this point.[1]

Whenever you find your finger-passages "out of form," recall this experiment.

The second way of Finger-use needs Hand-exertion.

When the finger is exerted in the *second* way (by its strong muscles), this demands a down-exertion of the hand each time the finger is used, as will be explained presently. Both ways also demand accurate adjustment of the Forearm Rotational-stress, as you will also realize later on.

B. The HAND and how to use it:

4. To enable the finger to do its work efficiently with the key (as just indicated), you must exert the hand downwards upon it, *each time* momentarily and individually with each finger, during the moment of Key-descent, so as to form a stable Basis or Foundation for its action.

NOTE. — To talk of "*Anchorages*" or "*Fixations*" in this connection, is only a vague and misleading way of stating the plain fact, that a certain portion of our playing-limb must either be (invisibly) exerted or left lax, so as to form a stable and secure Foundation or Basis for the exertion or movement of other portions. Definite statements are here needed: as to *which* portions of a limb to leave *passive* or supported, and which to *exert*. That alone will help us. Whereas, merely to *name the point* (or joint or hinge) where the limb must be immobile during the act of touch, does not in the least inform us *how* to produce such immobility (or "Anchorage" or "Fixation") or stable Foundation from which to exert our limb effectively. We are not in the least instructed *what* to do, nor WHAT *not to do*, by being directed to *render immobile* (for the moment) certain of our *bodily hinges!*

To be told to render such and such a bodily-hinge immobile, or set, or "fixed" or "anchored," can only lead to *stiffness*, and general technical incapacity. The term "Fixation" should therefore be strictly banished from the Pianist's vocabulary. It is incalculably harmful; and "anchorage," though not so evilly-suggestive, is little better; while, as pointed out, both are quite uninformative as to the cause of well doing — as to *what we have to do* to produce such needed Stable Foundations for our work against the key.

See also Chapter XIV, "On Nomenclature."

[1] *See* Chapter VIII, "On the Holding of Notes"; also Additional Note XIII, "The Flat and Bent Fingers."

It is clear that without such *help from the hand* (visible or *invisible*) there is no foundation for the finger to work against — for you cannot apply the "strong" muscles of the finger (*see* ¶ 3 and ¶ 42) without also exerting the hand; and without such hand-help, finger action *alone* is too uncertain and feeble.[1]

Also, *vice versa*, it is obvious that you cannot bring your hand-force to bear upon the key, without a corresponding exertion of the intervening finger — visible or *invisible* as the case may be.

NOTE. — Indeed, it would be a great convenience, at the Piano, if we had a separate hand for each finger; much bad technique would be impossible! But as we only have one hand available for each set of five fingers, so we must be careful to use it *five times as often* as we do the fingers, since that one hand has to do duty, individually, for each one of these five fingers!

We need ten hands

Whenever a so-called "finger-passage" is not clear-cut, or powerful enough, always recall the fact that you really need ten hands! The fault is corrected instantly if you correctly apply the hand-force (not *Movement!*) each time individually for each finger — unless you are holding yourself stiffly rotationally! *See* ¶ 18, and also Chapter VI, "On Forearm Rotation."

Finger *v.* Hand Movement.

5. Now, with this muscular combination (of Finger-force and Hand-force) you have two optional MOVEMENTS available.

(*a*) A movement of the finger alone — while the exertion of the hand remains *invisible*, or,

(*b*) a movement of the hand instead, while the finger-exertion may here remain quite hidden from view.

When the finger provides the *movement*, this is called "Finger-touch," although the *action* is here compounded of *exertions* both of the hand and the finger; the first *invisible* but the second visible.[2]

Whereas, when the hand provides the actual *movement*, then it is called "Hand-touch," or in the old days, "Wrist-touch," although the action is here compounded of both finger and hand exertions — the *first* here *invisible*, but the second visible.

[1] *See* Additional Note X, "The Pure Finger-work *Myth*."

[2] *See* Chapter XIV, "On Nomenclature."

Such difference in *movement* is determined by one of these two exertions being slightly in excess of the other; thus when the hand-exertion is slightly in excess of its fellow, we have "Hand-touch"; whereas with the finger-exertion in excess, we have "Finger-touch."

NOTE. — This difference in MOVEMENT has little influence on the actual tone. It is merely a matter of convenience. Thus, for the quickest passages, the *shortest* lever, the finger, can more easily be reiterated than can be the hand along with the finger, since this forms a far longer lever.

When the *Tempo* of the passage is slow enough to allow of it, we may, instead, use movements of those still longer levers — the Forearm or the Whole arm. But the longer and heavier the lever the heavier also is the *mass of Inertia* you have to cope with; since more force is required to overcome the sluggishness of a larger mass than that of a smaller mass, and this materially affects the problem of choice of Movement. *See* Chap. VII, on Movements, and Chap. XIII, "On Position."

C. *THE ARM* and how it is needed.

— The Hand's Basis.

6. The Hand, when vigorously applied in helping the fingers, again in turn needs a stable basis for its operation. This basis is here needed at the Wrist-joint, else the Wrist-joint itself would give way upwards, under the stress of the reaction or recoil arising from the down-exertion of the hand and finger against the moving key.

For this purpose of Basis at the Wrist-joint, the *ARM* has to be employed; and it is available in *Six Distinct Ways*. Succinctly stated, these are as follows:

The six ways of Arm-functioning: —

I. The *Poised-arm* element
II. The *Forearm-rotation* element

III. Forearm weight.
IV. Whole arm weight.
V. Forearm down-exertion added to the full weight; and lastly
VI. Upper arm forward-drive along with Forearm down-exertion — usually the cause of all bad Tone.

The *first two* of these six ways of using the Arm are invariably needed, whatever the nature of the passage — they are COMPULSORY; whereas the last *four ways* of applying the Arm are needed *only during the moment of key-descent.* Choice here depends on the tone required; these last four ways are therefore OPTIONAL.

We will first consider the two COMPULSORY *arm conditions — the "Poised Arm" and the "Rotative Fore-arm," under* A *and* B, *as follows:*

7. A) **The Poised Arm.** You may "poise" (or balance) the whole arm by its raising muscles, causing it (as it were) to float above or on the keyboard. No part of its weight or force rests upon the keyboard *when the arm is* FULLY *poised* — or completely balanced by its own muscles. When fully (or nearly fully) poised, its *inertia,*[1] alone, suffices as a basis for the exertion of the hand-and-finger in light, rapid passages, etc. Also, thus poised, it serves, in *every* passage (*in between the sounding* of the notes), as Basis for the action of the fingers in holding down notes, as in "artificial" *legato*, etc.

NOTE. — *See* Chapter XI, "On Legato and Staccato."

Arm-vibration Touch:

8. In rapid "Agility" passages, where you must thus use the *fully-poised* arm continuously, the tone is produced by individually-timed *exertions of the finger and hand* (either exhibited as finger movement or as hand-movement), and the arm itself will here be sympathetically driven *into vibration* by reaction from these individual and momentary impulses of the finger-and-hand, against and with the keys. This constitutes "*Arm-vibration touch,*" and all rapid *but musical* passages should thus be played by arm-vibration touch, whether legato or not.

[1] That is: Sluggishness of response to a motion-impulse.

Weight-transfer Touch:

9. Whereas, with the Arm less fully poised, a measure of its weight may actually come to bear continuously (although gently) *upon the keybeds.*

This constitutes "*Weight-transfer*" or "*Passing-on*" touch. It also thus forms the basis of "Natural-legato," since it *compels* each finger in turn to hold down its note until relieved by the next finger. *See* ¶ 13.

NOTE. — These matters are fully elucidated in Chapter XI, "On Legato and Staccato"; Chapter VIII, "On the Holding of Notes"; and Chapter XII, "Weight-transfer and Arm-vibration Touches."

10. *All* successful Agility passages must necessarily be played *either* as "Arm-vibration" or as "Weight-transfer" touch; and speedy finger-passages form the very backbone of all *real* Piano-music.

Understanding of these matters is therefore of prime importance, and will be found fully dealt with in Chapter XII, which is wholly devoted to the further elucidation of these — the distinction between Weight-transfer touch and Arm-vibration touch. We will now further consider the Poised Arm Element.

11. With the arm fully poised the hand remains uninfluenced by its weight, and it can here lie quite loosely on the keyboard-*surface.*

12. The fully-poised condition of the arm may however be slightly modified in rapid finger passages, when played *forte;* a more substantial Basis is then needed for the rapidly succeeding but powerful finger-and-hand impulses, and the arm may then be allowed actually to rest *a little* on the Keyboard. *This is* feasible, provided the passage is sufficiently rapid to *prevent* such extra weight from coming to bear solidly and continuously on the Key-*beds.*

NOTE. — If, however, the degree of the weight thus borne along is allowed to *outbalance* the sum of the upward reactions experienced (from the rapidly succeeding momentary finger-and-hand impulses against the keys), then the weight will after all come to bear continuously upon the key-*beds*, and we shall thus lose the advantages of *Arm-vibration* touch, and shall instead have *Weight-transfer* touch, with all its disadvantages musically, as shown in the next paragraphs, and in Chapter XII.

Weight-transfer touch again:

13. We have seen (¶ 10) that with the *somewhat* less fully-poised arm-condition (or heavier form of "Resting") this weight comes to bear continuously *upon the key-beds*, and when purely passed on from Key-bed to Key-bed forms "Weight-transfer" or "Passing-on" Touch.

NOTE. — "Purely passed-on weight" here signifies *without* those *momentarily* applied individual impulses of the finger-and-hand which constitute Arm-vibration Touch.

Continuous Hand-exertions:

14. Realize, at once, the important fact, that any such continuously-resting Arm-weight on the Key-*beds* (as in Weight-transfer touch), although still light, in turn also compels you to EXERT YOUR HAND CONTINUOUSLY.[1]

In short: The main distinction between Weight-transfer and Arm-vibration lies in the CONTINUITY OR DISCONTINUITY of the exertion of the Hand. In Weight-transfer you have CONTINUOUSLY applied hand-pressures (the degree of which is determined by the amount of weight carried), whereas, with Arm-vibration, the hand-exertions are applied INDIVIDUALLY for each finger during key-descent only. This would indeed be much simpler, if we had TEN hands instead of two only!

15. Such continuously "passed-on" Weight AND Hand-force may again be slightly increased to correspond to the required degree of tone.

Continuous Rotatory stresses:

Moreover, such continuously passed-on Weight may here compel the Forearm rotational-stresses also to be *continuously*

[1] That is, your hand cannot here *lie loosely* upon the keys in between the sounding of the notes, as with the Arm-vibration type of touch, but must be *continuously exerted* (although lightly) in direct proportion to the degree of the continuously resting Arm-weight here allowed to be transferred from key-bed to key-bed.

applied for "*bunches*" of notes at a time proceeding in the same direction.[1]

16. Finally, the inevitable drawback in the use of "Weight-transfer" touch lies in the fact that it very materially interferes with *your ability to choose the tone* for each note *individually* — both with regard to loudness and duration, and thus to the detriment of your musical craftsmanship.

17. In short, with "Passing-on" (or Weight-transfer) touch, we can practically only have "Mass-production" effects — swirls of *crescendo* and *diminuendo*, produced by the respective gradual increases or decreases of this passed-on Weight-basis. Therefore strictly avoid "Weight-transfer" touch for all passages which need every note to be *musically individualized* — that is, for all *melodic* passages; since melodic passages always require meticulous *selectivity* of tone and duration for every note. All this is further elaborated in Chapter XII under "Weight-transfer *v.* Arm-vibration."

B) The Forearm Rotation Element

Forearm Rotatory Stresses mostly *invisible:*

18. Forearm rotatory exertions and relaxations must be adjusted to every note you play. They are either repeated or reversed from note to note. Mostly, however, they are applied WITHOUT *any outward indication whatever of their presence or absence.* The Forearm Rotation Element applies all through your playing, and either makes or mars it. Without its application your hand would stand upright on the keyboard (with thumb up) instead of lying prone upon it.[2]

Indeed, you cannot touch the Piano without its incidence. It

[1] Hence have arisen those fantastic "Undulatory" and "Curvilinear" *theories* of touch first put forward in the dark ages of piano-teaching, when everything was tentative, owing to the fundamental muscular facts not having been grasped, since Eye-evidence was alone depended upon — theories resuscitated, however, by some recent writers!

[2] Unless you purposely play without any Forearm rotational exertion — and therefore with your hand sideways, as recommended in my "Child's First Steps" and "Nine Steps towards Finger-individualization," which refer to.

is needed for all single notes, octaves, chords, and for singing passages as well as for every note in the speediest of Agility "finger" passages, whatever the form or type of touch employed. It is required equally for loud or soft playing, for *staccato* and *legato*, and however slow or quick the passage. Most ruined playing is to be traced to ignorance of its inexorable laws.

Understanding and mastery of Rotation is therefore usually the solution of most "finger-work" troubles. Attention to it indeed largely constitutes "L'art de délier les doigts," or "Fingerfertigkeit," to quote CZERNY.[1]

Of all the six forms of Arm-use or condition here enumerated, Forearm Rotation is the most important. It therefore needs far more detailed elucidation than is desirable at this stage, hence it receives a separate Chapter to itself further on — Chapter VI.

The Four Optional Forms of Arm-use:

19. *As already noted, the first two forms of Arm-use (the Poised arm and the Rotative arm) are* COMPULSORY *in every passage, whatever its nature, whereas the remaining* FOUR WAYS *are* OPTIONAL.

20. These last *four* (optional) ways of arm-use are applied *only during* the *moment of each individual Key-descent*. They are required where the poised arm condition, alone, does *not* offer a sufficiently substantial Basis for the work of the finger and hand. Choice, therefore, here largely depends on the kind of tone required.

We will now consider these *last four propositions* in further detail, under I, II, III, and IV, as follows: —

I) Forearm Weight.

21. You can, during key-descent, set free (or "lapse") the *weight of the forearm* ONLY, as a Basis for the exertions of the finger and hand. This comparatively light weight (of the Fore-

[1] But do not forget that you also usually need "ten hands"! *See* Note, page 25.

arm only) is very suitable for light chords, etc., where no great resonance is needed, and where the general musical effect is to be lightsome and delicate.

Movement *re* Condition again

Realize, however, that this *release* of the upholding muscles of the forearm does not NECESSARILY entail any *actual movement* or "fall" of the arm.

NOTE. — It seems incredible that anyone could be so dense as to misunderstand or misinterpret my teachings as to the Element of Weight. Recent authors, however, seem to believe that I refer to *Movement*, when, instead, I refer to those *invisible* changes of state in the limb, whence arise the phenomena of Weight *set free*. Apparently, I presumed too much on the intelligence of my earlier readers!

"Arm off" not necessarily a Movement:

Anyway, let it now be clearly understood that when I speak of "Arm off" it does *not* mean that the arm should be raised-up into the air! All I wish to convey by "Arm off" is that *the incidence of this weight* is here *to be omitted;* and, therefore, that the arm should here assume or resume its *poised condition* — through its self-supporting muscles coming into action.

"Arm-on" also not necessarily a Movement.

Again, when I direct that the Arm-weight is to be "lapsed," this does *not* mean that the arm is necessarily actually to *FALL* or move, but that the arm, for the moment, is to be left unsupported by its muscles (to the needed degree), so that this weight, ***invisibly*** *supported* and countered *by the exertion of the hand and fingers*, may thus serve as a *Basis* for their action.

Indeed, the full weight of the arm can be applied (and mostly should be) without the slightest outward or visible indication of its presence.[1]

[1] Such misunderstandings are on a level with one that occurred recently in class. After a lecture of mine on these very points, a member of the class at her next lesson asked me to explain "How can one possibly play *legato* if one takes one's arm 'off'?" — and illustrated her question *by sliding her hand and arm* "OFF" — *the keyboard!* This came from a quite intelligent woman! But she had probably only listened to half I said; all the ideas were new to her, and of course she had been brought up under the sway of that paralyzing fetish of *Movement* — which always seems to throw a dark pall over the sufferer's intelligence.

II) Whole-arm Weight.

22. In order to obtain louder effects, you need greater stability (or Basis) for your finger-and-hand actions than Forearm-weight alone can give; you here need the weight of the *whole* Arm (both of the upper-arm and forearm) *more or less liberally* released. With a medium-sized arm this will offer ample basis for *cantando* and *cantabile*-tone in single notes, and for some chord-effects.[1] Or No. III may be used — *see* page 35.

23. Good Singing-tone, in the making, *feels as if* Weight-release "produced" the tone. Weight alone, however, does not really occasion it. Remember, Weight only serves as a Basis, and it must correspond to the desired *exertion* of the finger and hand.

Movements are optional:

Only *one* of these three Elements of touch-*construction* need be *visible* during the act of touch — that is, visible *either* as Finger, or Hand or Arm *movement;* the other two remaining invisible.

NOTE. — Moreover, you may prompt into being this three-fold combination (of Arm, Hand and Finger for singing tone) in *two ways* — either by thinking of the sensation of the *Weight-release*, or of the *Exertions* implied.

Weight *v.* Muscularly-"*initiated*" Touch

Thus (1), you may call up the *feeling of the release* of the Arm-weight, and rely on the finger and hand to do their work by sympathetic reflex-action, owing to the Weight being left unsupported — but see that they *do their work!* Or (2), you may call up the *sensation of the work being done* (by finger-and-hand exertion) and thus allow the required Weight-lapse (No, no, not Movement!) to occur, owing to the sympathetic or co-ordinated sense of the need of a Basis.

This distinction I called "Weight-initiated" *v.* "Muscularly-initiated" touch in "The Act of Touch." It is further dealt with under ¶ 34 of this Chapter. Also *see* "The Act of Touch" itself, pages 162–164, and also page 198.

Cantabile needs both good tone and *legato*

[1] *Cantabile*, however, not only implies good carrying tone, or tonal contrast, but also needs good *legato*. It is through the legato and super-legato (*legatissimo*) inflections of Duration, that *cantabile* achieves its charm.

Both Weight and Exertion need Timing:

24. Moreover, realize, that to produce a telling, vital tone, it does not suffice merely to provide the correct Weight and corresponding exertions. On the contrary, effectively to make use of such weight and exertion you must always carefully direct and *time* your *finger and hand exertions* along with the Weight release. That is, you must insist on giving the *proper acceleration* TO THE KEY during its short journey downwards — in short, you must "*think the key*" unremittingly.

Also, remember that this acceleration must always be "at increasing ratio" during the flash-like process of key-descent.[1]

First learn to play *with* Weight, then without.

25. Thus you must first carefully learn to supply Weight (visibly or invisibly as the case may require), and then you must as carefully learn to OMIT it at the right moment, and on the right occasion.

NOTE. — Thus, the very first step at the keyboard is to play by Weight-release only, *pp*, as shown in my "Child's First Steps" and "Nine Steps towards Finger-individualization." Only when this principle has been grasped for chord and melody-playing, may you proceed to play with "Weight-off" — as required for Agility-passages.

Heavy Resting-weight kills Music.

26. Arm-weight, allowed to rest too heavily upon the keyboard *in-between-the-sounding of the notes*, inevitably does infinite harm both technically and musically. It will certainly mar all Agility and clearness, and cause "stickiness"; and it will also render every passage, thus misplayed, thoroughly dull and uninteresting musically, since such solidly-resting weight precludes that nice *choice* of the tone-colour for each note, so imperatively needed if the result is to be Music-making.[2]

Hence, you must learn correctly to apply the arm, and must

[1] *See* ¶ 35, and also ¶¶ 11, 12 and 13 of Chapter II.

[2] *Vide* ¶ 10, on Weight-transfer Touch, and ¶ 9, on Arm-vibration Touch; and also Chapter XII on this subject.

learn also to *avoid* its incidence on the Keyboard, when not needed.

Indeed, the arm may badly mar technique as well as make it!

NOTE. — More harm, in fact, has been done (and also, unhappily is still being done) by such false ideas of Weight-transfer touch, than was done in the past by a deliberate striking or hitting the keys down with its vaunted "little hammerette" action of the fingers. Indeed, all teaching that recommends various *more or less heavy grades of passed-on Arm-weight* — or "*Schwere Tastenbelastung*" — should be strictly shunned. This more recent form of German mis-teaching (copied by recent writers who ought to know better) has done incalculable harm, and has crippled almost irretrievably many a would-be and promising pianist; in fact it has done as much harm (and perhaps more) than the older folly of forced finger-lifting.

False Weight-transfer Touch

The question of Weight-transfer (where it should be used, and where not) is fully elaborated in Chapter XII.

III) Forearm Down-force with Upper-arm Weight.

27. For fullest tone, both in Singing passages and everywhere else, you need a still more substantial basis than the fullest *Arm-weight* can supply, unaided. Here you must learn to *add* a *down-exertion* of the Forearm *to* the previously discussed momentary Weight-release of the whole arm. That is, you must *leave free* the weight of the whole arm, while you nevertheless *exert* your Forearm downwards; that is, a down-*exertion* of the Forearm *in addition to* this whole-arm Weight.

Use of the Forearm lever:

NOTE. — This conjoint Forearm down-exertion with released Weight is needed for a certain *penetrating* singing-tone. Pure Weight-release does not suffice here. This exertion of the Forearm downwards is again quite a natural action. It is really a *lifting* action! For it is similar to the natural use of the bannisters as a help in mounting the stairs. The Shoulder, therefore, in this case becomes the Basis for your playing action — it is *lifted* against, and thus, through your shoulder, the whole mass of your body (quietly resting on the chair) becomes the ultimate Basis.

Use of the Forearm lever

28. The main secret of producing large tone without harshness lies in this down-exertion of the forearm in conjunction with a FREE UPPER-ARM.[1]

[1] No doubt, we may also on rare occasions *add* a light *downward* (and backward) *exertion* of the *upper-arm*, thus helping the Elbow *backwards*. But remember,

IV) Upper-arm Forward-dig.

— The form of Arm-use to be *avoided*.

29. Finally, we see that a *fourth* optional Form of Arm-use is possible. It is one, however, that should be *carefully avoided* — unless used very lightly indeed. Here, along with the down-exertion of the Forearm, you *drive forwards* with the Upper-arm, instead of leaving it lax as in No. III. It *feels* (and is) a horrible digging action into the keyboard with arm and elbow, and the Elbow feels thoroughly rigid during its perpetration.

30. This last (and *undesirable*) form of Arm-condition, the *fourth*, at once calls for more amplified consideration, as it forms one of the worst and most frequent causes of bad tone, and perhaps more often spoils musicality of effect than any of the many other possible forms of misdemeanor at the Pianoforte.

It is only too frequently heard in the playing of otherwise quite good pianists, and even popular artists. (Only the very rare, truly musical player avoids it consistently.)

NOTE. — Many artists, while achieving perfect beauty in *cantabiles* up to *mf* (by means of No. III genre of tone-production), unfortunately reverse all this, and apply the upper-arm *forward-drive* (the No. IV, and bad genre of tone) when they try to play a real *forte*. The *Additional Note*, No. IV, "On Beauty and Ugliness in Touch," is important in this connection (the use and misuse of the third and fourth optional ways of Arm-use) and this should therefore be carefully studied.

31. *Certainly*, this fourth way of Arm-use is the easiest, most natural — and *nastiest* — way of obtaining plenty of *noise* from the Piano. It is, in fact, an instinctive action in Self-defence![1]

---

when this action is properly produced, the Elbow still feels *perfectly free and elastic*, and tends to fall back, and thus *pulls* the fingers upon their keys. Also, do not forget in the meantime to *intend*, time, and aim that due *acceleration* of the key during each Key-descent, without which good and controlled tone remains impossible.

[1] Recall its helpfulness, should you have the misfortune to be attacked in some lonely lane one night! In that case, *do* use your pianistically strong arm just in this way behind your fist, and you can easily deliver a splendidly effective knock-out blow! But avoid delivering such musically catastrophic knock-out blows upon the inoffensive strings of your Piano — if you

Jujutsu at the Piano

Its application in fact forms a strong confutation of that quasi-scientific folly, the assertion that "quality-differences" cannot be produced by any treatment we may mete out to the Key.

An experiment on Quality-contrasts

NOTE. — The fine experiments on this point by the American Steel and Wire Company's acoustical department under Professor William Braid White, have anyway proved that quality-differences *do* arise with differences of touch; although, so far, these experiments have only shown them to arise in conjunction with variations in Tone-*intensity*. Whether they cannot be given *without* change in tone-intensity still remains to be decided. This matter is elaborated in the previously alluded to *Additional Nòte*, No. IV, "On Beauty and Ugliness in Touch." . . . As an experiment, in the meantime, try a *crescendo* on a repeated single note, or chord, first in this horrible way (with an upper-arm forward-jerk along with Down-forearm and thrusting finger-and-hand exertion), and then play the *crescendo* again, but with a properly free Upper-arm and Elbow, and clinging-finger, along with the necessary Forearm down-exertion to bring the tone up beyond a mere *forte*. It is irrefutably convincing which is the *wrong way of treating the Pianoforte*, and which is the *right way!*

But, as insisted upon in this *Additional Note*, No. IV, it really does not signify whether you ascribe the difference between good and bad effect to *quality*-differences, or to an over-forcing of the action in playing *too loudly*. The fact remains, that if you wish to behave in a civilized way at the Piano, you must learn to avoid the No. IV tone-destroying type of touch, and must instead make a habit of No. III, the true tone-producing method.

Moreover, be sure to make the suggested experiment with a really *hard*-hammered Piano — since a soft hammer materially hides such gross maltreatment.

Soft *v.* hard hammer

Indeed it is from an instinct of self-preservation, that all Piano-makers are provoked to provide hammers with felts *far too soft*, and which therefore tend to nullify our colouring efforts. It is naturally resorted to by the makers, to protect their good name from the onslaught of the forward-driving Piano-wrecker.

The softer the hammer presented to the player, however, the harder is he compelled to learn to "drive," so as to obtain some measure of contrast, or colouring; and the better the player succeeds in this, the more does the maker try to counter him by still softer hammers! And so the struggle continues, like the fight between gun and ironside in the Navy!

Realize, here, that the most musical Piano is the one that *can*, at will, be made to sound *quite harsh* — within reason! Whereas, the most *un-musical* Piano is precisely the one that turns a pleasant face, however badly you pommel it!

---

would like it to remain in condition, or your hearer a friend! Such forward-drive touch, with its destructive resistless onslaught, is bound to knock the strings out of tune in the shortest possible time, even if you apply it with only moderate force. Whereas, if you apply it really viciously, you are likely to break strings and even hammer-shanks. Its only recommendation therefore is, that it is good for trade!

A soft-hammered Piano, with its pretty agreeable "ready-made" tone (as CHOPIN used to say) is a quite inartistic instrument. It is absolutely disheartening to the musical artist who has *learnt to* USE *his instrument rightly*, and who is out to play with all possible shades of colouring. It is disheartening, just precisely because any real measure of *quality*-differences (as I prefer to call them) are almost unattainable with such woollen-blanket type of hammer.

"Ready-made" tone useless artistically

I, myself, when testing a new student's ear, always use the crescendo and decrescendo experiment previously noted, with its repeated chord played both ways alternately, and it is curious to note, that the *colour*-ear is far more frequently met with than the *pitch*-ear.

The obvious moral of this is, that if you wish to make the musical section of your public happy, carefully refrain from No. IV type of tone *mal*-production, and *always* rely upon No. III, even for your fullest *fortes*.

Forward-drive occasionally appropriate:

32. This objectionable No. IV type of arm-combination nevertheless occasionally finds its use. Gently, it can be applied with good effect, for producing certain "dry" effects; and for that comparatively rare effect, a true *staccatissimo*, it serves admirably — used thus *gently*. It is also responsible for certain special colour effects — for instance, that gentle little knock, suggestive of distant "Horns," is produced in this way.[1]

Upper-arm forward for *ppp*:

33. Also, strangely enough, this *forward* action of the upper-arm can actually help us to obtain the *very lightest* effects. But to succeed in this, we must carefully avoid *any vestige of Fore-arm down-drive* with it, and indeed must also almost eliminate all forearm weight.

Thus, when you lightly exert the upper-arm *forward* (away from you) you really *lift its weight off the keyboard* — visibly or invisibly, as the case may be, and you can thus achieve light-

[1] A pupil of mine, however, suggests that this "Horn" effect is partly owing to a form of "half-pedalling" produced in this way by the fingers themselves, instead of by the toes — and that the slight knock delivered with this stiffish hand and fingers causes a slight momentary rebound of the key with its damper. Possibly he is right, and it seems to be a plausible explanation.

Horn imitations

ness to any degree. But do not overdo this trick, else you will miss your notes!

As two noteworthy instances of its application you will find that it is the only way of playing with certainty the *up-beat* (the opening note) of Beethoven's Sonata in A, Op. 2; and also the first note of the Fugue in the last movement of his Sonata in A, Op. 101.

Beethoven, Op. 2, No. 2:

From Op. 101:

Weight-transfer or Passing-on Touch Again.

34. Arm weight, moreover, as we have seen in ¶¶ 10 and 13, can also be correctly applied for tone-production while *continuously* (but lightly) resting on the keyboard for certain light, soft effects. *See* Chapter XII on this subject. Also Note under ¶ 26 of this present Chapter.

The Truth about Weight-touch.

— "Free-fall of Arm" fallacy:

35. Do not imagine that it is by an actual *fall* of the weight that tone is produced, and that "the greater the weight the quicker the *speed*." That is a total misapprehension, and quite untrue physically. An ounce falls with precisely the same

speed as a ton — although the *impact* of a ton is a vastly different matter from the impact of an ounce!

Weight is needed solely as a Basis. True, the *height* from which a weight falls would influence the speed, for a weight gathers speed as it falls. But this fact cannot be taken advantage of in playing the Piano — since such "free fall" of the arm would preclude our attaining any musical certainty. The reason being, that if you "drop" your arm uncontrolled upon the key, you cannot possibly *feel and judge* how much force is needed *by that key* for that particularly desired tone — and it always *should* be a desired tone. Nor can you thus provide the due degree of *acceleration* needed during Key-descent. Such uncontrolled drop of the arm would instead reduce everything to mere guesswork and good luck — or more probably, bad luck!
It is altogether alien to the expression of Music-sense. Therefore, never let your arm drop or fall upon the keys uncontrolled by its upholding muscles.

36. Deliberately to instruct the student to "*drop the arm from a greater height the louder the required tone*" is therefore sheer folly, and constitutes thoroughly bad, mischievous teaching.[1]

_Re_ a supposed _drop_ of the Arm

NOTE. — Some two years ago an author published the following really comical statements as to my teaching of "Weight": — "A further defect that arose lay in the *Uncontrolled* use of the weight; too much insistence on *complete* instead of gradual and balanced relaxation of the controlling muscles was the cause of this, and the result too often a hard tone. . . . Matthay's maximum of tone was limited by the amount that could be obtained by weight and its speed *from different heights*."

This, among other fabrications as to my teachings, was also copied (possibly without investigation) in a more recent compilation. To attribute to me such folly as that the key should ever be *struck* or *hit down* by a Weight "dropped" from a greater or lesser height, is so incredibly stupid and comic that it hardly needs serious contradiction; yet there may be many who have never read "The Act of Touch"; or who may have glanced through it as cursorily and unintelligently as these authors seem to have done, and who therefore might accept such misstatements as truth! Other authors may or may not have taught such nonsense as this about Weight, but nothing I have ever written, said, or suggested could be thus misconstrued. Particularly when it is remembered that I have in-

[1] *See* the extra Note on "Arm-fall," on the next page.

sisted all along (perhaps *ad nauseam!*) that one cannot possibly play musically if one *hits* the Key down, either by Weight, or in any other way.

My reiterations on all these points however still seem to have been too infrequent to overcome the resisting obtuseness of some minds, complacently smothered by the old obsession of *Movement*, when confronted with an analysis of the *Invisible* in Touch — the thing that really matters! *See* ¶ 35 on "*The Truth about Weight.*"

Arm-drop real, or seeming

EXTRA NOTE. — As a matter of fact, a good-sized arm, really "dropped" from a height of say eighteen inches or so from above the keyboard, and taken by a resisting finger and hand, would probably smash the strings or the hammer or even the finger! If in doubt as to the truth of this, try it on your own Piano — but not on mine! The fact is, that again the eye is the deceiver. A freely descending arm certainly *looks like* a true "fall" or drop. A musical player, however, never adopts such mis-touch. Instead, he always *controls* the descent of the weight (by the *up*-muscles of his arm) so as to reach the surface of the keys with *insufficient* speed to knock the keys down. That is, he is careful to reach the key with not enough impact to *preclude* his taking hold *upon* the key, and depressing it as he *feels* its need during descent.

In short, you must always give the necessary access of force *when* and *after* the key is met, and finger and hand can then provide the required proper acceleration by their *guided* co-operation — although all this may remain quite *invisible.*

Ample movement of Arm, when advantageous:

37. When playing *forte* by arm-*movement*, it is an advantage to allow your arm to descend and subside from some little distance. The *inertia* (sluggishness) of its mass is thus in a measure overcome as a *preliminary* to the actual tone-producing act — which, remember, must never begin until the surface of the keyboard is reached. Therefore, even in this case, you must reach the keys quite gently — so that you can still judge the resistance met with from them.

Weight does not *produce* tone directly:

38. Moreover, realize that Weight never really *produces* the tone. As already insisted upon, Weight can but form a *Basis* for the activities of the Finger and Hand. Arm-weight could only be said to "produce" the tone, if allowed to subside with the key *unaided by any intervening exertion* of finger and hand. This is manifestly impossible; therefore (as I pointed out in "The Act of Touch"), whenever you apply Weight never forget *to use* (exert) both hand and finger.

NOTE. — The only case when Weight may be said to "produce" tone is, when you play with your *fist* sideways, as shown in No. I of my "*Nine Steps towards Finger Individualization*," — the four-page pamphlet issued by the Oxford University Press. Here, certainly, your whole arm and fist descend *with* the Keys and produce the required *pp* tone — if relaxed precisely to the needed extent. This alone exemplifies tone-excitation purely by Weight-descent — although a vestige of hand exertion, *sideways*, must participate even here! The moment, however, that you place your finger-tips upon the keys (as in "*Step IV*"), that moment your fingers and hand are compelled actively to *respond* (by reflex action) to what is felt as an impending descent of the Weight, and they then (in response) *actively* (exertionally) support that Weight upon the descending keys — arm, hand and fingers here descending as a whole. This *visual* effect has led to the stupid mistake made by some, that finger and hand are *not exerted* in "Weight-touch"!

The sole case of Tone-production by Weight-release!

Moreover, if the finger and hand exertions are slightly in excess of the Arm-weight released, then they will *move* instead of the Arm. The Weight (or Arm) will therefore *not be allowed to descend at all* here — although its influence thus invisibly supplies the finger and hand with the required Basis for their action. Hence it is also clear, that although we call such process "Weight-touch," yet, truly speaking, "Weight-touch" really is touch by finger-and-hand exertions, although these are prompted into action by the Weight-release.

Weight-touch does not imply *non-exertion* of Finger and Hand

The true function of Weight:

In short, as already reiterated so often, the function of Weight in playing is solely that of Basis, whether it moves or not; that is, its function always is but to form a stable foundation, sufficient to resist the reactions of finger-and-hand exertions, so that these can be effectively applied to the Key.

Weight-initiated *v.* Muscularly-initiated Weight-touch.[1]

39. This is a psychological distinction rather than a physical one. It implies that the triple combination of Weight *versus* finger-and-hand exertion required for singing-tone can be *prompted* into co-operation *in two ways*. You can either (1) give your mind to the *sensation* of Weight-release of the arm; or (2) give your mind to the *sensation* of Work-to-be-done by the finger-and-hand.

The *timing* of this complete Triple-combination will thus

[1] Already indicated in Note to ¶ 26 of this Chapter.

ensue somewhat differently, and will slightly affect the quality of the resultant touch-action. If you think of the sensation of *Weight-lapse*, the needed finger-and-hand exertions arise in response to it by reflex action, and are therefore slightly laggard in their response; whereas, if you recall the sensation of *work* being done (by finger and hand) then the *Weight*-response will be infinitesimally delayed in its incidence. The first will lead to better key-*acceleration* than the last, and therefore the tone will be "rounder" and "sharper" respectively. The difference is like slightly changing the "timing" of the magneto of your motor-car engine. Some will aver that there can be but little difference in the actual sound-quality arising from this distinction in touch. Possibly there may not be much, but the difference in *sensation* is quite marked — and therefore matters, since it leads to material (though subtle) differences *musically;* and such subtle distinctions in musical effect are everything, when we have risen beyond the mere strumming stage, and are out really to express the spiritual in Music.

The Dual Nature of the Muscular Equipment.

40. The researches and discoveries of the Australian physiologist, the late Dr. JOHN HUNTER (as already indicated in ¶3 of this Chapter), have important bearing on our work as Piano teachers. They indeed strikingly corroborate the teachings of "The Act of Touch" in many particulars; and the importance of his discovery of the *dual* nature of our muscular equipment cannot be overrated.

John Hunter's discoveries

NOTE. — These discoveries were first made known in a lecture delivered at London University in January, 1925, by Professor G. Elliot-Smith, and commented upon by Sir Oliver Lodge in his Résumé (in *The Daily News*) of the previous year's "Memorable" doings, as "*one of the biggest in possibilities that has been done for a long time.*" Dr. Elliot-Smith referred to the "culmination of the researches into muscular movement made by a brilliant young Australian, Dr. John Hunter," who had died recently in London upon the eve of describing his discoveries in a series of lectures. "Hunter showed" (said Dr. Elliot-Smith) "first that *the muscular system is* DUAL, *one kind of muscle doing the actual work, and another maintaining position when the work is done.* To illustrate: An oyster closes its shell with 'A' muscle, and keeps it closed with 'B' muscle. This diminishes fatigue and prevents jerkiness."

41. This discovery, that we possess two distinct sets of muscles for the *same* limb-action, one by which to do the serious work of a limb, and the other by which to do the light work, is most important, for we find this applies again and again in our Piano-work.

NOTE. — Do not confuse this duality of muscle *for a particular purpose* with that implied by muscles with *antagonistic* function.

Examples of this Duality:

42. *As instances:* (*a*) to raise your arm you are aware of the necessary muscular exertion, but to retain it raised seems no effort at all — because the "small" muscles alone then remain active. (*b*) To *sound* notes we have to use the "strong" flexor muscles of the fingers situated on the forearm, a fact we become conscious of by the sensation of tension through and at the lower side of the wrist-joint.[1] Whereas, we can and should hold the Keys down quite lightly, after the sounding, by using only the activity of the "small" (or weak) muscles inside the hand — the "lumbricales." (*c*) Much of the failure to understand how Forearm rotational actions can help or mar playing, arises from the fact that we can so easily recognize that an *exertion is necessary* to turn the hand into its playing position, — for we then use the strong rotatory muscles. Whereas, to *maintain* the hand in its thus turned-over position, we find that the *small* or weak muscles fulfill this duty quite well; but we are apt to overlook this fact, and are then likely to be deceived into imagining that we are "doing nothing" muscularly! Whence arises the fault, that when we try to use a finger at the fifth-finger side of the hand after the thumb, we are likely wrongfully to *continue* this unperceived light action of the rotatory *small* muscles *towards the thumb* (even when we do not commit the worse error of continuing the "strong" muscles' action!) and we shall thus inevitably impede

[1] *See* Chapter VIII on "The Holding of Notes," also page 23, ¶ 3.

the exertion of those other fingers by destroying their rotative Basis. And so, also, has arisen all that folly as to the supposed "weakness" of the 4th and 5th fingers! They are bound to be amply strong if only we do not impede their action by continuing this faulty but invisible rotatory exertion towards the thumb — when it should be discontinued.[1]

43 These discoveries in fact clarify and simplify the *explanation* — and the doing — of much that seemed somewhat difficult before. For instance, we used to think that in making a strong effort with the fingers and then *continuing it lightly* (as one should for tenuto or legato) that this implied *reducing* the same exertion to the precise minimum needed; whereas, we now realize, that *at first* we must exert *both* sets of the finger flexing-muscles concerned, but must then simply *cease all activity*, completely and promptly, of the powerful muscles, while carrying-on *solely* with the "weak" ones — a complete cutting-out process quite easy in comparison to the first.

Further Examples and Experiments on Strong *v.* Weak muscular-action:

44. Experiment and satisfy yourself on these points thus: —

I. Realize that the difference between holding your arm *nicely* "poised," and holding it clumsily and stiffly, depends precisely on this distinction. Evidently the arm *should be sustained* solely by its *weak* "up"-muscles — ample for the purpose, and *not* by the strong exertion you must employ, say, when pulling a tree up by its roots! As another instance: you *cannot continue* the comparatively strong exertion needed to lift your arm, when you afterwards try to keep it *stationary* half-way up, *unless* you then also employ an *antagonistic* exertion thus to keep it immovable — *against* this wrongly-continued exertion of the raising-muscles. What you must learn to do, is gently to raise the arm by its "strong"

[1] All this is fully explained in Chapter VI under "Forearm Rotation."

and weak muscles, and then sustain it in that position *solely by its "weak" muscles* left active, and while *cutting out* the strong muscles. Try both methods; it is instructive.

II. Again, you will vitiate that light "tap" of the forearm, sometimes required, if you use the *same* down-forearm exertion required of it, which you need when you help yourself upstairs by the bannisters! Or when you need it (moderately) for tone beyond *f* or *ff* as in that form of "arm-use" described earlier, under No. III. Try both methods!

III. Sound the notes of a finger-passage forcibly and correctly as needed in *forte*, but then wrongly *continue* the action of these powerful muscles (as well as the weak ones) *after* sounding the notes, and thus unmistakably *jam* your hand down upon the keybeds, while ruining the passage — just as all bad players do. Then play it again, properly, sounding the notes strongly, yet afterwards holding them down quite lightly — solely therefore by the "small" muscles of the fingers, and with the hand itself almost if not quite inactive — or only active with *its* own small muscles, and thus realize the absurdity of doing the thing wrongly.

IV. Or play an octave passage (or any double-notes passage) with the hand jammed down upon the keybeds, and then repeat it with the notes held down quite lightly — again solely by the "weak" muscles of hand and finger.

V. Or turn the hand over into its playing position, and hold it there firmly (and wrongly!) by a powerful rotatory exertion; and then again *leave* it there, apparently effortlessly — by the residual exertion only of its "weak" muscles.

Try both ways, and realize what is *really* implied by rotatory "adjustment."

Here, in fact, you have a root-difference between playing *easily* and playing with *the greatest possible difficulty* — as you would do, if you obeyed the old teachers! Experiment on the above lines, and convince yourself of the truth of these facts, and how you can encompass Ease.

Instinctive obedience to the Laws of Touch:

45. A *technical* genius (or so-called "Finger-talent") of course instinctively obeys all these laws (without knowing what they are) and he usually does not forget the right sensations by which to recall these right actions — unless, unhappily, his naturally-gained facility is *destroyed* by the old iniquitous misteaching to "*press down firmly upon the keybeds,*" or to "*strike the keys well*" with the "*little hammerette action*" or other such soul and musically-destructive ideas.[1]

Coda. The Merging of Touch-forms:

46. Here it is well at once to realize that all *touch-forms* can in application merge or dissolve one into the other. All forms of *Movement* as well as all forms of Touch *Construction* can thus be modified and approximated in practice.

A) Movement-merging:

47. Thus, any desirable combination may be used in place of well-defined *movements* solely of the finger, hand or arm (vertically or rotationally). That is, the movement may be a combination of finger and hand movements, or with vertical or rotational arm movements.

A proposed impossible "Reconciliation"

[1] Recently, it has even been tried to revive some of these pernicious teachings, and it has been claimed that there can be a "*Reconciliation*" between our present-day knowledge of the facts, and these now happily exploded ideas of Key-hitting and keybed *burying* of the tone-impulses. In fact, it is misdirected that one *should* press "deep" into the keybeds, "deep down," "past them" and "down to the floor!"

Obviously, there can be no possible "Reconciliation" between ideas thus diametrically contradictory — between *Knowledge* of the fundamental facts of Piano-playing and *Un*-knowledge of them! You must subscribe either to one or the other, and if you are possessed with the old pernicious out-of-date ideas and cannot wipe them out of your mind, then Natural Selection will very probably eliminate you musically, and thus put an end to your Piano-misdoings! *See* Additional Note, No. XIV, "An Impossible Reconciliation."

B) Touch-construction merging:

48. In the same way, the various kinds of Touch-*construction* may also coalesce. For instance: during key-descent, to the always necessary finger-and-hand exertions and forearm rotational-changes, you need not *solely* add forearm weight, or solely whole-arm weight, or solely forearm down-force along with upper-arm weight.

Instead, you may supply any desired in-between muscular-inflection or combination; and may omit drawing a sharp line of distinction between them when desirable — they may merge one into the other at will. But the distinctions exist none the less.

Weight-transfer and Arm-vibration also may merge:

49. In the same way, there need be no well-defined distinction between *Weight-transfer touch* and *Arm-vibration touch* in certain passages — again the two forms may coalesce in a measure. *Continuous* Weight-transfer may thus imperceptibly pass over into *individualized* Arm-vibration touch, and *vice versa.* It is like a walk gradually becoming a trot, and finally a run — but with the distinction that at the Piano we can modify the weight, so as to render the running *easier!*

Mentally, all the Touch-distinctions must remain clear:

50. Unless, however, you clearly understand all the various touch-elements and types discussed, and have them at your disposal in their *unadulterated* forms, you cannot *choose* the most appropriate for the passage in hand. For instance, you cannot fully realize the *musical* effect of a swift but *melodic* passage, if you allow a certain degree of weight-transfer musically to mar and *muddy* the needed pure, individualized Arm-vibration touch demanded in such passages — whether played resiliently or in true legato.

Carefully, therefore, master all these distinctions of Construction *and* Movement, and learn to apply them *separately* when needed, but also do not fear to combine them where that is desirable.

Technique itself must become subconscious:

51. In the meantime, realize that when all these things have been learnt, they must be forgotten! That is, having purposefully learnt to obey all these physical and physiological laws involved in Technique, they must be relegated to the SUBCONSCIOUSNESS before they can truly help you in purposeful Musical-performance.

Just as with any other language, all must be learnt; but a language cannot serve as a vehicle for expression until use of it has become second-nature — until it has become promptable by the Subconsciousness.[1]

Chapter VI

THE FOREARM-ROTATION ELEMENT

Preamble.

1. We must now undertake the further elucidation of this element — perhaps the most important of all pianistically, physiologically, and pedagogically. Hence this special chapter is

[1] In a recent compilation the claim is made of a world-reeling Discovery, viz., the teaching of Technique by means of "CONSCIOUS-*Mental-Muscular-Control.*" It is, however, conveniently overlooked that all this was taught in full detail nearly thirty years ago in *The Act of Touch.* True, I did not adopt it as a "slogan," etc. Unfortunately, it is also overlooked that I carefully warned the student, even then, that while all technical Correct Doing can and should thus be taught, yet he must not be satisfied until all this has been made into Habit, so that it is available for free artistic speech in his purposeful efforts to Make Music.

devoted to it; and if the keen-minded reader finds overmuch reiteration and repetition, he must kindly bear with me for the sake of his less keen-witted fellows.

2. Success or failure technically (and therefore musically) depends on a clear understanding and due mastery of these Forearm Rotatory-adjustments. Just here, however, we find perhaps more vagueness and misunderstanding than anywhere else. In spite of all that I have written and lectured on this very point, I am still persistently and stupidly misrepresented as dealing solely with rotatory MOVEMENTS — movements which had already been recognized and approved "for occasional use" in tremolos, etc., half a century ago! Whereas, throughout, I am referring to rotatory actions or stresses, inactions and reactions, mostly *unaccompanied by any movements whatsoever.*

Not Movements, but hidden actions.

3. Let us be quite clear then, to begin with, that my discoveries on this point do *not* refer merely to the actual rotatory *movements* before-mentioned, but, on the contrary, deal particularly with those *invisible* changes of state rotationally (momentary reversals or repetitions of stress and relaxation rotationally) which, although *unseen,* are needed for every note we play, whether we know of them or not, and ever have been needed, and ever will be — so long as keyboards are used. The fact is, that no player *ever has been* successful, nor could be, without the closest conscious or unconscious obedience to these very laws of Forearm-rotation, which although mostly *unseen* in their incidence, are nevertheless aurally and physically only too patent and inexorable.

4. As these all-important alternations and repetitions of rotational *stress* are comparatively rarely disclosed to the eye (being usually unaccompanied by *any rotational movement whatsoever*) and, being thus *hidden,* they have totally escaped attention or recognition, alike by players and teachers during all these past centuries of keyboard use.

Note. — The trouble all along has been, that since these *exertions* were not disclosed by movements, they completely escaped notice; and teachers of the past, unaware of these facts, were therefore unable to help their pupils easily to achieve technical mastery.

Correct *Doing* was therefore only achieved in rare cases by the musically and physically supersensitive, who were able to *sense* the physical needs through their own musical insistence, and through repeated experimental failure to ultimate success. But what a pitiable waste of time!

Successful players have always obeyed rotation:

5. Obviously, *all* players in the past, who successfully happened to master their instrument, must also have perfectly fulfilled these inexorable hidden changes in the Forearm stresses rotationally, although unaware they were obeying any natural laws. Yet such Master-artists (as always) were but few and far between; all the rest lumbered along with supposed irremediably "stiff" limbs, and supposed "weak" fourth and fifth fingers.

The ignorant use rotatory-exertions all the time:

6. Clearly realize that the fault of the unsuccessful player is *not* that he "does not use Rotation" (as often imagined!) but that, on the contrary, he *does* use Rotation most of the time *too much*, and does so violently and stiffly, and in fact has not learnt to OMIT rotatory-exertion when he should, and does not apply it *freely* when its application *is* needed. Indeed it cannot be reiterated too often, that without *freedom* rotationally — as everywhere else — there never has been any Easy Technique, nor can there be in the nature of things.

Forearm Rotation in daily avocations:

7. Moreover, Forearm rotatory-actions are not a special process, solely applicable for piano playing. Quite the contrary, for Forearm rotatory-exertions and relaxations are used everywhere in our daily lives. A few instances: You have to apply them when you bring your fork down to your plate, prongs downwards, and again when you bring your food to your mouth — unless you impolitely use your fork as a spoon! In writing, it is

the *invisible* rotatory exertion of your Forearm which turns your hand over, and which presses your pen upon the paper. You turn your door-handle, your key in its lock — you apply the rotational force *invisibly* until the door-handle or the key gives way, and discloses the true nature of the exertion in movement. Obviously, you wind your watch by *visibly* disclosed rotatory exertions. The screwdriver and the bradawl need Forearm rotatory-actions, both *visible* and *invisible*.[1]

You use it (mostly invisibly) when you play Tennis, Golf or Cricket; and you cannot hold your Billiard-cue without its constant help.

As a final example, you cannot properly press your bow on your Violin or 'Cello strings, without such *invisible* rotatory-exertion of the Forearm, freely given! Hence so much bad bowing, since this fact has been overlooked by teachers, through ignorance of such *invisible* rotatory actions.

Invisible rotatory-exertions and the Bow-arm

NOTE. — I have heard of Violinists and 'Cellists who despaired of attaining a free action of the bow-arm, but who, after only six weeks' accidental practice *at the Piano* of my "*First Solo Book*" and "*Pianist's First Music-making*," found, to their astonishment, that they had cured a life-long fault — rotational stiffness of the bow-arm, and had acquired a free, full tone!

8. There is, then, hardly any action in everyday life that does not largely depend upon visible or invisible Forearm rotatory-help; and when we come to so delicate an operation as Piano-playing, the least disobedience to its laws inevitably mars all our playing.

The Nature of the Action:

9. Yet, strictly speaking, there is *no such thing* as true Forearm rotation. Not "Rotation" in the sense that the Forearm itself rotates *as a whole*, with the Elbow as a pivot — as it seems to the eye.

[1] No doubt screws were given right-hand threads, because rotatory-actions and movements were found easier outwards (towards the little-finger side) than inwards (towards the thumb), and very possibly this fact influenced clock-makers to choose a "clockwise" movement for the hands on their dials!

The fact is, that you can only "rotate" the Forearm *at its wrist-end*, and the wrist-joint and hand turn along with it; and you can only rotate about half a turn. It is really a *twisting* process of the Forearm-bones.

10. The Forearm consists of two bones, normally lying side by side. These are pivoted both at the Elbow and at the Wrist-joints; you can feel their position by touching the elbow, and the hand at the wrist.

Now, when you turn (or "rotate") your hand into its playing position, palm downwards, you twist the outer of these two bones, the "radius," upon the inner bone, the "humerus," just as you can twist one finger over another. In this way you obtain that partial rotation of the wrist by which the hand is swung over into its playing position.

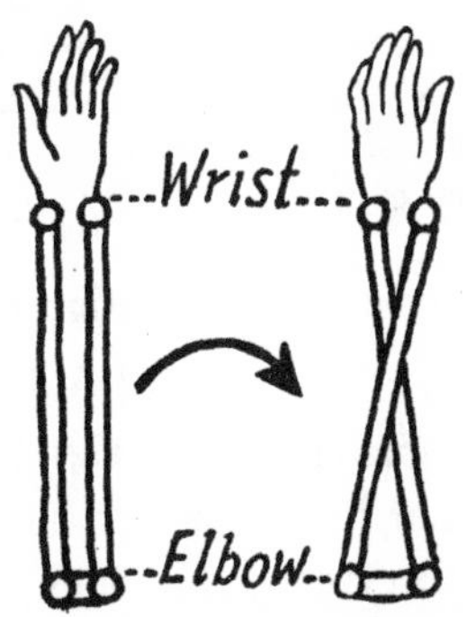

Diagrammatic Representation of the Two Forearm Bones of the Left Arm, before rotation and after.

11. Obviously, *everyone* (whether he understands Rotation or not) is *compelled* (and always has been compelled) to make this rotatory *movement* to bring his hand into the playing position, palm downwards. He is also compelled to *continue* a slight, although now *invisible*, exertion (rotationally) to retain his hand thus in level position; although the hand itself may in the meantime be lying quite loose and inactive on the keyboard. Moreover, to sound the thumb-note at all strongly, he is compelled momentarily to *increase* the rotatory-exertion of the Forearm inwards, so that the thumb may be amply helped to move its key down efficiently.

Again a double muscular action:

12. Evidently we also possess "strong" and "weak" muscles rotationally, just as in the case of the finger. The hand is evidently turned over into its playing-position (or "supination")

by the exertion of *both* the "strong" and "weak" muscles concerned in Forearm-rotation; whereas the "weak" muscles evidently suffice to retain it thus turned over, and the "strong" muscles may therefore promptly and completely stop work.

NOTE. — Obviously, it is this prompt and complete *cessation* of the *strong*, "inward-twisting" muscles that has led to the delusion that *no* muscular exertion is needed to retain the hand in its level playing position.

To help the thumb to sound its note (as already noted) a momentary action of the "strong" muscles is needed. The application of these "strong" muscles is therefore always intermittent and *momentary;* whereas the action of the "weak" muscles *may* be continuous for a time. Realize also, that even in *forte*, it is actually but a comparatively gentle exertion of the Forearm rotationally, that is needed. This is not noticeable unless attention is drawn to it. In fact, as already said, *none* of the exertions used in playing should ever be really violent. If they are, you may be sure you are playing stiffly, and badly!

Timing the cessation of Rotation:

13. Now, the trouble is, if this exertion *inwards* (momentarily required to help the thumb) is instead CONTINUED *at full strength*, then the Basis for the action of the *other fingers* is taken away from them; and they will then seem weak and incapable. Hence the invention of those thousands of futile exercises designed to overcome this supposed "weakness" of these fingers. Whereas we now know, that these supposed "weak" fingers are rendered quite "strong," the very moment this unneeded and paralyzing (but unseen) exertion rotatorily *towards the thumb* is ceased.

NOTE. — Such exertion towards the thumb may, however, be so very slight that we are likely to *overlook* it. Any exertion, nevertheless, *in the wrong direction*, will here inevitably impair the efficacy of the finger next used. Be sure therefore that you avoid any such *residue* of rotatory exertion in the *wrong direction*, even from the "weak" rotation muscles! It is owing to non-comprehension of this point that has arisen the superstition as to the supposed "weakness" of the fourth and fifth fingers at the Piano. Hence, also, so much sticky, clumsy and uncertain Technique, generally. Remember, these fingers are indeed rendered helpless so long as you continue a strong rotational exertion towards the thumb after it is played, and thus *deprive* those other fingers of the necessary *basis* for their action against their keys; whereas these fingers are instantly transformed into "strong" ones, provided that when you wish to use them you are careful to eliminate (inhibit, or cease) any residue of unneeded rotatory exertion *towards the thumb* — even of the "weak" rotation-muscles!

As a matter of fact, these supposed "weak" fingers themselves are naturally really stronger at the Piano than the thumb itself — *with its sideway action*, provided you do not spoil their effectiveness by leaving your forearm rotationally stiff, or even antagonistic to their well-being, pianistically.

Rotatory relaxation often suffices:

14. With the hand lying loosely on the keyboard the hand will quite naturally *roll upward* onto its side (with the little finger as a pivot) when you cease the slight rotatory exertion towards the thumb. Now, if at that very moment, however, you sufficiently exert the little finger, it will act as a strut, and will thus *prevent* the hand from rolling upward. You cannot see any rotatory movement, but you can *feel* the stress in the direction of the little finger, and how this is thereby helped.

15. For soft notes, *cessation* of all the rotatory exertion towards the thumb hence suffices to give the little finger the necessary *basis* for its work in sounding that soft note. But when more tone is required, then you must, BESIDES *ceasing the exertion towards the thumb*, also *add* a rotatory *exertion* towards the little-finger side, to enable you sufficiently to exert that finger.

The relationship of Rotatory-help to Rotatory Movement

NOTE. — To recapitulate: Be sure to realize through *experiment at the keyboard*, that if you *cease* the exertion Inwards (towards the thumb) this will leave the forearm and hand free to roll over Outwards (towards the little finger), and that this tumbling-over *tendency* of the forearm, thus caused *by relaxation*, can provide for more tone from your little finger than you would at first credit, with so little Basis for it. For greater tone, however, you must, in addition, *exert* the forearm outwards, although this rotative exertion is not necessarily displayed as *movement*, neither in this case nor the former one. As everywhere else in Technique, *movement* or its absence is no criterion whatever that you are doing rightly or wrongly. For instance, if you cease the rotatory exertion towards the thumb (as just discussed), the hand would naturally fall over to its side, but such rotatory movement will be *prevented* if you accurately time a sufficient exertion of the little finger (or other finger) at that moment, and you then have only a finger-*movement* with the key, while the rotational *relaxation* is not in the least disclosed to the eye.

That is, the rotatory change towards the little finger will not be *seen*, if you hide it by a *sufficient* exertion (and movement) of the little-finger, or fourth finger or any other finger at that moment. On the other hand, the exertion of the finger itself will be *hidden*, if you *outbalance* it during key-descent by a greater exertion (and movement rotationally) of the Forearm — and you then have rotative *movement* (or "Rotation-touch") in place of finger movement (or "finger-touch") with the key.[1] In slower passages (as beforesaid) actual rocking or rotatory movements may optionally be employed, but in really quick passages there is no time for such. In short: Finger-*movements* are usually preferable in quick passages, but of course with the proper individual Forearm-stresses invisibly applied, along with the exertion of each individual finger.

Direction of Rotatory-help:

16. Realize next, that the *direction* of rotatory help is always *from* the finger last used, and *towards* the finger being used — and you must always supply such rotatory help with perfect *freedom*.

17. Thus, when a passage moves melodically alternately upwards and downwards, the rotational stresses are alternately Inwards and Outwards. Try the following: —

18. *Per contra*, when the melodic movement proceeds in the *same* direction, as in a straight-on five-finger exercise, then you must *repeat* your rotative stresses in the direction of the passage, instead of alternating them.

Now it is easy to realize that in repeating the same note you must repeat the same stress rotationally; yet it is not so easy when you have to repeat the same rotational stresses, but with *different fingers*. Thus: —

In the straight-on five-finger succession of notes, evidently you must help your thumb by a rotatory exertion Inwards — towards it — during the moment of moving the key. But when you use your index-finger after it, you must reverse all this — the Inward rotatory exertion must cease,

[1] *See* Chapter XIV, "On Nomenclature."

and a *relaxation* Outwards (or even an *exertion* Outwards) must replace the Inward-stress while you depress the key with that index-finger. For the next note (played by the middle-finger) the index-finger *serves as a pivot* (from either the surface or depressed level of the keyboard), and rotational help for it is again outwards; therefore you must *repeat* what you did for the last note. The ring-finger needs another similar *repetition* of the outward rotational-impulse (with pivot on third finger), and the fifth finger likewise (from fourth finger). Thus, after the thumb (with its Inward rotation) you have *four* Outward impulses (or stresses) rotationally; and when returning (*after* the little finger with its Outward impulse) you must then provide *four* inward impulses rotationally to help these fingers. *Refer* to the Examples given on p. 22 of EPITOME.

19. Taken slowly, you can show these stresses by actual rotatory *movements* each time, as directed. The hand, in this case, *turns back* (each time) before each rotatory-*movement*, and then turns again in the direction of (*and along with*) the next finger you play.

20. In a quick passage, however, such rotatory-*movements* cannot be attempted — there is not time for them.

Instead, the rotational-stresses are here completely disguised, hidden and replaced by *finger movements*. Nevertheless, you must supply the necessary help individually for each note by *invisible* forearm rotative exertions or relaxations, precisely as you do when you allow actual rotative *movements* to accompany each note.

21. The law hence becomes clear, that the *direction* of rotation (whether accompanied by actual rotatory-movement or not) is always *in the Direction of the new finger* and *away from* the last finger, which each time becomes the pivot for the new action.

NOTE. — Thus, when you play the Middle-finger *after* the Thumb, rotational help is given to it *outwards*, whereas when you play it after the Little-finger, rotational help is *inwards* — towards the Thumb.

Rotatory direction with thumb under a finger:

22. The rule applies with equal force when you turn a finger over the thumb, unexpected although it may seem. Therefore, to help a finger turned over the thumb, you must still give the invisible or visible rotatory help *outwards* (towards the little-finger side), in spite of the fact that the note sounded by the finger is on the wrong side of the thumb.

Thus, in a shake played with a finger turned over the thumb, you should give alternate rotations Inwards and Outwards — whether visible or not. Thus: —

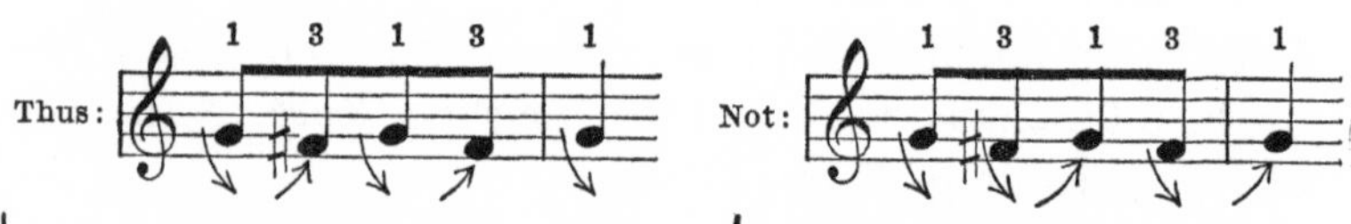

↘ here signifies Rotation towards thumb, and ↗ signifies Rotation towards little finger

Try it with rotation supplied first in the correct direction and then in the wrong direction. It is quite convincing!

Bad Scales:

23. Much scale-playing, etc., is uneven and sticky, because this rule has not been grasped.

This rule, however, is precisely reversed when you turn a *long finger over a short one*, as in double-notes scales, etc. Hence, when the middle-finger is turned over the fifth, you must here help the middle-finger by a rotational-stress towards the *thumb*-side!

24. In the Epitome I have noted the *first steps* towards acquiring this required co-ordination between Forearm and Finger, and it is useless to reprint them here.

Note. — These First Steps (for Young and Old) are more fully dealt with in my "*Nine Steps towards Finger-individualization*" (Oxford University Press); "*Child's First Steps*" (Joseph Williams); "*Pianist's First Music Making*" (Oxford University Press) and "*First Solo Book*," etc. (Oxford University Press).

Some additional warnings may, however, here be useful:

The purpose of Rotation:

25. In the meantime, do not forget to bear in mind the ultimate *purpose* of these rotational stresses and relaxations. Whether allowed to become visible as actual *rocking* movements or not, the purpose is to *help the fingers* in their work by correct rotational stresses, and not to impede them by wrong ones. Therefore, do not forget *to exert the fingers themselves.* If you forget that, all is lost!

Rotation-stresses must be given freely:

26. Remember, the rotatory possibilities of the forearm must always be applied at their free-est. That is, always *without* the exertion of *both* "pronation" and "supination" muscles at the same moment — in plain English, without exerting the forearm rotationally *both outwards and inwards at the same moment* — which would create a technique-destroying muscular conflict. You must contrive to send your *nerve-message* solely to one set of muscles, and must not allow some of it to leak or stray over to the opposite *or "antagonistic" side.*

NOTE. — In short, when you use *your arm* rotationally, be sure to exert it *only* in the required direction, and strictly inhibit the opposite exertion of it.

Passages by similar motion made "difficult" by rotatory conflict:

27. Such antagonistic action is, however, very likely to arise in passages where the two hands move by *similar motion* melodically. Here the rotatory impulses are needed for the most part in *contrary* direction in the two hands. Hence such passages are often found not so easy to play as to write! The *direction* of rotation is confused by the two hands moving alike melodically — and our ear actually may mislead us here. Hence "stiffening" ensues. This difficulty vanishes forthwith when this rotatory *contrariness* is duly recognized.

28. Moreover, this tendency thus to make "difficulties" may also supervene when the two hands are not played simultaneously, but when a melodically-alike passage is repeated in close succession by the two hands, as in a canon.

Also applies, when hands played in succession

NOTE. — Play through the first sixteen bars of Bach's C-sharp major Prelude, from the first Book of the Forty-eight; and you will feel that there is a great temptation to play the theme in its left-hand version with the *same* rotatory impulses as before used for the right hand, thus leading to its impairment and your confusion!

Passages by contrary motion first:

29. Because of these reasons, co-ordination between forearm rotation and fingers should first be studied *in passages needing a reversal*, rotationally, each time from note to note; and when the hands are first played together, passages should be chosen, so far as possible, which need the rotational help in *similar* direction in both hands, and which, therefore, move melodically *by contrary motion.*

30. In the early stages — both in the case of a real beginner, and, in the far worse case, of one who has been playing upside-down technically for years, this practice of passages by contrary motion melodically, and with constant reversals from note to note, rotationally, should be insisted upon for a while — since in this way the rotatory adjustments are more likely to be provided correctly, almost instinctively. Studies and pieces which exemplify such conditions should therefore be chosen. Music for the student, at this early stage, should also be *written* in accordance with these principles.

NOTE. — I have myself tried to set a good example for composers in this respect, but it is not easy to evolve interesting matter under such onerous restrictions. The reader may, however, be referred to my "*Playthings for Little Players,*" Book I, and my "*First Solo Book*" (Oxford University Press). Several numbers in these works conform quite strictly to these rather severe restrictions. The *Preface* to these sets of little pieces fully explains these desirable restrictions. Also, in "*The Pianist's First Music Making*" (Oxford University Press), the dry first steps are made interesting by the addition of a Duet accompaniment, for the teacher. These I consider to be quite a manifestation of genius on the part of my collaborator here — Felix Swinstead.

Stiffness possible, while apparently passive:

31. It is even possible to make this mistake of antagonistic and self-defeating rotational actions, while your hand, itself, lies quite loosely and inactive upon the keyboard. Try it! Let your hand lie loosely on the keyboard-surface, and see whether your forearm is really quite free rotationally, and is not perhaps slightly stiffened-up.[1] This rotatively "free" condition of the forearm is always a pleasant sensation — or absence of sensation — to a Pianist, since it gives him confidence that he is going to play easily — and is not going to play with irksome, troublesome technical restraint.

Upper-arm *re* Forearm Rotation:

32. Another and perhaps important warning is, never to substitute *upper*-arm rotation-stresses where those of the Forearm are called for.

33. Understand the distinction: It is possible to bring your hand into playing *position* by raising the upper arm and elbow sideways and outwards with the hand upon the keyboard. Thus the sockets of the two forearm bones *at the elbow* are themselves turned outwards, and brought almost perpendicularly one over the other.

True, you *could* try to help the thumb to sound its note in this — ridiculous — way; but to substitute such clumsy action in place of the natural and easy one of Forearm-rotation is obvious folly!

Note. — It is necessary, however, to allude to this possibility, since a comparatively recent author has seriously suggested this Upper-arm rotatory process (with its digging action) *in place of* Forearm-rotation — which he pronounces to

[1] *Free* from all antagonistic exertion, but *not* without that slight exertion of the "*small*" muscles, required to keep the hand in its level position!

be "impossible in quick passages"! — and since copied elsewhere. This, of course, only proves that the author has had no inkling of the real meaning of my Forearm-rotation teaching; and imagines it to refer solely to rotational *Movements*, as so wildly misunderstood also by some not unrecent German writers! *See Additional Note III*, "On Forearm-rotation Misunderstandings," etc.

Upper-arm *v.* Forearm-rotation Test:

34. If you are not quite sure of this distinction between Upper- and Fore-arm rotation, refer to the following convincing "Test-exercises":

1. Fold your arm in front of your chest. Poise it nicely and freely. Now rotate the forearm, while thus in front of you, as easily and freely as you *should* do when executing a tolerably quick tremolo. With the arm thus bent at right angles, you are bound to use solely *forearm* rotation, and Upper-arm rotation is altogether "cut out" for the time being.
2. Next, stretch your whole arm straight out in front of you, and again, with the Forearm only, execute your free and easy tremolo movements.
3. And now, instead of this comfortable Forearm-rotatory tremolo, try to substitute a twisting of the whole arm from the shoulder-socket — Upper-arm rotation. Although you may partially succeed in doing this (but accompanied by very ugly and clumsy circular movements of the Elbow itself), you will still find that the Forearm rotatory-vibration is incomparably more easy and natural.
4. Now apply the rotatory tremolo *of the Forearm* to the keyboard itself, *via* any two fingers.

Finally, again try to execute it instead by means of Upper-arm rotation, and the folly of this mistake is amusingly evident — for it would need a circling elbow, and would be sure to be stiff at that! Carefully eliminate any such false and ugly technique from your technical scheme.[1]

[1] *See* "Additional Note," No. III, "On Rotation-misunderstandings," where these experiments are amplified.

Octaves, etc., need Rotation *invisibly* provided:

35. FOR OCTAVES, and passages in double-notes (double-thirds, sixths, etc.), the law is, that the rotatory conditions must be *remade each time*, individually, for each double-note effect; but in the meantime *do not forget* the required exertions of the two fingers concerned! Double-third passages, rotationally, are often a cross between octave and single note playing. In some places the rotational effect has merely to be repeated, whereas in others a *single finger* acts as a pivot, and the rule as to single notes, rotationally, then supervenes. Difficulty in octave passage playing is most frequently traceable to disobedience of this law. *Remake* the required set of conditions each time for each octave, and the difficulty forthwith vanishes. Give sufficient rotatory-exertion each time towards the thumb to enable this adequately to sound its note; and also, be sure to provide for each successive octave, individually, the exertion each time of the thumb *and* little finger during key-descent.

The folly of "hand-forming" for octaves

NOTE. — The hand cannot be *"formed"* for the octave passage, as the old teachers so fondly imagined — and hence wrought so much mischief technically. To attempt any setting or *"fixation"* of the fingers, would only result in stiff fingers and hands, unable to do their work, and a stiff forearm unable to fulfill its duties. In the old days, only geniuses could play so-called "lightning octaves" — because their healthy instinct compelled them to disobey their teachers! Nowadays, however, every student can and should be directly taught this "great secret" — of gliding along the surface of the keyboard, and for each octave remaking a momentary rotational exertion to help the momentary finger-and-hand exertions.

"Finger-work" defined:

36. We realize, then, that not only is there *no* "Finger-technique" without Hand- and Arm-help in some form or other, but also, that the *Forearm rotatory help* must always be provided for every note played, whatever the form of touch used.

NOTE. — So-called "Finger-work" is never finger-exertion only, but always implies finger-exertions either invisibly or visibly backed up by Forearm rotative-stresses and hand-exertions, *plus* the *other* arm elements, when and where required.

Or, we might go even further, and define "Finger" passage-work as consisting of: —

"*Individually applied FOREARM-rotation impulses TRANSMITTED to the keyboard by the OBEDIENT exertion of the finger and hand for each note,*"— that is: Forearm-rotational and Hand-and-Finger impulses accurately *timed* for each key-descent, and optionally helped by the other arm elements when required.

Rotatory Movements:

37. As to rotatory *movements* themselves (as indicated earlier) these are optional. During slow passages they are not only harmless, but may even be particularly helpful. Whereas, in quick passages they may become a hindrance, and even impossible, and finger-*movements* must here be substituted — but do not in the meantime lose the benefit of the INVISIBLE rotational help given individually for each note.

38. Whether, in the end, you choose to exhibit rotative Movements in a passage, or instead choose finger or hand Movements, depends upon which of these three components you place in the ascendant at the moment.

NOTE. — For further information on Rotation, read the *Additional Note*, No. III, and also refer to "*Forearm-Rotation*" and "*Child's First Steps*" (Joseph Williams). Also "*First Solo Book*" (with its Preface); "*Playthings for Little Players*" (two books), and "*Pianist's First Music Making*" (three books) and "*Nine Steps towards Finger-Individualization*" (Oxford University Press).

Rotational Analysis of passages:

39. Finally, since correct Rotation is so all-important, whenever a passage "goes doubtfully" play it through once or twice so slowly that you can *analyse and re-analyse* the DIRECTION of the succession of its rotatory-impulses. Do this so slowly that you can *actually* rock the hand from side to side for each note — a rolling or rocking movement *towards* each note, after first rocking backwards. Thus you impress upon your mind

the *direction* of the rotational help which eventually you have to provide *invisibly* and WITHOUT actual *rotatory movement*, and yet correct in the incidence of its rotational stresses for every note.

NOTE. — As there has been a good deal of misunderstanding (and worse) as to the true nature of the Forearm-rotation Element (and apparently still is in some benighted quarters), I *again* refer the interested reader to the *Additional Note*, No. III, which fully deals with all the points raised.

Chapter VII

ON THE MOVEMENTS OF TOUCH

— *during and before Key-descent*

1. Ample preliminary movements *to* the key are not to be discouraged, provided the *Tempo* of the passage admits of such. Often they are quite helpful when used in the right way.

Right and Wrong ways of reaching the Key:

The right way is to reach the keys always quite gently with your finger-tips. The resistance of the key can then be gauged on the way down; whereas, the wrong way is to "lift" the fingers, etc., "so that the key may be hit down" — a now exploded theory of the past.

2. Remember, it is only after your finger-tip has reached the surface of the key that the true tone-producing action must "follow-on." There need not necessarily be any break between the *two distinct* activities of reaching the key and bringing the same into motion. The finger-movement *to* the key should always be quite light; whereas, the tone-producing stress *during* the "follow-on" may be quite forcible at times.

3. Thus, for instance, when you turn your hand over into its playing position, your thumb reaches the key-surface quite gently; but to sound its note, the forearm rotatory exertion as well as the thumb exertion must both be materially increased during the moment of Key-descent.[1]

4. The Movement *during* key-descent may, in this case, be either a movement of the thumb, or of the forearm rotationally. Movement of the *Thumb* results when its exertion outbalances that of the Forearm; whereas an actual rotatory movement of the Forearm results when that element is in the ascendant.

Finger-lifting and striking:

To teach finger-lifting so as to be able to "strike" better, was one of the worst fallacies and superstitions of the teachers of the Past; and this, because it precludes any judging of the key's resistance, and therefore also precludes musical playing—if really carried out.

Reiterated notes:

5. For *quickly reiterated* notes do not leave the surface of the key at all; and for very soft effects do not even allow the keys to rise fully to surface-level.

6. If you have already formed the habit of ridiculously pulling up your fingers, it is best for a time never to raise the tips beyond key-level, until you have made a saner habit—that of taking hold *upon* the key so that you can use it to make Music.

NOTE.—The really musical pupil of course never did obey such injunctions, and his ear and his instincts instead forced him to play correctly, in spite of his "teaching"!

7. For a slow succession of notes, the whole arm (or the forearm only) may be moved; for quicker passages, the hand; and for the quickest, finger-movement only is available.

[1] Neither the "strong" muscles of the Forearm, rotationally, need participate until the key is reached, nor those of the finger.

8. Further details of Movement are given in the *Epitome*, Section VII, page 27, to which refer. Also *see* Note to ¶12 of next chapter.

***Test movements not* necessarily essential:**

9. Certain vertical movements of the wrist-joint, with hand on the keyboard and elbow quiescent, are recommended in my "Relaxation Studies" in learning to "aim" the tone-producing impulse required in "Weight-touch."[1] I find, however, that these *testing movements* have been misunderstood by some (or purposely misinterpreted) to signify that I insist on such movements as a *necessary* part of the technical process! Must I repeat for the *n*th time that such up-and-down movements of the wrist have been suggested only as *test*-movements *during the learning stage*, and that I have NOT recommended them during actual performance except as an occasional reference-test for freedom?

The exercises in question certainly form an admirable way of acquiring that necessary co-ordination (and *timing* during key-descent) between finger-and-hand exertion and lapse of arm-weight, needed to ensure success technically — but they are *not* a necessary part of Technique.

NOTE. — The full weight of the arm (full lapse of the arm) can indeed be quite well applied during tone-production without showing the slightest hint of any *movement* of the arm or wrist whatever! The arm can be either fully or partially relaxed irrespective of any actual *movement* of it — provided the finger-and-hand exertions are ample and are properly *timed* — or "aimed" to the tone.

The same question arises with regard to the constant reversals and repetitions of the Forearm-rotational conditions required from note to note. They *may* be allowed to become evident as actual movements, or they may be *totally hidden from view*, while a *movement* of the finger only may be substituted. In fact, most of the processes of tone-production need not be disclosed as movements, and *vice versa*, visible, actual *movements* form no sure indication of the actual processes employed or needed in Touch.

---

[1] *See* Section II, page 9, *Relaxation Studies* (Bosworth).

Chapter VIII

THE PROCESS OF HOLDING NOTES DOWN

— *the Right way and the Wrong way.*

1. As important as the proper *sounding* of notes is also the proper mode of holding them down once they are sounded.

2. All accuracy, musically, and ease in keyboard progression is instantly ruined if you hold notes down wrongly, by continuing the *same* force needed to sound them — except in *pp*; it will ruin Agility, and accuracy of tone-response to your wish. As already insisted upon, however powerfully you may need to move the key down, once it is down it must be held quite lightly. This is a first law of Technique.

3. Now recall that you can only satisfactorily sound a note when you actuate the finger by its "strong" muscles — which are situated on the forearm. During the flash of key-descent you will therefore quite properly feel a *slight tension* on the underside of the wrist-joint.

4. But in sounding the note you are *also* using the "small" muscles of the finger, which are situated on the inside of the hand.

Notes held only by the weak muscles:

Now, it is imperative to learn to hold notes down *solely* by continuing the action of these last, the so-called "small" muscles (or "lumbricales") of the finger.[1]

5. Remember, precisely the same applies with regard to the Hand. When helping the finger-exertion by hand-exertion during key-descent, you may use the "strong" flexor muscles of the

[1] *See* Chapter V, ¶40 — on the late John Hunter's discoveries of the Dual nature of the muscular equipment. Herein lies a great part of the secret of good, easy technique.

hand; whereas to hold the notes down these are no longer required.

6. The moment, therefore, that you have completed the action of sounding a note, you must instantly cease the action of the "strong" muscles — with their slight straining across the wrist, underneath; and you must fulfil the holding of that note in *tenuto* or *legato* solely by the "weak" (or "small") muscles, with complete cessation therefore of the strain across the wrist-joint, and it will then *feel* as if the holding were done on the underside of the fingers themselves — in fact, it may seem as if there were no effort at all!

Simplicity of transition from powerful to gentle effort:

7. This complete and accurately-timed TRANSITION from the powerful sounding-effort to the gentle holding-effort, which I have shown to be requisite for all musical playing, seemed a rather complex process before the advent of Dr. John Hunter's wonderful discovery of the *dual* nature of the muscular equipment.[1]

We now see why this *transition* is a perfectly natural process, perfectly simple, neat, and easy to control.

Thus, to recapitulate: in sounding the note, we can quite forcibly apply both the "strong" and "weak" sets of in-folding ("flexing") muscles both of the finger AND hand, and we can nevertheless completely cease the action of the *strong* flexors (both of finger and hand) at the right moment, and then carry on solely with the *weak* ones to hold our note down — a perfectly simple process!

Briefly: exert your finger and hand as fully as you like during Key-descent to attain that duly required acceleration just up to the point of sound, and then completely cease all that work, and hold on to the key solely by that gentle elastic action of finger and hand which leaves knuckles, wrist, and fingers quite elastic.

[1] *See* again Note to ¶ 40 of Chapter V.

In other words: Exert the strong flexors both of the finger and hand during key-descent, but *hold* the notes solely by the continuance of the weak ones.

NOTE. — Remember that excellent example of the Oyster, quoted by *Hunter*, and it should not prove an insuperable difficulty for an intelligent would-be Piano-student to learn thus to sound a note rightly, and yet hold it correctly afterwards even at his first lesson!

8. This law of holding lightly (by means solely of the "weak" finger muscles) applies equally, whether you hold the notes fully depressed (as for Tenuto or Legato) or whether you hold the notes instead *at their surface-level*, as in *staccato*, and in all light Agility passages.

Tests for holding rightly:

9. The TEST for correct action in this respect is found in watching for *mobility* at the *knuckle-joint*. If you can freely sway the knuckle of the hand up-and-down while holding the notes down, this proves that you are using the right finger-muscles — the "small" ones; whereas, the slightest impediment in this floating, vertical movement at the Knuckle, is proof that you are using the wrong ones. Frequently test in this way, even during the actual performance of passages.[1]

NOTE. — But this does not mean that you *must* always sway the knuckles up and down while playing! Such swaying merely serves as a visible TEST to ensure knuckle-mobility — which last is usually *invisible*.

10. To demonstrate the possibility of this two-fold action, experiment as follows: —

Clench your hand somewhat firmly, pressing your finger-tips well into the palm of your hand. Notice, that while you continue doing this, there is *a slight strain* across the wrist, on its under-side. Now move the hand slightly and very carefully up-and-down, and you will notice this tension better. Now completely *relax* this straining across the wrist-joint, while

[1] *See* ¶ 13, on the holding-notes Test.

still leaving the tips of your fingers gently in contact with the palm of your hand. It is solely this second form of quite light, gentle pressure that is required of your fingers, when you hold down the notes of your Pianoforte correctly.

You can also test for this correct holding of notes, by seeing whether the knuckles can float up-and-down while you hold the notes down.

Further Tests:

11. Test also for mobility at the wrist-joint. There must never be any so-called (and mis-called) "fixing." Such "fixing" *should* instead imply the sufficient exertion only of the folding-in muscles of the fingers, during the moment of key-descent, in conjunction with a down-exertion of the hand when required, and should never be allowed to degenerate into a general stiffening or fixing of the whole limb (owing to the use of antagonistic muscles) which inevitably destroys all Technique.

12. In my "Relaxation Studies" are described many other tests and exercises to assist in the acquisition of requisite skill in this particular respect. Very helpful are the *first two* quoted in Section I of that work.[1]

The Undulatory, Curvilinear, or "Kurven" Theories of Touch

Note. — These forward-and-backward Tests of the Arm, and up-and-down swayings of the Wrist-joint, which I there recommend (in my *Relaxation Studies*) solely as *tests*, are no doubt akin to the puerile "undulatory Theories of Touch" of some recent writers; but, whereas I put these (and rotational *Movements*) forward in 1911 as occasional Tests for Freedom at the knuckles and wrist-joint, these "undulatory theories" have been seriously proposed as an integral part (and explanation) of the processes of Touch in general!

As indicated elsewhere, these undulatory theories are obviously again the result of trying to analyse touch from the outside — from the movements exhibited by successful players. Almost every artist sooner or later develops certain amiable little fads of movement, quite unessential, but which he has accidentally associated with the sense of freedom in certain passages; such harmless movements are of course actually of the same nature as these very Tests, here alluded to. They are adopted by such artists simply as *Tests* for freedom at the knuckle and

[1] "*Relaxation Studies*," page 4, etc. (Bosworth).

wrist and for rotation, and which are therefore movements quite extraneous to the Act of Touch itself. The incapable analyst, however, comes on the scene (himself probably quite incapable of playing rightly) and imagines that these quite unessential movements form "The Great Secret" of the witnessed artist's success! And the poor student is then instructed when playing certain rising successions of notes (such as the ascending five-finger exercise) that he must wave his arms forwards, upwards, and roundwise (rotationally), and must, for the descending succession of notes, reverse these wriggles, and unwind himself.

But there is nothing new under the sun! Even LUDWIG DEPPE (born 1828), who was valiantly trying to break away from the horribly stiff pedagogy then in vogue, is found still using such empirical "Suggestion-devices" in his "Kurven" Theories — curvilinear (or "undulatory") up-and-down and rotational swayings, which he imagined to be a necessary part of the process of playing Arpeggios, etc.!

While such movements might optionally accompany passages successfully played, imitation of such (sometimes amiable) fads will certainly not necessarily conduce to the acquisition of correct habits of Key-treatment, nor do they give any inkling of the things that matter. Moreover, the fact is, that the public *does not enjoy them*, and is apt to become restless under the infliction.

The "Holding-notes" Test-exercise:

13. Perhaps the most important and useful of such Technical Tests are the age-known "*Holding-notes Exercises*." They must, however, be practised *correctly* in the way shown in my aforesaid "*Relaxation Studies*." Practised *wrongly*, as they mostly were in the past — with the notes held down "firmly" as we were told to do — they are bound to prove more baneful than any other *mis*-practised exercises. In fact, thus practised, they would tend to build up a sure bar to one's ever acquiring a correct Technique!

NOTE. — Holding the notes "at surface level" was certainly a step forward, but even with this improvement, the "Holding-notes" exercise is still bound to be dangerous, since one can hold one's hand quite stiffly while thus executing it!

The *only safeguard* is to insist on the test for freedom *at the knuckle-joint*. The proper mode of practice is fully explained in *Set* XIV, pp. 106 and 107 of these "*Relaxation Studies*" of mine, which see.

14. The most efficacious positions of this holding-notes Test are the three following ones, and they cover the ground.

Sound the *sf* note quite strongly by the *strong* finger muscles (and hand-exertion also) — but then at once hold it quite lightly by the *small* finger-muscles, so lightly indeed that your *knuckles* can be swayed up-and-down freely *as a Test* while you sound the subsequent notes. *See* next page:

15. The "*Throw-off*" and "*Float-off*" Test-exercises — and others — quoted under *Set* III, pages 24–33 of these "Relaxation Studies," incidentally also serve this very same purpose.

Chapter IX

THE BENT AND FLAT FINGER-ACTIONS

1. There are two quite opposite forms of finger-action possible, as already described in Chapter IV, ¶ 2, etc. Formerly this difference was but vaguely understood. Hence arose the terms "Bent-finger" and "Flat-finger," because of the *visual* difference when the finger is much raised from the keyboard, in its preliminary movement. *See* Chapter V, ¶ 2.

2. The point to understand is, that you can move towards the key and with the key, in two quite distinct and opposite ways. With either of these two actions, however, once the finger has fulfilled its movement, and the key is down, your finger *may* actually be equally more or less flat or bent. *See* the photographs given on page 34 of the Epitome.

A curling or uncurling action:

3. Thus, (*a*) you can exert or move your finger in a folding or curling-in direction; or (*b*) you can do the opposite thing, and open-out or uncurl the finger as it moves towards and with the key.

4. With the *folding-in* action against the key, you will in a measure exert a pulling or clinging action upon the key with the finger-tips; hence its designation "clinging-touch" (or flat-finger) because, if you lift the finger well beforehand, you will then start this folding-in action with the finger in a more or less straightened-out or flat preliminary position.

Clinging-finger, a gripping action:

5. This folding-in or "clinging" action is the most natural and generally useful one at the Piano. It is precisely the same action of the finger as in all our ordinary avocations when we grip hold of anything. It is the same action as folding your finger-tips into the palm of your hand; but at the Piano this complete folding-in of the finger is baulked, since the keyboard intervenes.

The Bent-finger unbends in moving down:

6. With the opposite action — the *unfolding* or opening-out action, you will, on the contrary, thrust or shove with your finger against the key — in place of that pulling of it towards you, which you experience with the "clinging" form of touch.

In this shoving, or *thrusting* action (as I have called it), if you start from a well-raised position, you will find that the finger is more or less fully bent or curved — hence its name; but when you move down towards (and with) the key, you actually open it out, or uncurl it, more or less. The nail-phalange (or nail-joint), however, here remains more or less vertical throughout.

7. This *thrusting* action of the finger is more artificial and complex than is the clinging or gripping action; and this, because when you descend towards (and with) the key by this

form of finger-action, you have actually to *raise* the two outermost portions of the finger (the nail and middle phalanges), *relatively to* the descending knuckle-phalange — indeed, a much more complex and conflicting action when compared to the natural gripping process of clinging or flat finger.[1]

Bent-finger needs Elbow forward:

8. Moreover, the bent or thrusting finger-action, being in the nature of a thrust or shove, has this disadvantage, that it needs, as a basis for its shove, either a forwardly poised or actually forwardly exerted *upper-arm*, or Elbow.[2]

In this case, however, you totally cut out any assistance from Upper-arm *weight*. Whereas with the clinging-finger, the Upper-arm can be relaxed more or less fully, thus providing a far more satisfactory basis for (pleasant) tone-making than does the "straight from the shoulder" action or bent finger, with its more or less forward driven Upper-arm and downward-acting Forearm.

9. As already pointed out (Chapter V, ¶33) this forwardly-poised Upper-arm, with its thrusting finger, is however sometimes required for soft light passages, since the weight is thus taken off the keyboard — provided you avoid any fore-arm *down-exertion* in the meantime.

With such poised condition of the Upper-arm you may *optionally* employ either "flat" or "bent" finger.

10. Note also, that with the clinging action you *may* have the finger almost or completely flat, straight, and therefore fully elastic, where a certain tone-quality or delicate tone-control demands this; whereas, with the thrusting finger-action the finger *must* remain more or less arched to the last — and therefore, more or less rigid, and inelastic — physically and tonally. *See* the photos of Finger-position given on page 34 of the EPITOME.

[1] In ordinary life, this thrusting action of the finger is rarely employed, except when pushing something away, or playing at marbles, etc.!

[2] No, this does NOT mean necessarily a *Movement* forward of the Elbow!

NOTE. — I myself, personally, hardly ever use anything but Flat-finger. Being gifted with really strong fingers, I can make quite a fine harsh noise when I wish it, even with the elastically-disposed Clinging finger!

Also, when I need a penetrating singing tone, I contract the clinging-finger well inwards until it is fully arched when the Key is down. This, however, does *not* constitute Bent-finger-action, although to the eye it may seem like it. *Forte* passages played by the old-fashioned rigid, bent finger sound an abomination to me, personally. But these things are matters of Taste, — either good, or bad!

The tonal effect of Flat *v.* Bent

For neat, sharp, "dry" (*i.e.* fully staccato) effects, the use of the Bent-finger is certainly appropriate, and such effects cannot so easily be produced by the Flat-finger.

A Recapitulation of Arm-condition *v.* Finger-condition:

11. Here recall, as shown in Chapter V under "The Six Arm-conditions," that these two opposite forms of finger-use also demand a correspondingly opposite *attitude* or *condition* of the Upper-arm, more or less marked according to the amount of tone. Thus: when you use the Clinging-finger, the implied *tendency* (not Movement!) of the Upper-arm is to fall away from the keyboard — while thus setting its whole weight more or less completely free (as a basis for the pulling action of the finger-tip against the key) during the moment of its descent.

12. For full tone in chords, or cantando and cantabile, this relaxation of the Upper-arm is more or less complete during each separate act of tone-touch.

13. For *fortissimo*,[1] you must *add* to this Relaxation of the Upper-arm also the down-exertion of the Forearm, during the moment of key-depression. But remember, you must nevertheless leave free the Upper-arm (with elastic Elbow therefore) when you thus employ this down-force (or *lifting-exertion!*) of the Forearm against the moving key, else your tone will become forced and ugly, and you will certainly lose all nicety of tone-control.

14. Remember also, that for very light passages, and also when holding notes down, or when feeling your way along the surface of the keyboard, that the nicely *poised* Upper-arm serves

[1] And also for certain penetrating singing tones.

best. In rapid passages there is no option, as there is not time for those *separate* lapses of the arm, which can be used in slower passages.

NOTE. — But with the "poised" arm, naturally the amount of tone available is far smaller than with *separate* Arm-lapses, etc., for each note; this is the reason why you cannot play rapid finger-passages with the same degree of tone as you can give in chords and *cantabiles*.

The tonal advantage of alternate hands for alternate notes

Hence also, the device of taking alternate notes in a rapid passage with *alternate hands*. The passage, technically, is thus at *half the speed* of its Sound-effect; and separate lapses of arm-weight here become possible for each note, with a correspondingly greater volume of tone.

15. With the *thrusting* action of the finger, the Upper-arm *condition* is bound to be of the "forward" type. Although no *movement* may here be visible, the *condition* of the Upper-arm is that of a push-forward, more or less.

NOTE. — In soft passages this may need merely a forward-poised Arm — with its *tendency* to *lift* the Upper-arm and Elbow forwards and upwards. For *fortes*, however, the tone cannot be thus produced without a marked forward-forcing exertion of the upper-arm, — a forward-swinging exertion. This, again, may be given without any *movement* to divulge or indicate its presence, since the arm-force may be completely taken up by the implicated finger, and may thus be hidden from view. Remember, however, that this forward pressure of the Upper-arm, while quite invisible, may yet *destroy* all tonal beauty, or nicety of tone-control.

16. Moreover, recall again, that with the Thrusting-finger you *cannot* have the help of upper-arm Weight, since you are supporting it off the keyboard! Due to this, is the curious contradiction, that this very condition of the Upper-arm (thus poised forwards) can also give you the *lightest possible effects* — provided you avoid any straight-down action of the Forearm in conjunction with this forward poise of the Upper-arm. *Refer* again to Chapter V.

Playing on tip-toe:

17. Very light and gossamer effects are in fact best produced by the arm in this fully poised condition, while the fingers, as it

were, *play on tip-toe.* With flat-topped fingers (as my own) one can play such delicately-light passages on the *very top* of the finger — with nails almost (or really) touching the keys; the finger being here so greatly curved that the nail-joint may actually be slightly bent inwards. With sharp-pointed fingers, however, this ballet-dancing device is impracticable!

18. As an example of its application, take those little "echo" effects required in an already soft passage, such as in the F minor Study of Chopin's, Op. 25, No. 2: —

The arm is here *so light* that the hand is "just bounced along" by the light *tip-toe* impulses of the fingers — and forearm, rotationally. Much of the eerie effect (as it should be) of the *Finale* of Chopin's B Flat Minor Sonata also depends on this particularly subtle kind of finger-technique. *See* Additional Note, No. XVIII, "An Alternate *ppp* Method."

19. You will have realized, that *except* in very light passage work you cannot help the Unfolding or Thrusting-finger by this forward action of the Upper-arm without also applying the Down-exertion of the Forearm, more or less forcibly.

It follows, if you do employ this triple combination at all *forcibly* (that is, with elbow forward and down-exertion of the forearm along with the thrusting finger), that you are then bound to produce a hard, harsh, nasty tone, more or less uncontrolled, since the whole limb is here in a totally inelastic, ungiving condition.

NOTE. — This hard, machine-like playing (or strumming?) seems to be the ideal of some so-called artists. The notes are just spat out like so many cherry stones, without inflection, and the result has nothing to do with the expression of Musical-feeling. The Radio and Gramophone, however, may perhaps be gradually educating the public to expect something better than this typewriter kind of playing. Perhaps, in the near future, the mere virtuoso will have to give way more and more to the true maker of Music!

Piano Typewriting

Duration also affected by these Finger-contrasts:

20. Moreover, in the same way that the flat (or clinging) Finger-technique (because of its elastic condition) renders easier that due *acceleration* of the key during descent (which therefore makes for delicacy of tone-control, and good quality), it also renders easier the attainment of *Non-abruptness in Duration-inflections*. That is, the elastic (flat) finger not only renders "gradual" key-descent easier, but it also influences key-ASCENT in the same way. With Thrusting-finger action one is therefore more likely to produce abrupt staccato than with Clinging-finger action; and abrupt staccatos (*Staccatissimos*) are comparatively rarely required, and may easily sound ugly and out of place.

21. Finally, remember, that both these ways of Finger-action can be achieved either by the application of the "small" muscles only, to hold the notes down, or in combination with a momentary use of the "strong" muscles, necessary to *produce* the tone.

Chapter X

HOW TO FIND THE RIGHT NOTES

Don't try to *see* the notes, *feel* them!

1. To find the right notes, however quick the passage, you must physically *feel your way*, and must do so each time FROM the last-played note, — you must sense the *Physical Intervals* on the keyboard as well as the *Melodic Intervals!* Thus successfully *feeling* your way along the keyboard from finger to finger, you gain perfect security, and *cannot* sound "wrong notes"!

NOTE. — The Blind are compelled thus to learn. Eyesight often proves an actual stumbling-block to one's Pianistic Education!

2. This "feel" of the surface of the keyboard depends mainly on the *true sense of touch* — the sense of contact.

3. This sense of *physical continuity* in passages should also apply in one's *Staccato*-passages, and equally in passages *broken between the hands.*

4. Thus, in all passages broken between the hands, be careful not to lose contact with the key *last played by one hand* until you have felt a place on the keyboard for the *first note of the next hand* — that is, until you have located the next note physically.[1]

5. Thus you attain a sense of physical-continuity and security during every passage. This *physical* continuity (corresponding to its musical continuity) may be felt either at the depressed level of the keyboard *in Legato*, or at surface-level in *Staccato;* and you also thus acquire a *physical* sense of the continuity of the phrase-unit itself.

Two examples, from Bach's "Chromatic Fantasia" and from my own "Moods of a Moment," are illustrations of this point, and follow on next page.

[1] Here refer to "*Musical Interpretation*" (Joseph Williams), Section II, page 51, for a full elaboration of this point, and all it implies.

From Bach's Chromatic Fantasia

From "Moods of a Moment," Matthay, Op. 11.

Thus, at the beginning of the above passage (from Bach's *Chromatic Fantasia*) do not quit the *D* with the left hand until your right-hand thumb has found its E, etc. Likewise, in the excerpt from "Moods of a Moment," *join* the thumbs and the ring-fingers respectively.

Take no "chances" in Skips and Octaves:

6. *Even in Skips* you must still feel your way along the keyboard — a *glissando,* as it were, at key-surface. This applies equally in Octave-passages — which, in a sense, consist of a succession of *glissando* skips. The rule to remember in Octave-playing is, that when the passage travels *outwards* (away from the centre of the keyboard), you must feel your way along with the thumb; whereas, when the passage moves *inwards*, then the fourth and fifth fingers must guide you.

7. We shall find that this is the main secret of cleanness in Octave-playing — in conjunction with proper *repetition* of the Forearm-rotation impulse, and finger-exertions individually given for each octave.

8. The double level of the keyboard (with its black and white keys) renders all this easier.

9. Until you gain this tactile sense of the keyboard you cannot play in a darkened room; and until you *can* play in a dark room your technique will ever remain unreliable, unsure and insecure.

On Lateral movements:

10. To enable you to move from note to note on the keyboard, you have to supply *sideway* (or horizontal) movements of the fingers, hand and arm — both of the upper-arm and the forearm. As these movements are visible, they are too obvious to need much explanation.[1]

11. There are, however, *three* points to notice: —

In skips

1. In taking skips within the compass of two octaves it is best NOT *to move the Elbow* (and Upper-arm), but to leave that stationary. To succeed in this, you must, before beginning the skip, turn the elbow out sufficiently, to enable you to reach the *furthest-out* note conveniently. *See* Octave-playing, ¶ 35, Chapter VI.

In turning over thumb, etc.

2. When your fingers have to be turned over your thumb (or *vice versa*) this requires a movement of the *hand* — with the thumb stationary. Whereas, when you move the thumb under a stationary finger, this requires a movement (sideways) both of the *wrist* and *forearm*.

[1] Some of the apparently simplest actions, however, are quite complex. For instance, moving the right arm and hand up the Keyboard, from its centre, seems a simple enough action, yet it can only be accomplished, muscularly, by the harmonious blending of *four distinct* muscular movements! Thus, (1), you must rotate the Upper-arm outwards (Upper-arm rotation); this, alone, however, would swing your arm and hand right up from the Keyboard in a quarter-circle! (2), You must therefore transform this *up*-movement into a *horizontal* one, by *lowering* the forearm; but this would entail turning the hand over outwards, and

3. When playing scales, etc., it is best to have the Wrist turned somewhat "outwards"—away from you; this allows of your turning the fingers over the thumb without disturbing the relative position of wrist and forearm during the passage.

For scales, etc.

"From," yet "Towards":

12. While thus *physically* always feeling your way FROM the last note to the next, you must nevertheless never forget also *rhythmically* to think and foresee your way FORWARDS, as insisted upon earlier; that is, forwards towards tone in key-depression, towards the next pulse-place in quick passages, towards the phrase-climax, and towards the climax of the whole movement.

13. Briefly, to find the right notes, you must always play "*from*" the last note, while to ensure the right *time* and *rhythm* you must, nevertheless, also always think "*towards*" some rhythmical point or other ahead, while you are playing.

The Sense of "Resting":

14. Now all this implies a sense of RESTING on the keyboard during each phrase, section or musical unit.

15. Thus you may either rest (or lie) on the keyboard either at its *surface*-level or else at its *depressed*-level; and this brings us to the consideration of the problem of *Legato* and *Staccato*.

Chapter XI

HOW TO PLAY LEGATO AND STACCATO

1. Remember, you cannot sound a note at the Piano *without* EXERTING *your finger* to produce the down-movement of the key.[1]

can only be corrected, (3), by your rotating your forearm *inwards!* Finally, (4), to prevent the little finger being swept off the Keyboard, you have to turn the hand itself *inwards*, laterally.

[1] Except in the first steps of playing, as shown in my "Child's First Steps," and "Nine Steps towards Finger-individualization," where, instead, you sound the notes with the *side* of your hand.

2. Even for the very softest sound, you must still *exert* the finger — though very gently, and with no more force than will just suffice.

3. These two preliminary reminders may seem redundant, but they are not. The *exertion* of the finger is so often overlooked — as also the *exertion* of the hand to help it!

Staccato defined:

4. Now, a true *Staccato* should signify a note *without Duration.* Therefore the key must here be free to rebound the very moment that tone-production is completed, so that the damper can stop the sound instantaneously.

NOTE. — Colloquially, every passage that is not *legato* (or *tenuto*) is loosely termed "Staccato." But this is manifestly an error, since everything that is not a true *staccato* (or *staccatissimo*) is necessarily a *tenuto* of shorter or more complete duration.

Always, therefore, be on your guard, and look with suspicion on "staccato" marks, for they do not relieve you from the great care necessary to give the precise *degree of* DURATION to such supposed "staccato" notes, if you are out to make real Music.[1]

---

[1] Some students, it appears, find it difficult to grasp the distinction between the terms "Length" and "Duration" of a note. Realize that "Length" solely refers to the *space of time* covered by a *note-sign*, whereas "Duration" refers to the *proportion* of that length during which it is kept sounding. That is, the note-sign indicates a definite *quantity* of Time, but we do not necessarily prolong the sound to its full Time-value; we may cut it short, or may even extend it beyond its note-value — in *legatissimo*. It only forms one of the many anomalies of our musical notation!

Length *v.* Duration

Length is therefore a definite, compulsory quantity of Time, and may only be varied in a succession of notes, in Rubato or ritardando or accelerando, where the relative time-proportions of the notes nevertheless remain paramount. Whereas Duration (implying the contrast between Legato and Staccato) cannot be accurately noted in the text any more than can be the contrast between *forte* and *piano* — since all such contrasts are always largely a matter of Judgment and Taste as to degree, and are varied in a measure with the mood of the performer at the moment. A *rest*, on the other hand, is definite — except, again, that the Time-quantities can also be inflected in Rubato, etc., and that its *silence* may be encroached upon by a prolongation of a previous note's duration — at the taste of the performer.

In short, the length of Time between the beginning of a note and the beginning of the next note (or rest) is the same whether that first note be kept sounding its full Time-valse or not — and this last comes under the term of Duration.

The Act of Staccato:

5. A true Staccato implies that you must *accurately time* your tone-producing exertion, etc., to *cease* completely with the very moment of tone-emission, so that the key may here be free to rebound. You cannot thus cease each finger-action unless you *also* as accurately *time the cessation* of the help it receives from the hand and arm, during the moment of key-descent.

6. Staccato therefore implies, that you must *rest* very *lightly* on the keyboard, else you cannot accurately cease the finger-action (etc.), when needed.

7. In short, during Staccato, rest no more heavily on the keyboard than the keys will bear *at their surface-level.* If you rest thus lightly enough, you can succeed in playing *staccato,* always provided that you (as beforesaid) accurately *cease* the tone-producing impulses with the moment of tone-emission, so that keys and dampers may be free to rebound and "damp" each sound instantaneously.

The "Resting" in Agility-passages and Octave-passages:

8. Most AGILITY passages need this same light form of *Resting,* and also need equal accuracy in timing the complete cessation of the separate down-impulses with tone-emission. When your tone is dull in Agility-passages, the cure always is, to recall these facts of Staccato-resting, and accuracy of timing.

9. OCTAVE-PASSAGES equally need this *lightest form of Resting* — a *glissando* along the *surface* of the keyboard with a separate impulse for each octave.[1]

10. Now, to achieve this light form of Resting, your arm must be so nicely "poised" (or supported by its own muscles) that it floats over the keyboard, and thus allows the hand to

[1] *See* Chapter X, ¶ 6, and Chapter VI, ¶ 36, etc., on Octave-Playing; and for further directions as to octave-playing refer to the EPITOME, page 30, and also to the Section on Octave-playing, pages 91 to 99, in *Relaxation Studies* (Bosworth), where full instruction is given.

remain lying loosely and freely upon the keyboard at its *surface*-level, *between* the sounding of the notes.

The Act of Tenuto and Legato:

11. To obtain LEGATO — that is, the "natural" form of it — you must allow this Act of Resting to be *very slightly heavier*, but still quite light and gentle. Your finger will now be *compelled*, by this extra (but still light) weight, to hold down the notes until relieved by other fingers, or until you relieve the keyboard of this slight extra degree of continuously-resting Arm-weight.[1]

Natural or "compelled" Legato:

12. I have called this the "natural" (or *automatic*) form of Legato, since it is this continuous (but *light*) resting weight which here *compels* the fingers to "carry on" from finger to finger. It might also be termed *Compelled Legato* — because it is wrought or "compelled" by this slightly heavier, continuously-resting Weight.

Uncompelled or "artificial" Legato:

13. You can also obtain a Legato *without* this compelling action of Weight. You may, instead, employ the lightest form of Resting (precisely as needed for Staccato), and yet you can quite well hold the notes down. The notes are here held down by the continued action of the "small" muscles of your finger, directly prompted by your Will, and *not* here *compelled* to continue by the prompting of the heavier Resting, as considered in ¶¶10 and 11. This form of Legato I have called the ARTIFICIAL form of Legato.

14. With this "artificial" legato then, there is *not* sufficient Resting-weight to *compel* the finger to hold its note down, as in

[1] A recent writer advocates some two pounds or more of weight to remain thus heavily resting on the keyboard! A mistake made by BREITHAUPT and others of the German school — "schwere Tastenbelastung," they call it. As already pointed out, this teaching of a heavy weight carried along the keyboard or keybeds has wrecked many an aspiring Pianist. Avoid the error at all cost.

"natural" legato. And with this lighter Resting, the keys jump up, the moment you cease the light individual holding-action of the finger. This form of legato might therefore also be termed "*uncompelled*" legato, since it is *not* compelled by a continuously resting Weight.

NOTE. — There has been much misconception on this point. The distinction, however, is really quite simple; although, as everywhere else, a point will always appear "difficult," so long as it is not understood. Yet the difficulty never is in the fact; it always lies in the reader's insufficient alertness.

To help towards the understanding of this distinction between the two types of Legato, try the following experiments: —

Experiment in elucidation of "Natural" and "Artificial" Legato

(*a*) Place your feet almost under the chair you are sitting upon. Now, if someone were rude enough to try to pull that chair from under you, you would, instantly, but quite automatically, exert your legs, and would find yourself standing. Here you have a good analogy to "compelled" or natural Tenuto and Legato! Whereas, (*b*) if, while sitting on the chair like that, you press your feet against the floor (as in getting up), you will then also bring the weight of your body to bear upon the floor, but now only *so long as* (and to the extent) you willfully exert your legs. Here you have uncompelled, or "artificial," or *non-automatic* Legato!

On Duration-inflections:

15. Fluctuations (or inflections) of Legato and Tenuto (both in *staccato* and *legato* passages) are mostly produced in this last way — by the *individually* prompted holding of notes by the finger, that is, *without* the Continuous-weight compelling element.

This, in fact, is the form of Legato most often used. A true *Cantabile* is impossible without it, and so is BACH-playing. Natural legato, however, is easiest at first, yet this second or "artificial" type of Legato should be acquired as soon as possible, and in the end both types are often used simultaneously.

NOTE. — In passages which are on the whole Staccato, the varying durations of the notes, more or less marked (or waverings in the staccato of the passage), are best effected by such holding "without weight," rather than by a separate lapsing of weight for particular notes. Moreover, for *legatissimo* inflections, it is *the only way*. The notes are here "overlapped" not by individual increases in the Resting-weight (far too clumsy a way), but instead they are over-held by the needed fingers, *without* any "compelling" Weight.

Reminders as to Finger-actions and "Keybedding":

16. I have elsewhere explained the physiological difference in the action of the finger while producing the tone, and its subsequent light action in holding the notes — the "small" muscles of the finger here alone doing the work. *See* Chapter VIII, "On the Holding of Notes"; also, *Additional Note*, No. XII, "On Keybedding."

17. Remember, the pressure required on the keybed to hold a note down is not necessarily more than will suffice to sound the note *at its softest;* it is in fact slightly less, since it takes more force to move a limb than to keep it in position afterwards. But, as already indicated, it is often useful to use a *little more* pressure on the key-pads than actually necessary to hold the notes down. It gives one a sense of comfort to *feel* one is holding the note, and it helps to warn one to *let go* when time is up!

18. Also, as already insisted upon, this extra pressure does *not* constitute "keybedding." Remember, keybedding arises when you *mis*apply to the keybeds any force *intended to* PRODUCE the Tone. Keybedding implies that you have *ill-timed* your tone-making effort, and have in fact *buried* it upon the key-pads, instead of applying it *early enough* during Key-descent to fulfill its purpose — in Tone-production. So long as you keep separate in your mind the Act of tone-*making* and the Act of tone-*holding* there is no harm done. But you must always remember this distinction, else your efforts will fail to express your musical sense — whatever your endowments may be in that respect.[1]

[1] *See* ¶¶ 9 and 10 of Chapter IV.

Chapter XII

WEIGHT-TRANSFER AND ARM-VIBRATION TOUCHES

— *The true nature of all so-called "Finger-passages"*

1. Preamble: All rapid passages approximate either towards the "Arm-vibration" or "Weight-transfer" type of technique. Manifestly it must then be of extreme importance thoroughly to understand these matters, since all real Piano music so largely consists of such rapid (or "Agility") work, owing to the non-sustaining power of our instrument. Hence this Chapter is devoted to the further elucidation of these points.

What I mean by "Arm-vibration" and "Weight-transfer" is concisely defined in ¶¶ 8 and 9 of Chapter V, "The Physiological Details" — which see. Enough, to repeat here, that the distinction between the two mainly is: that with "Arm-vibration touch" the arm floats over the keys (and upon the keyboard) *at surface-level*, and the successive tones are produced by momentary (and individual) impulses from the finger and hand during key-descent — helped of course by the forearm rotationally; whereas, with "Weight-transfer," the arm is not so fully poised, and a certain light measure of its weight is passed on (as in Legato Resting) from *keybed to keybed*, and does not here cease with each act of tone-production.

In *slower* passages, however, instead of either of these forms of floating weight, it is possible to have as basis (for the finger and hand exertion) a *separate lapse* for each note from the normally "poised" (or self-sustained) condition of the arm — a great advantage, and a necessity where the larger tone-volumes are needed. In fact, this is "Third species of touch," as termed in "The Act of Touch." That is, the arm-*supporting* muscles are momentarily allowed to stop work during key-descent, and the arm-weight (thus set free during that moment) serves as a very substantial basis indeed, so that finger and hand can be effectively and fully exerted during the moment of key-acceleration. Or we may even add to this a momentary down-exertion of the forearm. Or we may use only forearm weight in place of whole-arm weight. All these points have already been noted in Chapter V under the "Six Possible Arm-conditions."

It is well to repeat, however, that although the arm does not necessarily show its momentary ponderous incidence by any movement, yet its whole weight (or more) may thus be available *during* the act of tone-production, while the normal condition of Arm-*poise* is instantly resumed upon its completion. All *cantandos* and *cantabiles* are thus played — even up to some considerable speed.

Beyond a certain speed, however, these separate arm-lapses (no, *not* Movements!) become impossible. Beyond such definite *tempo*, this "Third species" form of technique (with the arm separately lapsed for each note) gradually merges either into *Arm-vibration* touch, or into *Weight-transfer* (or "Passing-on") touch when the arm is left somewhat less fully supported, and some measure of its weight therefore then bears continuously upon the fingers, hand, and keybeds.

These matters must now be dealt with in greater detail.

2. Clearly, the two forms of "Resting" (legato and staccato *resting*) considered under "Legato and Staccato" in Chapter IX (arising from differences in the degree of the *Poised arm*) themselves form the main difference in basis between "*Weight-transfer*" (or "Passing-on") touch, and "Arm-vibration touch."

Definition of Weight-transfer touch.

3. We have seen, in Chapter V, ¶10, that the "*poised arm*," when not quite *fully* poised, may itself become a *Basis* for tone-production in rapid passages, while *continuously* (but still lightly) resting on the Keybeds — and that it thus forms "Weight-transfer touch." Now, such *continuously* resting weight, passed

on from finger to finger and keybed to keybed (as already pointed out earlier), also entails a continuously *active* (exerted) Hand, and may even entail continuous (although alternating) rotatory stresses of the Forearm.

4. Such continuously *passed-on* pressure applied from note to note (although slight) unfortunately greatly impairs our possibility to *choose* the tone or duration of each individual note, as already pointed out. The serious drawback of Weight-transfer touch is, that the successive sounds are hereby reduced *more or less* to a dead level of tone and duration, and therefore, under such form of technique, our passage-work will sound as musically dead as passages played on the Organ or Pianola, since the possibility of a Mind tonally operative and purposeful behind *each individual note* is here lacking.

All that is possible with Weight-transfer touch are *gradual* inflections of tone and duration — swirls of crescendos and diminuendos, and *gradual* changes in the degree of legato and staccato.

Weight-transfer, where inappropriate:

5. Musical passage-work, on the contrary, imperatively entails inflections from note to note — that is, the tone and duration of *each* note must be meticulously *chosen* with musical purpose.

Therefore, since such tonal *selectivity* is so greatly impaired and hampered (if not almost rendered impracticable in Weight-transfer touch), sternly avoid using it for *musically-alive* passages; instead (wherever practicable) use Arm-vibration touch, — with its *fully* poised arm and individually applied action, and its option therefore of tonal differentiation from note to note, as already repeatedly insisted upon.

6. The obvious moral is, that you should never play such melodically-musical passages *any quicker* than you *can* thus musically purpose each individual note, nor quicker therefore than you can apply such *arm-vibration* touch physically, since

beyond a certain definite rate of speed you are bound to lapse into "Weight-transfer touch," with its drawbacks musically. More on this point under ¶¶26, 27, and 28, further on.

NOTE. — Some otherwise excellent artists, however, often ignore this required keen musical and physical *individualizing* of the notes in Passage-work (which the Arm-vibration type of technique alone offers), and instead, they indolently lapse into convenient but banal Weight-transfer *Velocities!*

Weight-transfer always light:

7. Moreover, as already insisted upon, the weight *actually transferred from keybed to keybed* in Weight-transfer touch should always remain comparatively light, even during the production of those swirls of possible *crescendo* inflections. For the most part it should be little heavier than suffices to *sound* a note softly by Weight-touch.

At higher speed, extra weight possible

8. NOTE. — Moreover, as already anticipated in Chapter V, in high-speed passages a *somewhat greater modicum* of Resting-weight can be carried along in Weight-transfer Touch *without* this extra weight coming to bear solidly and deleteriously upon the Keybeds. Similarly, with Arm-vibration touch, during swift passages, some extra Resting-weight can be carried without impairing the efficacy of those individually-directed hand-and-finger impulses for (and with) each key, which Arm-vibration touch alone offers us, as demanded in rapid, but musical Passage-work.

The reason is, that at high speed of progression across the Keyboard a greater number of such impulses in a given time help to *support* the Resting-weight *off* the keybeds than at a *slower* speed. Thus *more weight* can be carried at *high speed,* without Arm-vibration touch (with its *floating* weight) deteriorating into Weight-transfer touch with its weight resting solidly *upon the keybeds*, and which would render Arm-vibration touch impracticable.

In short: the *louder* the passage (and the more energetic therefore these short-lived impulses of the finger-and-hand), the more readily can such extra weight be kept floating (or resting lightly) upon the keyboard.

An express train has been known actually to jump a small gap in a bridge at high speed! At slower speed the wheels would certainly have sunk in! *See* also the Note to ¶20 of this Chapter, and "On the Merging of Touch-forms" in Chapter V.

Weight-transference by cessation of the last-used finger:

9. Tone-production in Weight-transfer touch is effected by transferring the *basis* of light Resting-weight from finger to finger and keybed to keybed. This transference of weight is

effected by each finger in turn being prompted into exertion strictly *in response to* the accurately-timed CESSATION of the *previous* finger's work. Such reflex-action (in response to the weight thus *felt* to be "left in the lurch" as it were) is akin to the act of polite walking — and not stamping along, as a child does at first! Each leg in turn should be prompted into action by the *cessation* of the exertion of the previously-used leg. Experiment on these lines, both on the keyboard and on the floor, and the nature of this process immediately becomes apparent. Perhaps a better analogy than walking, however, is the process of stepping on to the *treads of a Treadmill.*[1] Now, if we step on to the treads of a treadmill, we find that each tread gives way AS we bring our weight upon it. The exertions *are the same* as used in walking upstairs, only instead of mounting any further up we are turning a wheel by the exertion of our legs. Here note, it is the *muscular exertion* which does the work, and we again realize how "Weight" (as everywhere in playing) serves only as a *Basis*, or stable *Foundation* (but *not* as a "Fixation"), so as to render effective the *work being done* by finger and hand.

A Walking Analogy

NOTE. — True, in the act of walking on level ground, we do transfer the *whole* weight of our bodies from foot to foot — we cannot do otherwise; whereas in "walking" on the Piano with our fingers, we must *never* carry along the whole, *fully*-released weight of our whole arm (or arm-*force* instead!) else our playing will certainly be crippled. Do not forget, therefore, that, even when most ponderous, only a comparatively *slight* release of the *whole* arm is required for such *Resting.*[2]

---

[1] We may gain some notion of this by trying to walk up a descending "escalator," or by watching the efforts of white mice in their revolving cage!

The Full-weight-transfer fallacy

[2] In Germany and elsewhere this was overlooked, as already pointed out, and the student was instructed to carry the *full* weight (or even full arm *force* — "Volle Spielbelastung") — from note to note without a break between! This grave misteaching has been responsible for many a broken-down student and player. Yet, even today, some misguided people are trying to revive this iniquity!

Obviously, playing under such hampering conditions not only renders the individualization of tone-inflection (tonal selectivity from note to note) impossible, but, as indicated, it has often ended in the unfortunate student being actually physically disabled.

On Key-bedding:

10. This again brings us back to the much misunderstood question of "keybedding." Merely carrying a measure of Weight on the Keybeds (as in Weight-transfer touch) does *not* constitute "Key-bedding" within the meaning of the Act.

As a matter of fact, I invented the term "keybedding" thirty years ago *as a term of* CENSURE, to denote quite another thing. "Keybedding" simply denotes the misapplication (or *mis-timing* on to the pads under the keys) *of the force intended to* PRODUCE SOUND. In other words, the force (weight, or muscular work) is here applied *too late* during key-descent to be effective in producing the intended key-*movement* and tone. As a result, the tone-intended force is "buried" on the keybeds, instead of creating tone. (*See* Footnote below,[1] also Additional Note, No. XII, "On Keybedding." *See* also ¶18, page 88.)

Legato Pressures:

11. Nevertheless (as pointed out earlier), it is sometimes desirable actually to provide a certain (but still *slight*) degree of continuous PRESSURE on the key-beds themselves. This however does *not* constitute "keybedding," and there is no harm, provided this continuous pressure is always *kept distinct from* the actual (momentary) tone-producing impulses.

Such gentle key-bed pressure may be, and indeed should be, quite legitimately and usefully applied to apprise us clearly how long

---

Many cases of such taught misdoing have come under our care to be cured; and we have had to act as a "Kuranstalt" for players crippled by this particular form of evil "method."

[1] A recent writer, after quite rightly stating that "the process of resting part of the weight of the arm on the keybeds must not be confounded with keybedding," yet continues quite wrongly thus — "which consists of *pressing* on the keybeds *by means of muscular energy*"*!*

This quotation hardly gives much "Sidelight" on this vital point. In the first place, it is quite impossible to press on the keybeds at all without such "definite muscular energy" of the fingers and hand; or does the writer imagine that arm-weight can possibly be applied to the keys *without* the intercession of Finger-exertion? — *and hand* exertion also?

we are holding those notes down. Thus applied, it forms quite good playing, and certainly does *not* constitute "keybedding," in its obnoxious sense. *See* Chapter XI, ¶17.

Again, it must nevertheless be reiterated, that such legitimate pressure on the key-beds must nevertheless be kept within reasonable bounds, whether the necessary finger-and-hand exertion is "compelled" by a Resting-weight or not, else it will of a certainty hamper Agility and destroy *tone-selectivity*. Moreover, remember *not* to use the "strong" muscles of the fingers and hand for such sustaining *pressure*, but only the "weak" or "small" finger muscles — as shown in Chapter VIII, "The Holding of Notes."

Weight-transfer touch, where appropriate and where not:

12. As to the appropriate application of Weight-transfer (or "Passing-on") touch, from what has already been inferred, it is only appropriate in soft passages *not* of a melodic character, not needing *tonal* rhythmical definition of their constituent notes — passages, the main purpose of which is to hide in a measure the non-sustaining powers of our instrument, by keeping the harmonies to the fore. "Weight-transfer" is needed for many soft accompanying passages and figurations, speedy arabesques, ornamental virtuosities, "filling-up" arpeggios and scales not of a melodic nature. As an instance of such accompanying figurations, perhaps best played by Weight-transfer touch, take this example from one of my own "Monothemes": —

Monothemes, No. 5, Tobias Matthay, Op. 13.

As a similar instance, all that fairy-like, atmospheric *ppp* accompaniment of Chopin's A Flat study, No. I, Op. 25, must thus be played — and also with the keys all played "from halfway down": —

Yet in the climax of this piece Weight-transfer again merges into Arm-vibration.

Most of Chopin's study in C, No. I, Op. 10, is also best thus played by Weight-transfer; yet where the harmonies become more important, and need more playing out, one must again use "Arm-vibration" touch, gradually exchanging from one into the other. Certain outstanding (or prominentized) notes of course need actual Weight-touch again, as shown in the Examples on the next page.

Chopin: Study in C, No. 1, Op. 10

Arm-vibration
Weight-transfer
8 va
Rubato
rit
accel

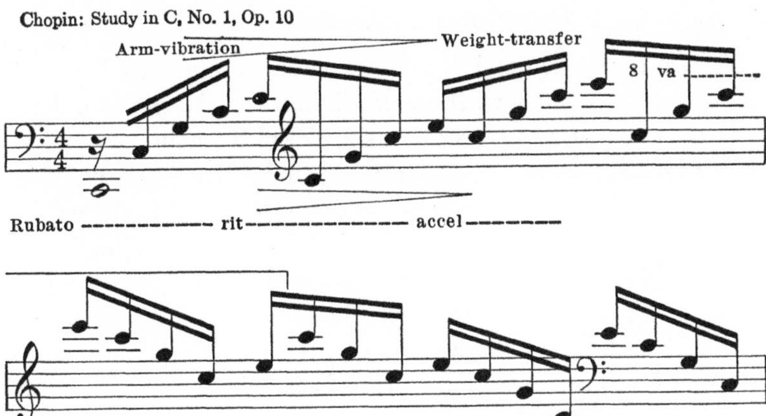

Here is another example (from my own Monothemes, No. 6) of such contrasts all within one phrase:—

Matthay: "Monothemes," No. 6

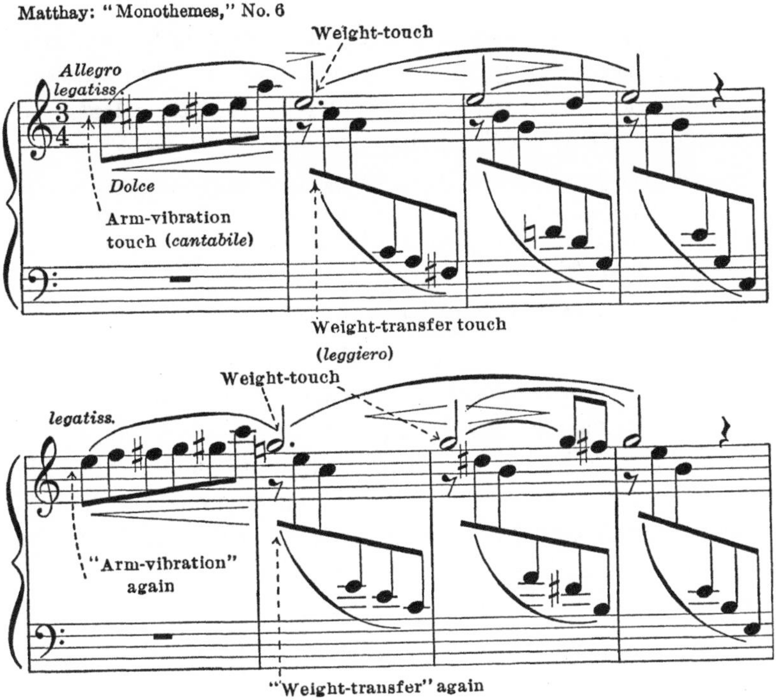

Weight-touch
Allegro legatiss.
Dolce
Arm-vibration touch (cantabile)
Weight-transfer touch (leggiero)
Weight-touch
legatiss.
"Arm-vibration" again
"Weight-transfer" again

Where to avoid Weight-transfer touch:

12. On the other hand, it is quite wrong to play rapid but yet melodic passages such as those of Chopin's C sharp minor Fantasie-Impromptu, or of his Fantasia, or the B minor Scherzo, as mere harmonic swirls of Passing-on touch, as indeed too often heard. Such swift Chopin passages are indeed in the nature of true Pianoforte *melodies*, and as such they need that individualized playing of the notes which Passing-on touch cannot supply. I feel this applies even in such pieces as his F minor study, Op. 25, No. 2, although this is too often misplayed and turned into mere musical (or unmusical) note-rattling.

Matters of Taste:

13. Here we enter upon the domain of Taste. The rhythmically indefinite and inflectionally flat effect of "Weight-transfer" may strongly appeal to one person for a particular Chopin or Debussy passage, whereas another may feel and wish that same passage to be fully alive and rhythmically-melodious, with inflections from note to note; but in that case *Arm-vibration touch* must be substituted.

NOTE. — Moreover, it is a good plan to practise through *all* Agility passages with Arm-vibration touch, also *staccatissimo*, even when Passing-on touch is to be applied ultimately. Anyway, it ensures their being played through slowly enough to be really *thought out!*

Where Weight-transfer is non-optional:

14. Finally, when we come to the melodic passage-work of *Bach*, *Mozart*, and *Beethoven*, then there is no option possible. To play such passages by "Weight-transfer" is a crime, and is indubitable proof of total musical blindness and insensibility. Yet it must be conceded that such vandalism is often enough committed by otherwise quite musical players; just as we find other artists trying to approximate Chopin to their correct Beethoven-playing!

NOTE. — How rarely does one find a Beethoven and Chopin player combined in the same person! Might one venture to suggest that this may perhaps largely be attributed to non-comprehension of the difference between the Weight-transfer and Arm-vibration types of technique? There have been, and are, exceptions. In the past, for instance, LISZT and ANTON RUBINSTEIN always kept their Chopin and Beethoven technique distinct, as it should be — just as distinct as the character of their Music.

15. Spread (or rolled) chords are usually and correctly played by such Weight-transfer (or "Passing-on") touch. As an instance, take the E flat chord study of Chopin's, Op. 10. Here each chord is an example of Weight-transfer. The melody notes, however, need individualized "Weight-touch," and where the Bass changes, those notes also need it: —

Chopin, Op. 10.

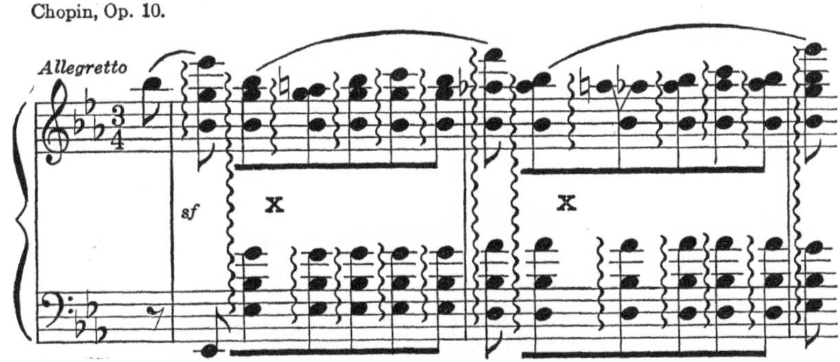

16. Moreover, for more *slowly spread chords*, etc., in place of such *pure* Passing-on touch, a certain degree of individualized finger-action is available when desirable, in addition to the weight transmitted from finger to finger.

NOTE. — But as a light hand-pressure is necessarily constant with the carried weight, the individualized finger-action is here analogous to stamping with the feet. Passages analogous to spread chords can also thus be slightly modified, and the musically deadening effect of passed-on weight thus somewhat mitigated. Passed-on weight, nevertheless, always remains a serious handicap, musically.

The Slur.

17. Pure Weight-transfer touch is also required, for instance, in playing the soft final note of the *ordinary* slur.[1] Here be sure that the new finger is prompted into action by the carefully

[1] *See* "The Slur or Couplet of Notes," Oxford University Press.

timed *cessation* of the *previous* finger's action, and this without any "individualized" action of its own, or of the hand, else that last note will not be so soft as intended.[1]

The "ordinary" slur:

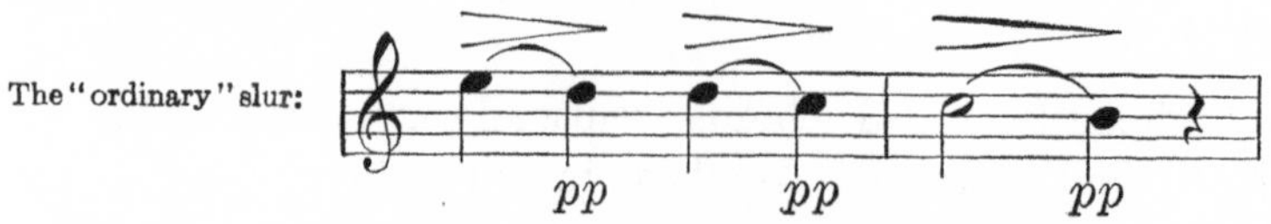

18. As a rule then, as already insisted upon, AVOID using Weight-transfer touch wherever possible, since it reduces your passage-work to the boring dead level of Pianola-like strumming, and instead use Arm-vibration touch whenever applicable.

Arm-vibration Touch.

Description:

19. This implies the lightest (or *staccato*) form of Resting. That is, the arm must be in its perfectly poised or balanced condition. The reiterated impulses of the finger and hand (given during key-descent only), assisted by the Forearm rotatory impulses, will (by reaction) here set the whole arm "vibrating," or trembling *in sympathy* with these individually applied finger-and-hand impulses against the keys; hence the term *Arm-vibration.* In Arm-vibration touch the hand is felt *beating upwards* against the wrist. In short: Arm-vibration means, that the Arm (in its finely-poised or balanced condition) is in rapid passages brought into *sympathetic vibration* by *reaction,* owing to the rapidly-reiterated but short-lived impulses of the Finger and Hand and rotative Forearm delivered against the key during each act of touch; the Finger-exertion here alone shows itself as Movement, while the hand and forearm rotative stresses may remain *quite invisible.*

NOTE. — As already emphasized in a previous Note (to ¶8), just as we have compared Weight-transfer touch to the act of *walking,* so we can compare Arm-vibration touch to the act of *running.* In running, the impulses of our legs against the ground suffice to keep our body *bouncing* along, and kept as it were floating in the air. Running, in fact, consists of a series of *jumps!*

---

[1] Here refer back to ¶9, page 92, where this is explained.

20. Thus, in *Arm-vibration* touch, if we really maintain the nicely poised condition of the arm, it will be kept bounced *off the keybeds*, kept floating off *them* (but not necessarily off the keyboard surface) by the closely reiterated kicks delivered by the fingers against the keybeds. Adjust the weight carefully, however, else instead of Arm-vibration touch you will again merge into Weight-transfer touch — with its weight transferred on the keybeds instead of *at surface-level of the keyboard* — as it should be in Arm-vibration touch.

21. In this vibratile condition, the *inertia* of the fully-poised arm serves as a quite sufficiently substantial basis for all quick passages needing tonal selectivity — both in the case of finger and hand Movement, and both for *forte* and *piano* passages.[1]

22. Moreover, since the tone for each note is here produced by the individually-applied impulses of the finger and *hand* (and rotative-forearm) you can here accurately and meticulously *select each tone and duration*, and can thus retain your listener's alert attention, however rapidly you play — provided you are not musically lazy, and can think quickly enough.

NOTE. — Remember, as already pointed out in ¶7, that in rapid *forte* Arm-vibration passages (just as in Weight-transfer touch), some extra weight can be carried without doing harm, because the arm is then kept in a state of flotation by the rapidly repeated, powerful impulses from hand and finger during key-descent. Moreover, a certain degree of *continuous* action of the "small" Hand-flexors may carry such continuous weight without impairing the individually directed impulses of the "strong" hand flexors. Thus we see, again, how easily Arm-vibration can approximate and merge into the Weight-transfer type of touch, and *vice versa*.

On Extra Weight possibilities

Refer to *Note* to ¶7, of this Chapter, and also to Chapter V, ¶48, "On the Merging of the Touch-forms."

Understand these possibilities, but do not worry over the precise point of balance where they should differentiate. In fact:

Understand Touch, but unless you have to diagnose faulty playing, *leave the selection to musical instinct.*

Never play the Piano *for the sake of using touches*, but use touches *for the sake of making Music!*

---

[1] *See* Note under next paragraph.

Arm-vibration fallacies:

23. This *sympathetically*-induced Vibration of the arm has, however, been misinterpreted by some recent writers (Breithaupt, etc.), who have seriously recommended that the fingers and hand should be "*shaken into vibration*" BY THE ARM, like using a flail — a mistake worthy of a *Till Eulenspiegel!*

NOTE. — This forms yet another glaring instance of mistaken diagnosis wrought by the precarious attempt to analyse the touch processes by observation of their outward (but so often misleading) manifestations of Movement. Indeed, the right and wrong actions here certainly *look* much alike — except to the highly practised eye. Be urgently warned against this mistake, since the result of trying to produce the vibration-effect *by Arm-initiative* will certainly provoke a very ugly form of technique. The correct effect may be likened to the vibration caused in the body of a stationary motor car with engine running — the car is here shaken *by the engine*, but it is not the engine that is shaken by the car! Correct arm-vibration touch feels *upwards* at the wrist, not downwards. The correct action may also be likened to the one used when carefully and neatly handling a pepper-pot — a vibrant action of the hand, and you would certainly spoil your lunch if you shook the pepper on to it by a *Breithauptian* Arm-initiated Vibration!

Arm-vibration legato:

24. To ensure musical playing you should (as already insisted upon) always choose this resilient form of touch for all Agility passages wherever possible.

Usually it is needed with "bouncing" keys — that is, *Staccato* in reality, although not easily recognizable as such by the ear at the speed. Nevertheless, this touch also admits of *Legato* — but necessarily only of the "artificial" type.[1]

Arm-vibration *v.* Arm-lapse:

25. Arm-vibration touch, in fact, is required for *all* musical passages taken at a greater speed *than will admit of* SEPARATE *arm-lapses* or *stresses* for each note individually, which last

[1] A reminder: Artificial or "uncompelled" legato means that there is here insufficient Resting-weight to *compel* the fingers into Legato. By the use of their "small" muscles the fingers can nevertheless quite well hold the notes down for *every* desired Duration-effect — such as Tenuto, Legato or even Legatissimo. *See* Chapter XI, "On Staccato and Legato."

are only possible at a comparatively slow Tempo — as already reiterated in the *Preamble* of this Chapter. Obviously, it is only in comparatively slow passages that you *can* thus help the individual notes by *separate* Arm-lapses and stresses.

The bane of excessive Speed:

26. Moreover (as already hinted in ¶ 6), you will find, when you try thus to *individualize* each note (as you *should* in all musical passage-work, by means of Arm-vibration touch), that *you cannot then play the passages quicker* than they were *thought* by the composer himself. Unless, of course, you throw overboard all musical self-respect, and instead use some form of Passing-on touch, when you certainly can, *and probably will,* play everything far beyond the intended Tempo![1]

Never quicker than musical thought:

27. Arm-vibration (to reiterate once again) is therefore the *staple* touch-form for all quick but musically-meant melodic passages, both soft and loud, such as you find, as beforesaid, in Bach, Mozart, Chopin, and Beethoven. It follows, from all this, that you must never play such "*Melos*" quicker than you *can* thus really think, time and *mean* the individual notes musically and physically.[2]

1 Many purely virtuoso-players evidently do so, for the sake of obtaining cheap applause from the musically undiscerning. A *real* composer, however, is necessarily a musical person, and hence must choose *Tempi* at which he *can* think and play his own music. As instances, try through, say, the G major Prelude, from the first book of "The forty-eight," or Chopin's F minor, C sharp minor or A minor studies, or his Prelude in B flat minor, or Fantasie-Impromptu, first by "Passing-on" touch (as musical *smears* taken at *unthinkable* speed) and then play them through again, really meaning every note — by means of Arm-vibration technique — and realize how immeasurably more musical is the effect for everyone concerned.

2 Remember, it is so easy to lapse musically, and to rattle through passages by Weight-transfer at great speed! The remedy is, to play *slower* and to try to think the musical value of each note.

A musical run sounds quicker than an *un*-thought one:

28. As a matter of fact, such passages actually *sound* quicker when thus *thought through* with vitally chosen and produced tones than when they are merely skimmed, rushed, and rattled through at an actually *quicker* tempo! The reason is, that you make the listener *attend* to *every note* if you yourself do so, and he is therefore far more *busy* than when you offer him but *smears* with a few landmarks thrown in!

NOTE. — Certainly, there are only too many cases where unmusicality of utterance is really owing simply to sheer musical insensibility, and there is no remedy then! Moreover, it is true that provided the weight passed-on is not too greatly excessive, you can, if gifted with strong fingers, *plough* your way through passages at any speed. Some indeed may regard this as a form of "Sport," but to the musically-sensitive listener it constitutes real musical misery. It is yet another of the many crimes committed in the name of *St. Cecilia!* Such playing does not constitute Music-making; it is only an exhibition of Sporting Athletics or Calisthenics, and is only applauded *as such*. *See* Additional Note, No. XVII, on Strong fingers *v.* Weak fingers — "Strong *v.* Weak Piano *voices*."

29. After all this, it is needless to repeat the warning *not* to try to play with a *quite heavy weight* continuously "*passed on*," or with "Schwere Spielbelastung," as actually advocated by certain comparatively recent German authors, and their ill-advised English imitators. Obviously, such misdoing not only precludes any intimate selectivity of Tone, but also renders all attempts at Agility clumsy, sticky, and in fact unattainable as a musical effect.

30. Coda — Summary of this Chapter:

The essential difference, then, between these two very distinct types of technique is, that with Weight-transfer a just sufficiently heavy weight rests continuously on the Keybeds, and tone is produced by each *finger* in turn *giving way* to the next in transferring this weight; whereas, with Arm-vibration the weight is insufficient to rest upon the KEYBEDS, and tone is produced by the individually-initiated and momentary action of each finger in turn, abetted by similarly individualized and momentary hand and forearm rotational impulses.

In brief, "Arm-vibration" implies that in place of a *continuous* Hand-exertion, the Hand-exertion must be supplied *separately* for each note, and must be as short-lived as in *Staccatissimo*, even in Legato.

Remember, you really need "ten hands"!

Chapter XIII

ON POSITION—AND MOVEMENT

1. Remember, good Position is the RESULTANT of correct balance in the forces used. The reverse does not hold good. You may obey all the orthodoxies of Position and yet the *invisible actuating* processes may be quite wrong, and you will play badly.

Provide the right muscular conditions, and Position (on the whole) will take care of itself. To stress Position calls attention to *results* instead of to the *causes* of the desired results. There are, however, some points it is well to consider. Thus:—

2. AVOID SITTING TOO CLOSE TO THE INSTRUMENT. Manifestly, if your upper-arm hangs straight down from the shoulder or even slants backwards, its weight cannot become available.[1]

It is best to sit sufficiently far away to allow the elbow to be moved in front of the body, so that you can easily reach the extreme limits of the keyboard. The best Elbow position is therefore with the *upper*-arm more or less sloping forward. Thus the free-set upper-arm Weight can exert a "pull" on the fingers when needed.

NOTE.—*See* my portrait at the Piano, page 46 of the "Epitome"; also that of *Anton Rubinstein* in "The Act of Touch," p. 305.

---

[1] If you sit too close you will be tempted to poke forward, and thus render all your playing stilted and uncomfortable and unpleasant.

3. As a matter of fact, the *whole* arm, if bent at the elbow, would balance itself by swinging the elbow *behind* the level of the body.

Try the following experiment: —

Open a penknife at right angles, and balance it with the tip of the blade between your finger and thumb, and you will find it will come to rest something like this at *b*): —

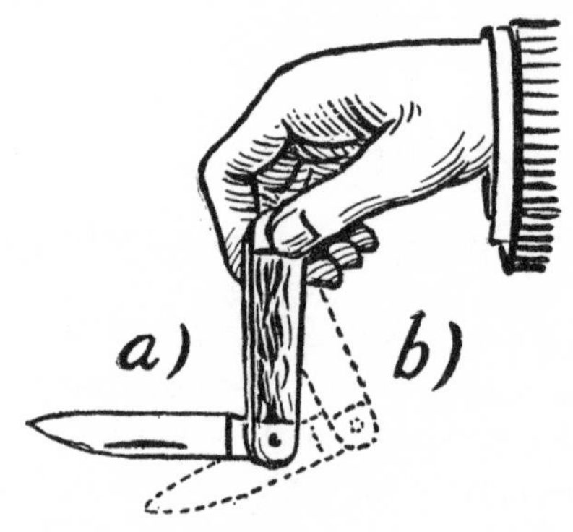

That is: the weight of the handle (upper-arm, *a*) is here pushed back by the weight of the hand and forearm, the blade, at *b*.

This is only a very rough representation of the whole-arm weight balance, but it is instructive. If you play with the upper-arm either straight down, or with the elbow actually swung back behind the body-line, you are almost bound to poke forward when you try to play loudly (with "thrusting" finger) and you will make a nasty noise instead of nice music.

4. Do not sit too high nor too low — the Elbow about level with the Keys. Sitting too high naturally suggests "Arm off"; this may *seem* to render running passages easier, but is likely to make you poke forward, with its usual dire results. Sitting too low suggests "Arm-lapse," and hence seems to render singing-passages easier. Lying back in a chair exercises a similarly beneficial suggestion-influence for weight-release in singing-tone; but it rather impedes Agility.

If, however, you provide the right muscular *conditions* you *can* play *all* passages in spite of the most exaggeratedly high or low position of the arm.

Nevertheless, a medium position is manifestly the most sensible one — Elbow about level with the keys. If you have a long *upper*-arm you are therefore compelled actually to use a higher seat than if born with a short upper-arm.[1]

Preliminary movements and Touch-movements distinct:

5. ALWAYS KEEP DISTINCT THE MOVEMENT *towards* A KEY AND THE MOVEMENT *with* IT. Always be over or upon the key before sounding it. The action *with* the key should always, so far as possible, be *vertical.* In extending the finger, or the hand, or the arm *towards* a key, therefore, be sure to keep that move-

[1] In a compilation on Piano Technique recently issued is a page of four illustrations supposed to show the different "positions" affected by the various "Schools"; thus, respectively: (1) "The Older Methods," (2) "Safonoff," (3) "Leschetizki," and (4) "*Matthay.*" The last illustrates an arm almost straightened-out and hanging down at an obtuse angle of about 45°, and with the keyboard indicated at a level rather lower than the hips!

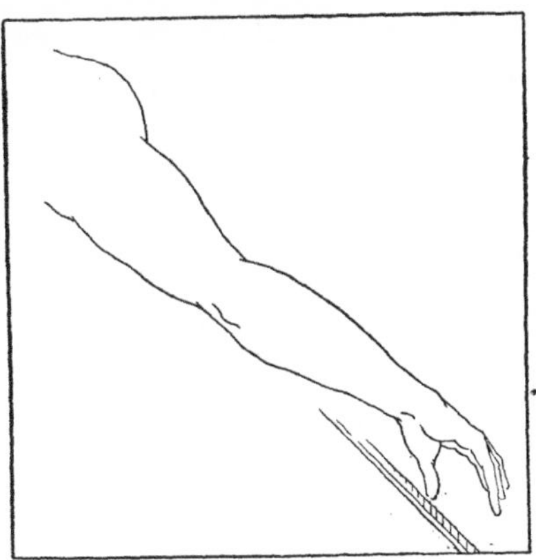

Is it really imagined that I instruct my pupils to play *standing* in front of the keyboard? — or seated on an Office-stool or Step-ladder! Misrepresentation such as this hardly seems appropriate in a book presumably meant to be seriously instructive.

ment or action *distinct from* the tone-producing one; else you will lose tone-control through the sideway pokes or stabs of the arm, etc. Not only will this spoil your option to select the tone, but it may even cause you to miss the notes altogether, or to split them. Therefore invariably keep the two movements distinct. This applies particularly when taking skips. Find your note first and *then* play it.[1]

Horizontal movements of Wrist and Hand:—

6. When turning the fingers over the thumb, the hand must be turned slightly *inwards* (or the wrist outwards) horizontally. Thus the nail-phalange of the thumb can remain in a straight line with its key, and you avoid sounding two notes with it. When playing a scale it is well to keep the hand turned inwards throughout the scale—both in ascending and in descending. This reduces *unnecessary* horizontal movements.

7. When, on the contrary, you turn a long finger over a shorter one, as in double-notes passages, all this is reversed, and you must then turn the Hand *outwards*—or Wrist *inwards*.

8. In Arpeggio playing, to-and-fro (horizontal) movements of the hand cannot be avoided altogether. These occur in conjunction with to-and-fro motions of the hand and forearm itself at the wrist-joint.

On Skips:

9. In skips within two octaves of compass, start *with the Elbow held sufficiently outwards.* This enables you to reach the outermost note *without* any Movement of the Elbow itself *during the skip.* This renders such skips less fatiguing and safer.[2]

Hand-position:

10. The much-debated position of the hand is mostly a personal equation. No two hands are alike, whereas the key-

[1] *See* ¶20, also ¶9, on the taking of skips.
[2] Also see ¶20 on this point.

board is inflexible. However, never really "hold in" the knuckles of the hand. A large hand, on the contrary, must indeed be made markedly *hollow* — with knuckles well raised above wrist and fingers. This position enables one easily to reach the keys with fingers and thumb, and avoids unnecessarily driving the longer fingers between the black keys. This also places one's finger-joints in a mechanically more advantageous position. Something like this is probably the most comfortable position for every hand.

The Wrist-level:

11. The level (or height) of the Wrist should be a resultant of the position and *condition* of the hand. With the hand and fingers arched as described above, the underside of the wrist is slightly lower than the Knuckles and Elbow; yet it may be somewhat higher or lower without harm.

Note. — Having a tolerably large hand myself, I am compelled mostly to use the "well-arched hand" to avoid sprawling my long fingers in between the black keys while keeping my thumb on the keys. This entails my usually *dropping my wrist* slightly below the level of the knuckles. Yet for certain passages, I may drop it still more, and for others raise it considerably! Also, for certain delicate singing tones, for the sake of the Elasticity it brings with it, I allow my fingers actually to *flatten* or straighten out — a precedent which, as already pointed out, Chopin himself provided.

The "Knuckles-in" fallacy:

12. The "knuckles-in" doctrine, or Method, is not only a total fallacy, but is also thoroughly harmful. To imagine that sunk-in knuckles give "more strength" is a delusion, only too likely to lead to stiffness and loss of finger-power. This delusion has been caused by an *illusion*. Thus: if you happen to be able to raise your fingers considerably *higher* than the level of your hand at the knuckles, then it will *seem* to you as if the knuckles were sunk-in. But the hand itself may for all that be level with the wrist, and *well* above key-level; therefore, after all, there is here no "sunk-in" knuckle! This illusion has been the cause of much misery to innocent and unwary students!

How to correct sunk-in knuckles and nail-joints:

13. If, however, your knuckles really do drop in while playing, possibly you are not exerting the fingers sufficiently to keep the knuckles *up*. Here the correction is simple — exert your fingers better! Or, the fault may be, that you are using too much down-force from hand and arm relatively to the fingers' reaction upwards from the key? The obvious correction here is, *do not spoil the balance!* The balance should be correct both ways — the finger-exertion should balance the basis provided for it by hand and arm.

14. In the same way, if your Nail-joint is inclined to turn in, try to correct this by exerting the nail-phalange more, relatively to the rest of the finger. This, however, may be a purely physical defect — maybe of the bones, muscles or tendons. In this case it is waste of time trying to alter it; it cannot be altered, and besides is of small moment. (*See* p. 170, *The Act of Touch.*)

NOTE. — One of the greatest woman-pianists of the last generation habitually played with all those nail-joints sunk in, and she had quite a colossal technique in spite of it! So those afflicted with this mal-position may take courage!

15. FINGER POSITION AND MOVEMENT have been fully discussed under "Flat and Bent Finger," Chapter IX; also Additional Note, No. XIII, which see.

A bent spine is ugly:

16. DO NOT SIT LIKE A HUNCHBACK. It is distinctly unhealthful, and of no profit technically. Besides, to see an ugly thing before him, is likely to make the listener imagine that the sounds also are ugly. Freely and *easily* keep your body erect, or nearly so. A slight leaning forwards from the hips is more comfortable for some; it was ANTON RUBINSTEIN's habit.[1]

17. Playing freely, with the constantly recurring relaxations of your upper-arm and shoulder, is likely to tempt you to *relax also the muscles that keep your body erect.* Have a care this does not happen.

[1] *See* the outlined figure of the Master on page 305 of *The Act of Touch.*

NOTE.—If you have fallen into this error, notice that the *pull* of the muscles and tendons that prevent your spine from collapsing can be felt at the lower part of your back. Make the necessary exertions there, and your body flattens out and rises from the stooping position.

Unnecessary Body and Arm movements:

18. DO NOT SWAY YOUR BODY AND ARMS UNNECESSARILY. Unnecessary movements of the body and arm are manifestly waste of energy; also they do not make for a sense of security. Moreover, the worst feature is, that such movements will attract the would-be listener's *Eye*-attention to your body, and will thus distract his *Ear*-attention from your Music-making.

NOTE.—Should you play stiffly and badly, you are almost compelled also to sit stiffly—and more or less immobile, since you feel you dare not move at all for fear of losing your place on the keyboard! Whereas, if you play freely you find you *can* move about considerably without any such precariousness of location. Nevertheless, do not allow this freedom to tempt you into wild movements!

19. WHEN YOU EMPLOY ROTATORY *MOVEMENTS* always let them be of the *Forearm*—not of the upper-arm.

The substitution of *Upper*-arm rotation, whether as action or as movement, as already pointed out, is a very clumsy thing and spoils Technique. It also entails circular movements of the Elbow like making a pudding—far too clumsy for use at the Piano!

20. FOR SKIPS WITHIN THE TWO-OCTAVE RANGE, as already noted, ¶9, place your Elbow *midway* between the two notes, so that you need not move the elbow itself sideways *during* the skip—it is unsafe and clumsy. All skips and sideway movements of the arm entail adjustments *of the hand* sideways, so that thumb or fifth finger may not be swept off the keyboard.[1]

Do not ape Movements:

21. EXTRANEOUS AND UNNECESSARY MOVEMENTS are often indulged in by artists—movements of the wrist, elbow and even

[1] Refer to ¶9 on the sideway movements of finger, hand, and arm with quiet elbow.

shoulder. Do not be misled by these. As already indicated, although harmless fads on the whole, they are *not* essential to the act of playing, but are in the nature of *test* movements, of the same nature as some of those given in my "*Relaxation Studies*" — tests by which the artist tries to recall the sense of freedom enjoyed when playing well.

NOTE. — As already pointed out, there have been attempts in the past to teach Technique empirically by deliberately adopting certain unessential movements in a forlorn hope to arrive at correct Doing by such roundabout ways — hence the "Curvilinear" and "Undulatory" Theories of Touch, probably first propounded by DEPPE.

The resuscitation of such exploded empiric ideas nowadays seems incredible, yet we find it being attempted!

22. In short, *do not ape the mere bodily mannerisms* of a great artist, but instead try to fulfill the correct *muscular conditions* just as he does — as needed and prompted by the dictates of his musical sense; then your playing may improve.

Obey facts, not make-believe fads! [1]

23. FINALLY, then, it is only by supplying a correct BALANCE between action and reaction that you will naturally acquire correct Position and Movement.

Moreover it is clear that *the Visible elements of Technique* — Position and Movement — are of quite insignificant importance compared with *the Invisible Elements* — the *actuating* muscular

Ugly and unnecessary Movements

[1] Among other things, one of my would-be critics charges me with actually *teaching* ugly movements of the Elbow, Wrist and Shoulder — supposed to be the result of "Rotation"! As I have just said, such movements are adopted by some artists as "*fads*," but they have nothing to do with my teaching — or the teaching of anyone else who understands the fundamental causes of Touch.

The delusion that freedom or exertion of the Forearm rotationally could or should induce rotatory (or "undulatory" or "curvilinear") movements *of the Elbow itself* is particularly amusing, since rotatory-movements of the Elbow obviously can only possibly ensue from Rotation of the UPPER-ARM itself, as shown earlier. This fallacy, among others with regard to Rotatory movements, is fully exposed in the *Additional Note*, No. III, on "Forearm-rotation Misunderstandings," etc.

changes in the *state* (stress and relaxation) of the various portions of the playing limb.

It is this last problem, primarily, which you have to learn to master. Only by doing so can you hope to produce your tones accurately in response to your musical wish, and can you succeed in true Music-making.[1]

Chapter XIV

NOMENCLATURE

On the Naming of Things

1. NOMENCLATURE of a thing is quite unimportant when compared to the actual *knowledge* of a thing. I may recognize a certain flower, may know its shape, colour, the number of petals, its habits of life, where it is to be found, and how it propagates itself; I may subsequently learn *its name*, but my real knowledge of the flower is not in the least bettered by the sound of its name, though it may seem so at the time. All I have learnt is how to allude to it and classify it when in communication with my fellows. Nomenclature (or Terminology) is a convenience, therefore, but the correct naming of things is no guarantee whatever that *the facts have been understood.*

Terms in the Past and Present:

2. When I wrote "The Act of Touch" I was faced with the difficulty that my fellow musicians and precursors had adopted certain terms to denote the *outward*, *visible* manifestations of

[1] For further details on Position, and illustrations, read Chapter XXIII of *The Act of Touch* (Longmans, Green & Co.).

the Act-of-sounding notes, but had almost completely ignored the underlying (and invisible) basic phenomena. To prevent confusion I had to retain the already accepted terms, but I also had *to add new terms* to designate the new knowledge of the causal facts.

3. "TOUCH" was one of these accepted terms, a generic term, including *everything* appertaining to the sounding of notes in playing.

4. Thus, in the past, we had "*forte* and *piano* Touch"; "*legato* and *staccato* Touch"; and "*arm*, *wrist*, and *finger* Touches" — to denote the various *movements* which *may accompany* the true processes of touch.

NOTE. — Later on, rotatory *movements* were also recognized as "Rollung" or "Rotatory Touch" — although there was still no glimmering presentiment that all these aural and visual effects are quite subsidiary to those *actuating* muscular stresses and relaxations which are quite hidden from the ear and eye, and only discernible and provable by correct deductions, and as *limb-sensations*.

5. To these terms of classification I therefore had to add and invent new ones, to denote *Touch-construction* — the physical *constitution* of the various processes of Tone-production, actuating stresses of limb, mostly invisible, which are the true cause of Touch in all its aspects, but which were ignored by the old teachers except in purely empirical suggestions. Hence the new terms: "*Species* of Touch" (the three species of Touch-*construction*), "*Weight-transfer* touch," and "*Arm-vibration* touch," etc.

The "Species" of Touch:

6. Thus we have: —

(*a*) "FIRST SPECIES" — of Touch-*construction*, denoting touch *produced solely by Finger-exertion*, with loose-lying hand, helped by individually (but *invisibly*) applied impulses from the Forearm rotationally. This allows only of Finger and Rotatory *movements*.

(*b*) "SECOND SPECIES" — where the actuating process consists of Finger-exertion, helped either visibly or invisibly by

Hand-*exertion* — and by the Forearm rotatively, of course. This may be accompanied either by Finger or hand *movements* — or by rotational ones.

(*c*) "THIRD SPECIES" — which includes the co-operation of the Arm-element — in one of the FOUR *optional* ways in which its vertical stress can be *individually* applied to help the Finger and Hand (and the Forearm rotationally) for each note.[1] Manifestly all forms of *Movement* are here possible during Key-descent — either Finger, Hand, Arm or Rotation "touches."

7. *Vice versa*, we now see that down-arm-*movement* must always imply some form of "Third Species"; whereas Hand-*movement* and Finger-*movement* may be built-up of any of the "Three Species."

8. In other words: All four forms of *Movement*, Finger, hand and arm (vertical as well as *rotational*) are available with "Third Species," whereas Arm-*movement* is cut out with "Second Species," and Hand *movement* also with "First Species." *See* Chapter XIX of "*The Act of Touch*," and an Additional Note on "The Distinction between Touch-species and Touch-movements" in "*Relaxation Studies*" (Bosworth and Co.).

NOTE. — Manifestly, the Forearm *rotational* Element cannot be classified as a "Fourth species," as a confused-minded writer has suggested. Since it *co-operates in all* of the three Species it cannot itself be a "Species." The *Poised* arm, for the same reason, also cannot possibly come under the appellation of a "Species of Touch," since it either operates *in between* the sounding of *all* notes (whatever the Touch-form) or is applied *continuously*, without break, as the basis of running passages where the lightest form of Resting is required. *See* Additional Note, No. IX: the distinction between the Visible and Invisible.

The terms *Arm-vibration* and *Weight-transfer* Touches.

9. *Arm-vibration touch* fundamentally consists of "Second Species," with its accurately timed individual finger *and hand* impulses for every note; but it may *approximate* either towards first species or third species — when it might be termed a "hybrid" touch.

[1] *Vide* The Arm element, under the headings I, II, III, IV, of Chapter V.

10. *Weight-transfer touch:* Here the stress of the continuously-resting weight practically wipes out that sensation of the *individualized* actions of the finger, hand and arm, whence has arisen the term "Species."

Those obsessed with Nomenclature might, however, rightly claim that there is an approximation to *third* Species when you derive your passed-on Weight from a slight relaxation of the Arm upholding muscles, in conjunction with the continuous Hand-pressure here needed; whereas, without Weight, but with Hand-pressure alone (but not too much of it, please!), there is an approximation to SECOND Species; and with the loose-lying hand alone it would certainly be FIRST Species. But is it worth driving this demon to such lengths? Particularly when we find that Arm-vibration and Weight-transfer touch so often merge into each other! *See* Chapter V, ¶ 48, "On the Merging of Touch-forms."

The place for First Species

NOTE. — As indicated in earlier Chapters, "First Species" is too precarious a proposition, anyway, to be practically available with our modern Piano-action, however well it may have sounded in Clavichord days. Possibly, however, one may thus play the alternative ***ppp*** shown in the Additional Note, No. XIX, and also thus play the first three ***pp*** notes of the so-called "slide." Indeed it might be called a very light form of Weight-transfer touch with Hand-weight only!

True "First Species" implies solely the use of the "small" finger-muscles, with loose-lying hand; since, if you use the "strong" muscles, this necessitates also the use of *Hand-exertion*, — but that is no longer First Species, but *Second* Species!

Optional terms:

11. No doubt, many another term might have served as well as "Species of Touch." For instance, one might have said "The three main species of *playing*," or "The three *kinds* of Touch-construction," or "The three *actuating* or three main *causation*-forms of Touch," etc.

Clichés *v.* technical Nomenclature:

12. As a matter of fact, I myself, in teaching Interpretation, hardly ever use any such terms of mere classification or catalogu-

ing of Touch. Instead, I constantly (where necessary) refer to the bare physical *facts* themselves, and use a multitude of concise clichés and ejaculations, which those of my readers who have patiently borne with me thus far can now easily appreciate, such as the following:—

> "Arm off"—lighter! "Elbow free!" "Weight, not Push-touch!" "Rotationally free"; or: "Rotational repetitions here, not alternations!" "More finger-grip!" "Knuckles free!" "Don't hold your notes down rigidly—only lightly by the 'small' finger muscles!" "Arm-vibration here—not Weight-transfer!" "Always hand behind the finger!" "Hand separately for each finger—imagine you have *ten* hands, not two only!" "Ten arms needed for Singing-tone!" "More than weight here—Fore-arm down-exertion needed!" Or: "Forearm-weight only for these light chords—not whole arm!" "Don't poke—never upper-arm forward with fore-arm downwards!" "Not *too late*—in key-descent!" "To the *tone*, not the floor!" "Not *staccatissimo*—always SOME duration even in 'staccato'!" "Choose—choose always every note!" "Choose Tone and choose Duration also!" "Listen for every note!" "Time every note!" "Listen inwardly, but also outwardly!" And perhaps my favourite one: "How MUCH?"—for every note; and: "Don't think of Technique—think of *Music!*"

Empiric phrases:

Such labels are useful in teaching; but notice that those here given always refer to actualities. They are a form of Tabloid-knowledge! They are in a totally different category from purely *empiric* phrases, which neither convey nor denote any true knowledge of facts, and are often directly misleading.

NOTE.—For instance, such dear old phrases as: "Press the key like ripe fruit"—for singing tone. Or "Snatch at the keys, like hot cinders"—for Staccato! Or "Press well into the key-beds"—an infallible way of killing all playing!

Caution however is needed even here, in the use of such Tabloid-clichés. Be sure that your pupil really does know to what they refer!

A teacher is so likely to assume that the pupil understands under such labeling the same knowledge as that possessed by the teacher. Hence a wise precaution is constantly to re-explain what such ejaculatory phrases *really signify;* else you may find to your dismay, later on, that the pupil has attached a totally wrong meaning to them!

NOTE. — Remember the example of my lecture-pupil, who thought that by "Arm-off!" I meant *sliding one's hands off the keyboard* — and naturally could not reconcile this with Legato playing! Not more stupid however than some "misunderstandings" of my teachings on this point alluded to elsewhere!

13. All this seems uncalled-for, since I insist on the unimportance of Terminology. Unfortunately, it is necessary to be explicit with these facts, since so many persist in confusing Touch-*construction* and *touch-movement* — the Invisible with the Visible!

NOTE. — Such confusion however (it must be repeated) has arisen solely from persistently mistaking the visible *movements* (the trappings of Touch) as the *Cause* of Touch, whereas the true causes and processes of Touch are mostly *invisible.* There can be no such "confusion" if this is clearly kept in mind.

In fact, there is no innate difficulty in comprehending the difference between Touch-RATIONALE and Touch-Movement. The difficulty usually arises from the presence of wrong Preconceptions — from long-standing habits of mis-regarding *movement* as the explanation of Touch.

Why Touch-facts sometimes seem difficult to grasp

The simple explanation is, that it is difficult to get rid of such particular mental misconceptions, like all other mental habits or aberrations. Obviously, the longer such false conceptions have lived in a mind, the harder are they to eradicate, and the harder for the sufferer (or the possessed!) to allow saner ideas to enter. This fetish with regard to Touch-*movements* (or reversal of Cause and Effect) is however just as childish as to imagine that it is the *visible* revolution of the wheels of a locomotive which *causes* the "puff, puff, puff" issuing from its funnel! No doubt, the child will presently experience quite a mental upheaval when he has to reverse all that, and learns to understand pistons and cylinders and steam pressures, etc.

A veteran or even middle-aged musician may likewise find it most uncomfortably confusing and difficult to rid himself of his thoroughly fixed but wrong notions of Movement as *being* Touch. But unless he has the necessary modicum of strength of mind to *budge* these wrong preconceptions, he cannot improve his teaching ways, or be a real teacher, in the sense now expected by the public.

Harmful Nomenclature:

14. While Nomenclature, classification or cataloguing is really then of little moment, nevertheless an *ill-chosen term* may do much harm. As indicated earlier, "Fixation" is a baneful term of this nature, since it is likely to suggest everything one should *not* do in playing! Obviously, it was invented by someone ignorant of the true Causal-conditions of good technique — evidently by someone who tried (as always, in the past) to analyse touch from its *visual* aspect. Also, in the past, incredible though it may seem now, it was thought that one *really* should *stiffen* one's knuckles, wrist, elbow (and even shoulder) during the act of tone-production — "so as to give firmness to one's touch!" Whereas, as demonstrated, what is needed, is, momentarily, a fully effective but elastic *steadying* of those hinges (or joints), when needed during the moment of key-propulsion.

Recoil must be countered, but not by "Fixation":

15. This required *steadying* of the joints, however, as demonstrated, you must never attempt to supply by any "Fixation" — or Tug-of-war derived from the simultaneous exertion of antagonistic or "contrary" muscles, the tendons from which run across those joints. On the contrary, as insisted upon earlier, this steadying — or resistance — or *Basis* you must supply by delivering a countering action from the *next adjacent* part of that limb.

NOTE. — As shown in Chapter V, to steady the *knuckle* momentarily, you must supply an invisible *down-exertion of the hand*, and thus *counter* the momentary recoil upwards felt at the knuckle owing to the finger's action against the key during its depression.

Again, to steady the *Wrist-joint*, you must there supply some form of down-stress *from the arm*, and thus counter and receive the recoil, there, of the hand's down-exertion when helping the finger against the moving key.

Yet all this remains invisible!

16. There never is any stiffening or "Fixation" in *good* playing — and never has been! Indeed, "Fixation" is always a sure indication of bad unresponsive technique. As said before, what

you must always provide, is a state of nice *balance* between Action and Reaction, that is all — but it is everything!

Knowledge of facts useful but not of Names:

17. Nomenclature, then, is a convenience, but is of no importance unless it conveys a *harmful* suggestion!

What does matter, is that you must learn to understand and supply the right *conditions* (and resulting movements) of those living levers of yours — the Upper-arm, Forearm, Hand and Fingers.

True understanding of the correct processes of Touch (mostly hidden from sight) will then assuredly help you in your endeavours to re-create Music to the full extent of your MUSICAL VISION.

CODA

CLEARLY then, the solution of the problems of Technique are not to be found in knowledge of Nomenclature, nor of Movement, nor of Position.

They are matters of *Mind* and *Muscle*, mostly Invisible, and therefore not soluble by Eye-analysis. To help yourself pianistically and musically you need:—

KNOWLEDGE AND UNDERSTANDING OF:—

Key-movement.

Key-attention.

The shortness of the act of tone-production.

The six ways of arm-use.

Finger-and-hand exertions individualized for each key-descent.

The distinction between the sounding and the holding of notes.

The inseparability of technique from the constant exercise of MUSICAL PURPOSE.

ADDITIONAL NOTES

Additional Note No. I

ON PRACTISING

PRACTISING does not consist (as so often supposed by teachers and students in the past, and even in these enlightened days by *some* teachers — and most students) in playing through a passage ten times, or twenty times, fifty times, a hundred, or even five hundred times, either slowly or quickly, and more or less *thoroughly wrongly*. But it consists in your trying to *find out all about that passage;* all about it musically and technically, the HOW of it — every note of it, for the sake of the Whole. It consists in your trying to find out precisely *where* its emotion and beauty lies, and what are the required inflections of Tone, of Duration and Time, to bring that beauty to the surface; and also what are the precise technical means which you must employ for that purpose — hence the "HOW" musically and the "HOW" technically. It implies consideration of *every note* before it is sounded, and hearing how it actually does sound. It means you must alertly *notice*, must find out, must analyse how and when each note should sound and how it does sound.

Moreover, you must *notice* how each note turns into each next note *horizontally* — that is, what the intervals are melodically and physically, and also, how each note fits in vertically with the notes of the other hand — *where* precisely they *meet* in Time — and all this is implied in the learning of the text — the mere "notes" of the passage; and all the while you must be recognizing better what musical value each note has with regard to all the other notes in the passage and the piece as a Whole — the greater or lesser musical importance or unimportance of each. Finally, playing itself, Performance, means actually doing this all the time — so that the musical beauty of the thought shall *come through.*

If your work is not on these lines, then it is merely strumming — a misuse of the keyboard as a typewriter. Instead, always try to make *Music.*

Additional Note No. II

AT THE BEGINNING

I have shown how I think a child should begin at the keyboard in my "Child's First Steps," and in the books complementary to that: "The Pianist's First Music Making" (with Swinstead's music), and also in my own "First Solo Book" and "Playthings for Little Players."[1]

One thing is learnt at a time. I begin by making the child sound notes at their softest with the side of his hand, by arm-release accurately timed *with* the key. It has however been recently suggested that this is far too complicated a *first* step for the beginner, as he has not only to learn to release his arm and to time its action, but also has to time all this *with the key.* At first, this argument of course seems perfectly logical; and the propounder therefore suggested that before touching the keyboard the child should learn not only to relax his whole arm, but learn also to do this as a *timed* action. I think, however, that this preliminary is not necessary in the case of the normal child. A child is not normally stiff; that usually comes to us later, through misuse of our muscular and mental systems!

1 "Child's First Steps" — *Joseph Williams;* the others by *The Oxford University Press.*

It is, however, overlooked that long before a child touches the Piano, he has already learnt not only to relax his arm when required, but *also to time such process*. For instance, he cannot comfortably allow his arm to descend to the table to take hold of his spoon (indeed a very early necessity) without neatly relaxing his arm, and also *accurately timing* such release to reach that spoon *when he wants to*. It is a timing lesson he is compelled to learn quite early in life![1] He also has to learn neatly at that moment to grip his spoon, somewhat like gripping hold of the Piano Key. Probably he will at first poke it into his eyes a few times, but there is nothing like adversity to teach one to be careful! Therefore, having already acquired these fundamental acts, when he comes to the Piano (after having been shown its mechanism — what remains, is to learn to associate this *timing* of the arm *along* with the key itself. Hence I consider that my "First Step" is quite vindicated as such, and clearly is the correct first step at the Piano in most cases. But in the case of an abnormal child, with inherited muscular tension, or in the case of adults who have fallen into bad habits, or have been mistaught, it may be better at first to learn the timing of the relaxations of the arm, etc., *away from the keyboard*. In all such cases, undoubtedly, it is easier to acquire a notion of freedom away from the *evil-suggestive* Pianoforte! Hence, it is precisely for such that many of my *Relaxation Studies* are arranged.

NOTE. — For instance, *see* Set V, "Hand-release"; Set VI, "Forearm-release"; Set VII, "Upper-arm release"; and Set VIII, for "Upper-arm release along with Forearm-down"; and, for the sake of learning to *time* these with the key, Set II of these *Relaxation Studies* (Bosworth & Co.).

[1] Unless learnt, every cup of tea would be spilt!

Additional Note No. III

FOREARM-ROTATION

Misunderstandings, Misrepresentations — and worse

Some years ago, a writer tried to denounce my teachings of Forearm-rotation on several indictments, and this denunciation has since been accepted as truth (apparently without investigation), adopted, and copied with frills by still more recent compilers of things technical.

Moreover, I find that some have gravely considered these stupid propositions. Such reiterated misunderstandings and misstatements of what I mean by "The Rotational Element" are naturally amusing to those who have successfully grasped the facts, particularly as these follies have been advanced by writers who proclaim their own scientific superiority. Such misrepresentations obviously condemn themselves; yet for the sake of any unscientific readers who might possibly be nonplussed and misled by what may appear to them as plausibility, it is perhaps worth while to clear them up forthwith.

Thus (I), it is falsely alleged that I advocate rotatory MOVEMENTS from note to note in quick passages; also that anything to do with Fore-arm rotation "must strictly be avoided" — except in the case of tremolandos and trills and such like.

Here is a passage from the earlier writer: —

> "To use the rotatory movement [N.B. *Movement*] of the forearm to play arpeggios or even extended passages such as Dominant sevenths, etc., is a mistake, and subversive of good technique. Some teachers [i.e., Matthayites] even go so far as to teach its use in five-finger exercises. Anything more unscientific, and indeed mistaken, than this it is difficult to imagine."

And here are some quotations from his apparent imitator and adaptor: —

> (*a*) "In all circumstances we must avoid in clear-cut finger work rotatory *action* whether 'visible' or 'invisible' since this is bound to interfere with pure finger articulation."

(*b*) "Since, however, the most valuable tone qualities (which must be pure and clear) require abstinence from rotary action and definite clear-cut finger action, our muscular system must be trained to *prevent* the participation of the former."

(*c*) "Rotation cannot *replace* finger work *because the tonal effect* is entirely different and in many cases inadequate."

"Cannot replace," is particularly amusing, since I have never suggested such nonsense.

(*d*) "No rotary movements, i.e., supinating and pronating movements, should be introduced except as *control* of the *supinating and pronating muscles.*"

How can a movement wrought by a muscle "control" that muscle?

"Nor should five-finger exercises, scales and arpeggios be taught on such principles as *moving* rotationally to each note."

(*e*) "Although our forearm must be *free* rotarily, in correct finger legato it must not be exerted in the rotary direction."

(*f*) "If we depress the key with a rotary Movement of the hand and arm to each note the key is struck *obliquely.*"

Obviously, it is again the Spectre of Movement that rears its head and is the misleader. Let us try to lay it once again.

Must I repeat for the *n*th time that my teachings with regard to Rotation do *not* refer solely or mainly to those quite unessential and purely optional *movements* which were indeed already recognized fifty years ago or more? — but that we are here mainly concerned with that really vital matter, the rationale of the material changes in the *state* or *condition* of the forearm rotationally, which either make or mar all technique, whatever its type — but which are mostly totally hidden from observation. It seems absurd constantly to have to reiterate such a point, self-evident as it is, once it has been really grasped. It is just as absurd as having to "explain," when discussing the manifestations of Force or Energy, that one is not at all necessarily referring to actual visible *movements.*[1]

[1] Possibly one might expect to find it difficult to "explain" such elementary matters even to so intelligent an animal as a clever horse, dog or cat — but surely one has a right to expect something better from a human intelligence?

This stubborn inability — or disinclination — to grasp the really quite simple (although *invisible*) facts of Rotation (as demonstrated) is just as futile as it would be to deny the fact of the *invisible exertions* of your arm upwards, when holding in front of your eyes this very book you are reading, "because" there is no visible *movement* upwards while you are steadily holding the book in its raised position, with hand turned backwards; or to be unable to realize that you *are*, in fact, all the while also exerting your forearm *rotationally*, outwardly (or "supinationally" if preferred!) so long as you continue thus to hold this very book *level* before your eyes — and although this continuous rotatory-twist remains totally hidden from your *eyes!*

Yet thus persistently is ignored the chasm between the previously *accepted* ideas of Rotation (as *visible movements* "occasionally applicable" in tremolos, etc.) and the true facts of Rotation as I have demonstrated them — those *invisible* muscular changes of state of the forearm (*invisible* rotational stresses) reversed or repeated from note to note, and imperative in all passages, quick or slow — stresses which have been correctly although unconsciously applied by *every* successful player, ever since the invention of the keyboard! [1]

The immanence of Forearm-Rotation in this sense (of *invisible* changes of state or condition of limb) will perforce remain a closed book to all and sundry who persist in misreading *Movement* into my explanations of the causal but invisible foundations of Touch.

(II). It is then seriously advocated that one should "*substitute*" UPPER-arm rotation (*i.e.* Elbow-rotation) in place of this much-condemned Forearm-rotation! And, in fact, that Upper-arm rotation *is* Forearm-rotation! All this, as Euclid

[1] True, I have pointed out, that for the sake of realizing the correct rotational *direction* from note to note, that it is well sometimes to take a passage slowly, thus giving the opportunity of analysing the rotational problems involved, by tentative *actual movement*-TESTS in this case. Nowhere, however, have I made the absurd statement that one should provide rotational *movements* for each note in rapid scale or arpeggio passages, as falsely asserted.

would say, is "absurd" — since it is quite impracticable, and untrue.

Upper-arm twist cannot possibly help the finger "instead of" Forearm-twist; it is impossible, because the forearm bones intervene, and any action of the upper-arm cannot therefore be transmitted to the keyboard *without* the exertion *also* of the forearm rotatory muscles concerned! Also, the Twist of the Upper-arm could only become available as a *hand and wrist twist* (*i.e.* forearm-rotation) provided the whole arm were kept *in a straight line* from shoulder to keyboard — with the arm *unbent!*

But we cannot play the Piano *without* our arms being bent at the elbow. Now, if we thus bend our arm, then any rotative action of the *upper*-arm inevitably tends to swing the whole of the forearm and hand upwards, *right away from* the keyboard! — describing a quarter-circle of movement upwards, and downwards again, when the upper-arm twist is reversed. On the other hand, if the fingers are forced to remain in contact with the keyboard (by an added *vertical*, up or down, action of the forearm itself, as the case may be), then the *elbow* itself will be sent into those ugly "curvilinear movements" which LISZT so rightly derided as "making omelette."

In proof of the invalidity of these contentions, try the following six experiments: —

1. Stretch your arm *straight out* from the shoulder, unbent at the Elbow. Now rotate the *upper*-arm (which involves rotation *of* the Elbow) and you find that this necessarily also induces a rotation of the hand and forearm.

2. With the arm thus *perfectly straightened* out, now bring your fingers upon the keyboard, and you may certainly be able to "help the fingers" by upper-arm rotation, but since the forearm intervenes, you are bound to use *forearm* rotatory exertions as well — else the upper-arm rotational exertion could not be transmitted to the keyboard!

Moreover, thus to enable you to assist the forearm rotatively by *upper*-arm rotation, you are compelled to sit at an impracticable distance away from the keyboard, else *you cannot keep your arm straight,* as would be necessary to encompass this unneeded and disconcerting "help" from the upper-arm.

3. Now repeat No. 1 experiment, *away from the Piano,* twisting hand and forearm (and elbow) by means of this clumsy upper-arm rotation — while keeping the arm straight out in front of you; and then, while still keeping the whole arm thus straightened-out, *substitute* FOREARM *rotation only* (in place of the previous upper-arm-rotation experiment) and realize how incomparably easier is this Forearm *movement.*

4. Next, place your thumb upon the keyboard in the ordinary playing position (with arm *bent*) and if you now really twist the *upper* arm "clockwise," but with Elbow *stationary,* you will find that your forearm is now swung *sideways* and up into the air — *right away from the keyboard.* Hence it is clear that you cannot help the little finger by such "upper-arm rotation" since the whole limb is moved sideways and lifted off the keyboard by it.[1]

5. Now, finally, try to insist on all the fingers remaining in contact with the keyboard, while you twist the upper-arm inwards and outwards in turn. You will now discover that this will *compel* an alternate outward and inward swing *of the Elbow* itself — the derided "Omelette" *movement!*

6. Test for *Upper* arm-rotation by grasping the two protruding ends of the Elbow between thumb and middle-finger.

(III.) Upper-arm rotational exertions, however, *are useful,* but not in the way imagined. When you take skips, by means of *horizontal* movements along the keyboard-surface, with elbow stationary, although these movements are apparently caused by forearm-swings sideways, yet you are really instead using *invisible* upper-arm twists; in fact you are here *countering*

[1] To prove this: open a penknife half-way. Rest the "Elbow" of this *bent arm* on a table, and twist the handle between the fingers and thumb, and the blade is seen to swing *sideways,* and also upwards, if this "elbow" is turned slightly outwards as in playing.

what *would be* the resultant up-and-down movements of the forearm by *an* INVISIBLE *alternate lowering and raising action* of the forearm itself, and thus *translating* the upper-arm twists into horizontal movements!

Of course, if some people prefer winding their watches by a clumsy upper-arm twisting action, instead of by normal forearm rotation, none can say them nay! Personally, I prefer winding mine by neat, easy, gentle *forearm*-twistings. And I like twisting-out my finger-passages at the Piano in a precisely similar manner, to help my finger and hand exertions, but mostly do so *without* any rotatory *movements* whatever — the fact which seems completely to baffle some unclear thinkers.

(IV.) Even a more amusing fallacy advanced by one writer (and duly subscribed to by the other) as a supposed "scientific" argument "against the use of Forearm rotational *movements*" (N.B. always Movements!) is that they are "*mechanically wrong*" — because (as falsely alleged) they form an application of Force "*at an oblique angle*," instead of vertically or in direct line with its required incidence. Copious diagrams are then used in the endeavour to enforce this supposed "scientific" incapacitation of the Forearm. Verily, if the blind lead the blind, both shall fall into the ditch!

Thus we read: —

"If then the rotatory forearm movement [N.B. always movement] be used, this fulcrum is not in direct line, as the leverage starts from an *oblique angle* position. . . ."

"The motion is oblique, and the leverage therefore has no direct fulcrum."

It does not seem to have dawned upon these investigators that the *movement* of the free end of any and every *lever* (since it moves on a fixed fulcrum) must inevitably be a path describing an "oblique angle," or, more correctly, *part of an Arc*, or circle.

Granted, it is correct enough to assert that a rotatory *movement*, whether caused by forearm or (if preferred) by upper-arm rotation, must be, for part of its journey downwards (*towards the surface of the key*), at an "oblique" angle — or, more correctly, at an angle describing part of an arc. Yet, when we come to the thing that matters, and consider the *invisible* rotative-*stress* (and in this case also *movement!*) *during* the moment of *doing work* (*i.e.* during the $\frac{3}{8}$ inch of Key-descent, this moment of the tone-producing process), we find that the direction of force is then practically *vertical* after all, and the degree of arc so small as to be negligible as a loss of power. In fact, the rotational force is here applied *more vertically* than in the case of Finger-action itself! — for in "clinging-touch" the finger-tip certainly does swing inwards (at an "angle" with the key) during tone-production; and in "thrusting-touch" the business-end of the knuckle-phalange also similarly swings round in part of an arc.

Indeed, if you swing your thumb towards its key from a *vertical* position (with the hand resting sideways, and with the little finger on a key as pivot) then, as depicted in these two books, the tip of the thumb will certainly describe a quarter-circular movement during the rotatory movement of the hand and forearm in bringing it into the playing position. (*See* Fig. 1, next page.) But then, one never should try to hit or strike a key down — not in this twentieth century, either by Forearm rotatory action, or finger action or in any other way — in spite of the instructions to the contrary by "the teachers of the old school"! No, the key must never be hit down, for that indeed is quite unmechanical! Instead, the tone-producing stress against and with the key must not be begun until the key itself has been reached — as insisted upon elsewhere. It follows, that during its short transit down *with the key* the thumb after all moves *practically vertically;* just as vertically in fact as do the fingers themselves at the keyboard; and although, theoretically, there is a slight curve inwards in all these cases, it is negligible as a practical proposition.

In short, the preliminary movement may describe quite a large part of an arc, whereas by the time the key is reached this curve becomes so small as to be negligible, and for practical purposes vertical with the key, as shown on the following page, Fig. 1.

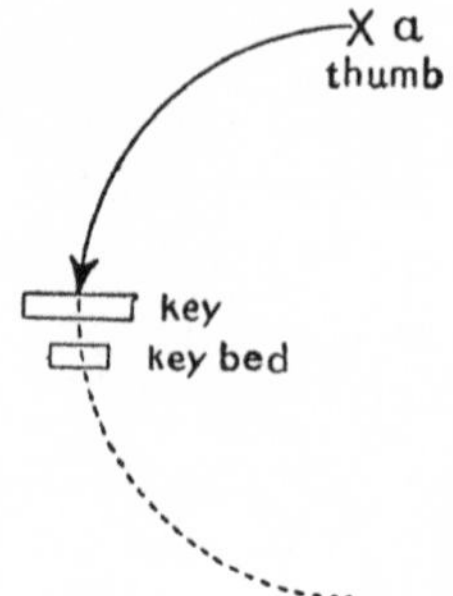

Fig. 1. — *a*, Tip of thumb raised off keyboard owing to the hand being turned up into its fully vertical position, with little finger resting on keyboard.

Moreover, it is clear that the same law must hold good in the action of any and every possible lever. Since a lever swings on a fulcrum, its "business-end" is bound to describe *part of an arc* — or "oblique angle" as alleged! According to these authors' dicta, then, it would seem that *all* levers must be "unmechanical" machines!

Levers, nevertheless, seem remarkably efficient! The reason is that their action is practically direct while actually doing work, a fact that seems to have escaped these scientists.

As a matter of fact, our end of the key-lever, being the free end of a lever, also swings in part of an arc — and moreover in an arc *opposite* to that of the finger actuating it.[1] Thus roughly: —

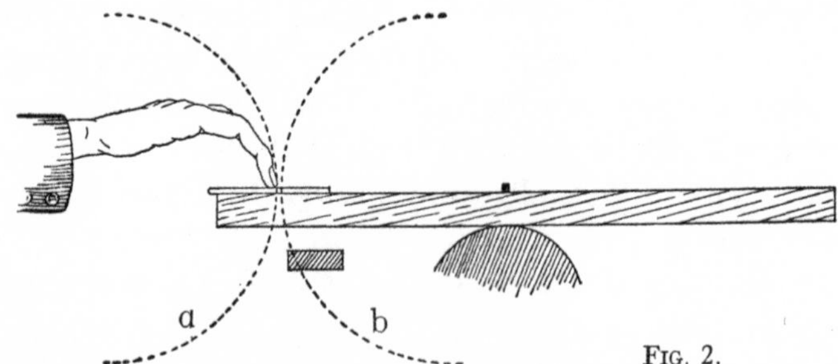

Fig. 2.

[1] Possibly, if our finger-tips were not padded as they are, we might therefore experience a considerable degree of friction. Possibly also this partly accounts for the unpleasant experience of playing with dry fingers; or playing on celluloid keys. *See* also the Photos C 1, 2, 3, on page 35 of the *Epitome*.

Perhaps the following may serve to make this matter clear even to those least-gifted with mechanical insight: —

Consider the motion of *one cog* of a cog-wheel transmitting power to another, as shown in Fig. 3 below. While the cog moves down towards its position for doing work, it describes a whole quarter of a circle of movement. It, however, only begins *to do work* when it engages with the cog on the opposite, *driven* wheel.

Certainly, it moves at an "obtuse angle" (as our authors describe that motion) *before* doing work, but notice that *while* the cog is actually transmitting power to its neighbour, the motion is practically vertical and direct, so small and negligible is the curve during that solely effective moment. Thus:

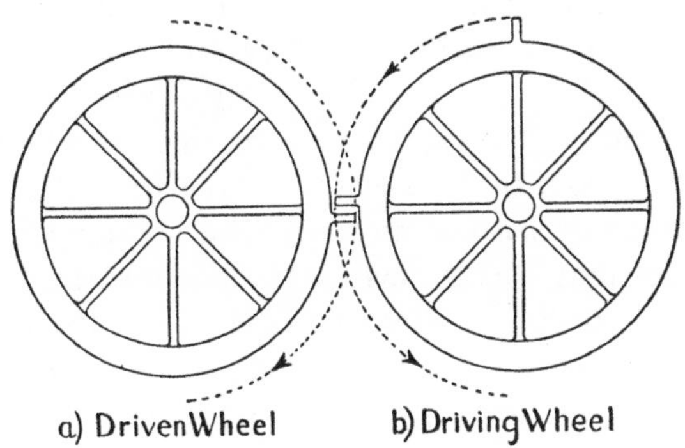

FIG. 3. — Showing the movement of one cog *before* and *while* doing work.

The action of your thumb, when helped by an actual rotatory *movement* of the Forearm, is identical with this; however large the preliminary distance travelled, and however large the portion of arc subtended, yet, while you are doing work *with* the key, the motion is quite comfortably vertical after all!

So it is to be hoped we shall hear no more of this absurdly *unmechanical* contention, that Rotatory *movements* (and *actions*) of the Forearm are in any way more "unmechanical" than are the Finger-actions themselves.

Finally, as to the assertion that the application of the *Fore-*

arm-rotation Element creates or induces "*ugly movements*" *of the Elbow itself*, etc., that is as *un*-scientific a proposition as could well be imagined. Here, again, the Spectre of Movement is the misleading genie. How can a twisting and untwisting of the bones of the forearm cause a movement OF the Elbow itself? The folly of this you can easily prove for yourself; thus: —

> Actually rotate the forearm freely, as in playing a *tremolo* by actual rotatory *movements*. Do it as violently as you like, yet the Elbow *remains perfectly quiescent* — provided you do your tremolo *freely* — as you should.[1]

Certainly, as I have pointed out in Chapter XIII, ¶ 21, there are some artists who have accidentally acquired various forms of unnecessary movement, to which, afterwards, they attach importance.[2] Such movements are but harmless fads. They may even prove useful, by recalling the feeling of freedom associated with Right Doing. Such extraneous movements, however, have nothing to do with the actualities of touch; and imitation of them will assuredly *not* lead to the wished-for results. Need it be pointed out that I have never anywhere advocated or countenanced such absurd, useless and unsightly movements? To lay them at my door cannot therefore be excused under the convenient terms of misunderstanding or misapprehension.[3]

As old as literature itself is the device of thinking to obtain

[1] True, if you wear a loose sleeve, the rotatory vibration of the forearm may induce a flopping about of part of that sleeve on your upper-arm. But no one, gifted with even a minimum of scientific investigatory power, should be misled by that into imagining that the upper-arm, *under* that sleeve, is also moving.

[2] PACHMANN, for instance, for one season affected a *tremolando on the depressed key*, averring that it improved his singing tone!

[3] Moreover, after asserting that the teaching of Rotation is responsible for much ugliness of movement, these very same writers then gravely advocate precisely such (previously condemned) "undulatory" movements, as *essentials* of the Touch-actions! We are in fact expected to welcome these unnecessary movements as things of Beauty and Joy-for-ever, when advanced under new and fascinating titles, such as: "*The Coffee mill*" — rotatory movements *of* the Elbow, "*The Caterpillar*" — up-and-down movements of the Wrist itself, and "*The Pump*" — up-and-down movements of the Shoulder. I leave it at that!

kudos by trying to find flaws in the teaching of the famous. And there are worse devices. One of these is to put false words into the victim's mouth, or false construction on what he actually has said, and then to demolish these false structures with a triumphant flourish of victorious superiority. This may be clever and ingenious — but it is not "cricket."

But "the Proof of the pudding is in the Eating." Indeed, most bad finger-passage playing must probably be attributed to non-apprehension of the simple facts of Rotation as I have shown them to be. Thousands of players all the world over have been cured by having learnt to understand them. And as John Adams, that great psychologist, has well said: —

> "*The ordinary person may lead a blameless life although unable to explain the true cause of error. For the teacher this is impossible. It is his business to understand the real causes of error and to be able to remove them!*"

For a Piano teacher not to understand the true bearing of this ever-present (but *invisible*) Rotation-Element is therefore unpardonable!

Additional Note No. IV

ON BEAUTY AND UGLINESS IN PIANO TOUCH

The following, from my pen, appeared in "The Music Teacher" of March, 1931: —

The Braid-White experiments of the American Steel Institute, to which Mr. Ernest Newman has recently called attention in an admirable article, and which were described fully in *The Music*

Teacher, are of extreme significance to every pianist, whether amateur or professional. Incidentally they prove the folly of key hitting and "striking," and the reason of the loss of power by so doing. But with regard to the question of quality-differences, recently published letters show that the deductions made from these experiments may easily be erroneous and quite misleading. Hence, in the interests of the musical public, a little clearing of the air may not be amiss.

It seems to be mistakenly assumed that these experiments prove quality-differences to be impossible, whereas in point of fact they triumphantly prove their existence; and, moreover, show them to arise from differences in the upper-partials or harsher harmonics, precisely as insisted upon in *The Act of Touch.*

Pseudo-scientists in the past have always tried to persuade us, musicians, that variations in the degree of loudness were the only possible ones, and that we, who insisted we could hear variations in the quality (or timbre) of the tone were suffering from foolish hallucinations. That is all changed now, and the tables are turned on our would-be traducers, for science declares that our ears did not deceive us. The false assumptions were based on the fact that the hammer, during the last thirty-second of an inch of its journey to the string, is thrown at it, and "therefore" only quantitative inflections were possible; quite overlooking the fact that the string has some say in the matter, and also that we are dealing with an elastic hammer-shank, which, when ill-used, may cause a raking of the hammer-head on the string, thus calling forth from it unparliamentary language! Other elements may also contribute — for instance, the key itself lies loosely on the key-frame and may jump.

That quality-differences are achievable by the act of touch your readers can easily prove for themselves by the two following experiments:

(1) Play a chord by a rigid drive forward of the whole arm — upper-arm (or elbow) exerted forward, while the forearm is exerted downwards. It is analogous to delivering a knock-out

blow in boxing. It certainly tends to kill music — and incidentally the instrument.

(2) Now instead, play a chord with the upper-arm (or elbow) lax, while the forearm may nevertheless be exerted downwards, and you will find it practically impossible to achieve a nasty noise.

It is best in both cases to repeat the chord in a *crescendo* and with pedal down, so as to eliminate any suspicion of durational contrast.

To produce the well-sounding effect you must be careful to *time* the necessary finger-and-hand exertion accurately in cooperation with the arm condition. It must all be done before it is *too late* in key-descent to have effect, and the tone must be attained by a proper acceleration *during* key-descent; in fact, an "acceleration" at geometrically increasing ratio — a law which applies in piano-touch just as much as in the case of every other exertion the object of which is to provoke Movement, such as rowing, tennis, golf or billiards. Give a jerk-action and you lose control and power, and at the piano it is the same — or worse.

These experiments should also be made on a "hard" hammered (bright toned) instrument. The very purpose of a *soft* hammer is to disguise in a measure the assaults of the tonally bad player, but it also largely deprives the sensitive player of colouring power.

Yet there is a fly in the ointment! These experiments also seem to prove that quality-differences can only arise along with quantity-differences; in fact, that every grade of tone-level also has its corresponding quality-inflection, so that harsh effects can only be attained by playing loudly enough, and that if we wish to avoid such, we must not go beyond a definite tone-amount.

But the experiments here are not at all convincing or final. Evidently the artists who experimented did play more harshly as they played louder; the records of the harmonics prove that. Yet that is no proof that other artists might not be able to show louder effects without so much harshness. Indeed, we find that there are many artists who charm us with the beauty of their tone in singing passages, here producing their tone as in No. 2 experiment, whereas the moment they attempt anything beyond a *forte* (or even *mf*) they change over to the type of touch indicated in No. 1 experiment, and thus become strident, or give dull thuds, which form a libel on the instrument used. Indeed, many famous artists mar their performances by such misdoings — and knowledge on their part of the No. 2 type of touch would greatly enhance the pleasure we receive from them.

Whatever is ultimately found to be the full explanation of the effects we hear, it can make no difference to the teaching of touch. If we misplay by using No. 1 type of touch, we shall certainly have comparatively little control over our tone-gradations, whereas with No. 2 type we can graduate the tone with perfect nicety down to an almost inaudible whisper — and consequently we thus have at our command a huge range of *crescendo* without reaching harshness. In fact, it is possible that the ultimate explanation may prove to be that with No. 2 type of Key-treatment, the whole range of tone, while ample, is given at a *lower level*, whereas with No. 1 it starts higher up in tone, and hence the tone has to be forced to create the desired contrasts.

The fact we have to realize is that if we act in one way the musical ear objects to the result as being ugly, whereas in the other way the result is acceptable.

The moral of all this is, whether you are merely a beginner-student or are one of the most famous of artists, at all costs avoid the forward-drive type of technique which so easily causes harshness and dull thuds and thus offends the susceptibilities of the musical ear.

We musicians, who love the beautiful in tone, can now work on unperturbed and even with more assurance than before. Or, if we belong to the order that subsists on musical mustard and cayenne, unalloyed, we also know how to ensure the ugliest possible effects.

The Ugly is very easy of attainment. It is the difficulty to attain beauty and subtlety that has called forth the adage: "*Art is long and Life is short.*"

No, quality-distinctions are not an illusion of the eye; they are often only too real — as Ear-pain! To master the No. 2 form of tone-making in *forte* is, therefore, the *gate* towards musical playing. Remember, you can still retain perfect mastery over tone-inflection when playing *forte*, so long as you leave *your upper arm (and elbow) free* when you have to add the necessary down-exertion of the forearm; and that it is then almost *impossible* for you to make a really nasty noise.[1] Whatever the ultimate explanation of the effect, you will thus play your *forte* and *fortissimo* with a full, pleasant tone, even on a hard-hammered Piano, and it will actually sound REALLY *louder* than with the forced variety! And although your tone will not sound noisy close up (just as in the case of a badly produced voice), it will carry well, will "fill" the concert-hall with a large volume of sound, and will make the instrument sound at its best and not at its worst and dullest, and twangiest! Nomenclature signifies no more here than anywhere else. It does not matter in the least whether you accept the beautiful effect as representing "good quality" of sound, or whether you call it "un-forced," or "un-loud," or "XYZ" tone, the fact is that you will fail to reach the full height, musically, of which you might be capable, unless you have mastered these facts!

[1] Refer to No. III of the four *optional* forms of arm-use, p. 35, Chapter V.

Additional Note No. V

EFFECTIVE AND INEFFECTIVE FINGER-WORK

It is often mistakenly assumed that Finger-passages, to be effective, must be *very loud*.[1] There is no greater mistake! Indeed, for BEETHOVEN passages, a certain degree of tone and ruggedness is often requisite — and plenty of legato also. But effectiveness does not depend on the quantity of tone. It really depends on good, true "finger-individualization." Now this implies in the first instance the accurate *timing* of each action — that is, the accurate foreseeing of each note's due musical place; and secondly, the physical timing of the tone-producing action itself — the separate timing of the *hand* and forearm-rotational impulses along with the finger, so that the work shall be completed *early* enough during Key-descent.

Therefore the ability to play successful finger-passages mainly depends on such accuracy in *timing*, since the forces used are else wasted on the beds under the keys, as indeed they so often are by the inexpert.[2] Hence, also, the utility of *practising* all passages *staccatissimo*.

Ultimately, however, the effectiveness of passage-work depends on the degree of *Musical Purpose* felt with every key used. The artisan (we will not say "artist"!) who strums through his passages automatically, just like a Pianola — however loudly and quickly he does so — has no real chance of artistic life nowadays against the true artist, whose whole soul is concerned in *making beautiful* and significant the succession of notes he employs. True, when you are condemned to play on a soft-hammered instrument, you may be sorely tempted to force your way through the felts in order to obtain some brilliance and

[1] *See* Additional Note, No. XVII, "On Strong *v.* Weak Fingers."

[2] There are some gifted with Samson-like muscles, however, who can nimbly get over the ground and play quite loudly in spite of much wrong-doing in this respect!

colour; but the best remedy in such predicament is, not to behave like a bad artist, but instead, to refuse to play on an abomination to which the makers are compelled to resort as a protection against Piano-smashers and Non-artists.[1]

Additional Note No. VI

PIANOLA *VERSUS* HUMAN PASSAGE-WORK

The Pianola and the Pianist

Mr. Ernest Newman, in an article in a *Sunday Times* of October, 1929, pleaded for a revival of the Pianola, and the following letter from me which he published on October 27 under the heading "MR. MATTHAY REPLIES," explains itself: —

Sir, Mr. Ernest Newman has written a stirring article in your last issue. We must all thank him for "giving us furiously to think" but we pianists and teachers must be allowed to protest against some of his dicta.

He asserts that it takes years of "leathering away at exercises" before you can play notes in rapid succession by hand, whereas, with the Pianola you can achieve this at once and at any speed.

All depends here on what we accept as worthy of the name of "playing" — that is the crux of the matter.

Now, the great charm and fascination of a Chopin passage, for instance, lies in the fact that you can with your fingers inflect each and every note you play as to Tone, Duration, and Time. It is this *individualization* of sounds which renders a

[1] Indeed, if you have an arm like a blacksmith's you *can* drive your way through the softest hammer — incidentally, ruining its purpose. But every Piano-maker, who knows his vocation, will nevertheless be willing to provide the *hard* Hammer (*with its full range of colour*) for every true artist whom he can trust not to misrepresent his instrument.

The next *Note* on "Pianola *v.* Human Passage-work" confirms this one.

passage played by the musical player so infinitely more interesting than when strummed through by the Unmusical and Unthinking.

Some years ago I attended a lecture, with musical illustrations on the Pianola. I had anticipated that the rapid passage-work might perhaps sound almost as well as when played by hand; but that the true failure would arise in the slow movements. It was quite the reverse! In the slow movements the operator had time to alter tone, duration and time from note to note. The result was not altogether unpleasant — but it most obviously needed highly skilled use of the levers and bellows, which must have cost the operator much "leathering" at the Pianola, and training as a musician. When, however, he came to a *Chopin* G flat study the effect was utterly boring — a total burlesque of Music. The succession of the notes was here far too quick to admit of any lever manipulation for each individual note, and only mass-production effects were available, hence the irritating dullness of the result.

Clearly, then, it is infinitely more difficult to render a passage *musically* acceptable through the Pianola than by hand. Therefore, the quickest and only way to learn to use the keyboard is patiently to acquire the use of your own fingers, hand and arm, and *Mind*, if you honestly wish to make Music. This does not nowadays imply "leathering away at exercises" — *wrongly* — for years! No doubt that was so in Mr. Newman's youth. Nowadays, however, a child is at once put straight on the right road, and if musical can achieve fluency and musicality in rapid passages without any of the drudgery Mr. Newman deplores, and is directly shown *through the practice of actual music* how to use the Piano as a musical instrument — and not as a typing machine.

While inserting my letter, Mr. Newman made further comments on the subject, and I sent the following letter, which, however, he did not insert; but in fact dropped the subject: —

October 31, 1929.

Dear Mr. Newman,

Thank you for inserting my letter. In your comments thereon you remark:

> "Some of the excellencies" in hand playing may be "purely imaginary." "The player fancies he is doing all sorts of wonderful things that exist only in his will and wish to do them; they do not materialize for the listener."

I quite agree there is some truth in this, but the whole truth is not quite as you put it. Pianists, certainly, sometimes do things which do not "come over." For instance, I have seen players lift themselves off their seats in frantic endeavours to make tone — *wrongly!* The fact, moreover, is, that a really musical and subtle player often uses inflections so delicate that they escape some listeners, simply because their ears (and minds) are too dull to notice them, and the message goes over their heads. Indeed, "it takes a genius to appreciate a genius" — fully; and it takes the really musical to appreciate musical playing to the full.

These divergencies of ear, or lack of it, no doubt largely account for those extreme divergencies of opinion where really musical players are concerned.

I fear that Pianola practice will hardly help to sharpen the ear in these respects.[1]

Cordially yours,
TOBIAS MATTHAY

[1] I might have added: In fact, we know of cases where most delicately musical artists have received apparently spiteful criticisms in London papers and have actually been accused of "lack of colouring"! Whereas, the critic may have been quite honest, but too dull-eared to *hear* the delicate nuances by which the player aroused his more musical listeners to ecstasy. One of these dullards advised CASALS (after a wonderful performance of a Bach Concerto) not to "waste his time over such mechanical stuff"!

Additional Note No. VII

REPRODUCED *VERSUS* SELF-PRODUCED MUSIC

"The Man and the Machine," and the Future of Piano Teaching

This article appeared in the *Daily Telegraph* of Jan. 4, 1930. It explains itself:—

WHEN the pianola first appeared on the scene many piano teachers foresaw therein the doom of their profession, but it proved to be a false alarm. There is, however, a real menace at present. The gramophone and wireless have come to stay.

True, so far, reproduction gives but a faint semblance of actual performance, and the pianoforte comes off worst of all. Colouring has to be whittled down at both ends. The engineer has to cut down the *fortes* to prevent "blasting," and he has to heighten the delicate nuances or nothing comes through. So we receive but a pale reproduction of a real performance, and the fine *subtle* artist's doings are reduced to pale shadows, and he seems little better than his quite ordinary fellows.

The Real Menace.

But it is safe to predict that the microphone will yet be immensely improved, and that it will in the end give us equal definition of the lowest bass as of the highest treble, and will adjust itself to all extremes of tone-gradation.

The real menace, however, does not lie in the wireless and gramophone reproduction itself, however perfected it may be. The danger is in the very likely misinterpretation of the whole situation by the layman. He may ask why, as a few bits of wire and a crystal (or valve) or a clock and a whirl-table give him quite a considerable degree of musical delectation in the home, he should spend money on educating his children to give performances far less adequate than those so conveniently provided.

This will seem an irrefutable argument, and he may, therefore, in ignorance, condemn his children to forego one of the greatest joys of existence — self-expression musically. Indeed, it is a great happiness to listen to good music adequately performed, but it is not the same joy as that of personal music-making, however humble the effort; and personal creation, artistically, is an inextinguishable impulse in the human breast.

The woodcut, the lithograph, and the etching have not extinguished painting, and the layman cheerfully pays school fees for lessons in drawing and painting, in spite of the far better pictures on his walls, or even in his newspaper, than any his children can achieve. Witnessing a tennis tournament of the greatest players does not give one the same joy as one's own miserable attempts. The splendid results achieved by our camera do not compare with our own perhaps very crude sketching attempts. The supreme artistry of a Pavlova and Karsavina do not deter papa from spending money on dancing lessons.

Moreover, learning to make music (on the right lines) is a very potent form of general education, far more potent than has so far been conceded by educationists, although the pendulum has indeed begun to swing in the right direction, and music is now officially recognized as a school subject even in our country. Music-making — I do not mean strumming — indeed always demands such keen attention *rhythmically* that it forms a most direct means of realizing what is meant by Concentration of Mind, which is fundamentally a *rhythmical* act; even granting that we must learn to re-apply this act for each distinct subject, as some psychologists contend. To quote from a psychology lecture of my own: —

"It seems to me that to make him learn to perceive the beautiful through sound is a far more direct way of educating the individual (in the true sense of that word) than, for instance, by making him automatically repeat yards and miles of words, formulas and phrases, an unthinking repetition of which cannot seriously be expected to better him one jot as a sentient human being, or to bring him into closer touch with the Universe."

Music and Education.

"This last point should, indeed, be insisted upon by musicians, for there still is a tendency among education-authorities to belittle the truly practical utility of our art as a direct form of education. Indeed, they fail to realize what a very strong factor the pursuit of every art, and our own art particularly, can be in bettering the life of the race."

Seen from the right angle there is every reason, then, why the lay mind should not condemn the child to non-participation in personal music-making, and it is, indeed, the urgent duty of every music teacher to insist on these facts, and thus help to save Music and his profession from a possible temporary partial eclipse.

I emphasized the same points in my Annual Speech on our Prize Day at Queen's Hall, in July, 1930, and a reprint of part of this follows, as Note No. VIII. I am also glad to find that in America a strong propaganda is being carried on with the same purpose in view, under the auspices of Harold Bauer and others.

Additional Note No. VIII

A PLEA FOR MUSIC-MAKING

The following is an *excerpt* from my Queen's Hall Speech at the Annual Prize-distribution and Concert of July, 1930. After alluding to the continued success of the School, I spoke as follows: —

While all this is most cheering, there is, however, another side to which I feel it is urgent I should allude, and which "gives one to think."

For the first time in the history of this School — and this year IT HAS REACHED ITS TWENTY-FIFTH BIRTHDAY — a quarter of a century of existence — for the first time the ANNUAL INCREASE in the total studentship has ceased; and, in fact, we have to confess to an actual slight drop in our numbers. Such set-back, however, is the experience of every music school in the country at this moment, and I fear others are worse off than we are. It is also the same tale all over Europe, and even from America we hear that 27½% of the musicians there are out of work!

These are signs that cause the gravest anxiety to us, leaders of the profession here, and elsewhere. It is not wise to bury our heads in the sand, and try to ignore them. These hard facts must be bravely faced, and, if possible, they must be modified by the efforts of all of us who profess to be TRUE LOVERS OF MUSIC.

Music, indeed, is at the parting of the ways. One of these may lead to greater appreciation of the great potentialities of music, while the other may lead to the most disastrous consequences, and may even endanger the very existence of the Art of Music in the future. Depression of trade, high taxation, the Wall Street and Hatry episodes, and the motor-car have contributed, but these may all prove to be but passing phases. The real menace, however, comes from the RADIO and the GRAMOPHONE. Here, on the one side, it is clear that knowledge of the literature of music is, at the moment, being enormously furthered by these agencies. But, on the other hand, unless we look clearly ahead, and ACT (all of us), we may presently find the door to musical progress closed. At best, the pale effects inevitable with a mechanical diaphragm are no more like the emotional effects of true, real, musical performance than are lithographic reproductions like real paintings. The public perfectly well understands the difference here — and the lithograph serves but as a stimulus to induce us to make the effort to see the original masterpiece.

The case with Music, however, is different. For the public MAY easily BE MISLED. Many may fancy that the real thing HAS been experienced, when, after all, but a faint semblance of Music has been presented. And however charming a record may be at first hearing, repetition of it soon palls, since nothing new is being said. It is, therefore, every music-lover's bounden duty to insist on the fact that actual performance is a vastly more rousing experience, emotionally, than ever can be obtained from the best of loud speakers or earphones, else the layman may imagine he has heard all that music has had to offer him — when he has become BORED by the mass of feeble music-imitations and mechanical repetitions he has heard at his own fireside.

Moreover, there is the fact TO INSIST UPON, that Self-expression, however tentative and inadequate, is a vastly greater influence æsthetically, educationally and morally, than ever can be mere listening, even the listening to real performances. Here it is not possible to overestimate the extreme value of personal musical striving in any scheme of general education as a fine direct mental discipline, and as an opening-up of the mind to things Beautiful.

I therefore plead that every child should be given the advantage of music-instruction in some form or other of actual performance, *as part of every school curriculum.*

Public opinion must be roused, and must force our Education Boards and Councils to recognize Music as a truly serious means of education. True, something already has been done — but in wide-awake America more has been done. Why not here? Surely the serious cultivation of Music will tend to make better and happier citizens of our children, the grown-ups of the future, and the Wireless and the Gramophone will then indeed help instead of hinder Music — and civilization.

Such words coming from the Principal of a thriving Music School may seem somewhat discouraging. Discouragement, however, is far from my intention. I am still an optimist! I firmly believe in the future of Music. In fact, there will always be a large section of the public that will insist upon personal self-expression through Music, and this public will indeed need the help both of the performer and teacher — so there is still hope for our profession! And there is always ROOM AT THE TOP.

After this S.O.S. to save Music, I need add but a few words of appeal for our STUDENTS' AID FUND. Without an interpreter Music ever remains dumb. The average person cannot read a score as he reads a book, and never will. The perpetuation of Music therefore immediately depends on the pursuit of it BY PERSONS OF TALENT, etc.

Additional Note No. IX

THE DISTINCTION BETWEEN THE VISIBLE AND INVISIBLE IN PIANO PLAYING

The following, which appeared in *The Music Teacher* of April, 1929, fully explains itself: —

I have followed with much interest the admirable articles of Mr. A. C. and am thoroughly in sympathy with them; therefore I am sorry that I must ask you to allow me to correct a misquotation he has inadvertently made. It is, however, a point on which there has been much non-apprehension in the past, and still appears to be, if one may judge from the errors perpetrated in recent piratical publications. Hence in the interest of your readers it would seem desirable for me to make this correction.

Mr. C. quotes me as speaking of "First species (*or* Finger-touch)," "Second species (*or* Hand-touch)," and "Third species (*or* Arm-touch)," etc.; and emphasizes this mistaken "or" by suggesting I should have catalogued Rotatory *movements* as a "Fourth *species*" of touch! Now I have never written anything so confusing and contradictory! On the contrary, from the very beginning, I have tried my best to prevent my readers from confusing these two quite distinct facts — the Visible *movements* of the limb with the Invisible *actions* of the limb. Indeed I wrote an extra chapter in my "Commentaries" and in "Relaxation Studies" in order to make this matter clear. To confuse these two distinct sets of facts as so often done, is just as absurd as to imagine that the wheels by the use of which a car is propelled are *the source* of the motive-power! We see "the wheels go round," but it is the *hidden* engine which does the work. We cannot be good chauffeurs unless the engine has no mysteries for us! I feel sure Mr. C. has not made this mistake, but his misquotation or misstatement may mislead others.

Old-fashioned Teaching.

In the old days musicians only recognized "*legato* and *staccato* touches" and "finger, wrist and arm touches" while they completely ignored the action of the engine! That is precisely what I essayed to set right in *The Act of Touch.* But, for obvious reasons, I had to retain the "finger, hand and arm-touch" nomenclature to denote the already recognized three main forms of *visible movement* which *may* accompany the act of tone-production. "Touch" is the generic term covering the whole ground, whereas "finger, hand and arm touch" refers solely to the particular kind of *movement* manifested. Therefore I had to invent the term "*Species* of Touch" in order to classify the three broad distinctions of *muscular combination* (action and inaction of limb) which provide the key-moving energy and are therefore the true cause of the effects — the "engine" in fact! Broadly speaking this engine-action may take the following forms: (1) You may have Arm-touch, that is, visible arm-

movement. This is bound to imply for each movement and sound a *change* in the condition (or state) of the upholding or down-pulling muscles of the arm itself to allow of the movement, and, combined with this, *invisible* exertions of the finger and hand are necessary. Or (2) you may have Hand-touch — that is, *visible* hand movement. This necessarily implies change in the actuating muscles of the hand, and the finger-exertion in conjunction therewith, although these changes again remain *invisible.* Moreover, when the hand itself thus moves and is exerted in the act of tone-production, you have the choice of two conditions: either (*a*) no change in the poised condition of the arm (which implies no change in the sustaining muscles of the arm), or (*b*) you may allow the weight of the arm (whole arm or forearm, etc.) to take effect along with the invisible finger and hand *exertion,* and the actual *movement* of the hand itself. In short, "hand"-touch may consist either of "second or third species" of touch-*construction,* state or constitution — call it what you like.

Finger-Touch.

Finally, coming to so-called "Finger-Touch" (that is, visible *movement* of the finger itself), you here have all three "species" of touch-constitution available. This means that, when you employ finger-*movement,* this may consist either solely of an exertion of the finger itself ("first species") or you may add thereto an *invisible* exertion of the hand ("second species"), or finally you may add thereto an *invisible* arm-basis, in its several available ways. Yet all these three totally diverse forms of action (or "species") here come under the heading of so-called "Finger-touch," because only the finger is seen to *move.*

Moreover, Arm-basis in the *production* of tone may itself be one of *four* distinct kinds: you may either (*a*) allow the weight of the whole arm (visibly or invisibly) to help during the act of tone-production; or (*b*) the weight of the forearm only; or (*c*) you may combine with the full relaxation of the upper-arm a down-exertion of the forearm (both invisible) to enable you to produce your fullest *forte* without harshness; or finally (*d*) you may instead *invisibly* drive forward with the upper arm while giving this down-exertion of the forearm. This last combination is, however, sure to produce a viciously hard tone in *fortes*, and should never be used except quite gently, for light, "dry" effects. If you are fond of nomenclature these four forms of arm-help (during the act of touch) might be classified as four "sub-species."

There is also to be considered that constant condition of the arm in between the successive tone-producing acts, in its nicely poised or balanced condition, which enables you lightly to remain in contact with the keyboard, and forms the physical basis of phrasing; it also forms the basis of "Arm-vibration touch" (used for most finger passages), a hybrid between second and third species.

Forearm Rotation.

Finally, along with all this, whatever the "species" of the forms of touch, and also whatever the Movements of touch, you must correctly employ the most important element of all, that is, the Forearm Rotative Element which applies *everywhere*, although mostly *invisible*, because not necessarily accompanied by any actual visible rotatory movement. For you cannot provide either finger, hand or arm-movement, or any kind or "species" of tone-production without the intervention of this twisting or untwisting function of the forearm — changes or repetition of action or inaction as the case may be — but required for every note you play, if you wish to play as easily as you can, and not as difficult-ly as you can! Now this Rotation-element, although usually hidden from observation, may also sometimes be allowed to display itself in actual rotative movements. As, however, this Forearm-rotatory element is necessarily implied in *all* forms of movement as well as in all forms of "touch-species" (touch-construction) it cannot also be considered to be a separate "Fourth species," as Mr. C. suggests — a Rotation-*Species* of touch! That would be like speaking of three different "species" of bird, such as the Eagle, Dove and Sparrow, and then speak of "bird" as a "fourth species"!

"Rotation-Touch."

But I fully agree with him when he urges that we should adopt the term "Rotation-*Touch*" when we accompany the ***usually invisible*** rotative changes and repetitions with actual movements. Indeed, I suggested this nomenclature twenty-five years ago in my *Act of Touch*, p. 189, section 32. Evidently he overlooked this! Here is the passage: —

"Production of tone may be accompanied by an actual tilting or rolling movement of the hand in connection with a partial rotation of the forearm. These adjustments of the forearm, at other times invisible, are here rendered visible. Such movement has been termed 'sidestroke' by some of the German teachers. A far less objectionable term for this variety of movement is, however, found in '*Forearm-Rotation-Touch*,' which, while describing it more accurately, also eliminates the word 'stroke' — so misleading when applied to any form of Touch."

A Summary.

A little Summary of all this seems desirable here.

The forms of visible *Movement* available are: —

Finger, Hand and Arm Touch, and the last may be either whole-arm movement, Forearm movement or Forearm-rotatory movement.

The forms of invisible *Touch-Construction* or "species" available during the moment of Tone-production are: —

(1) Finger exertion only, with loose-lying hand and poised arm.

(2) Hand exertion added to the Finger exertion and poised arm.

(3) Arm-basis along with Finger- and Hand-exertion. This arm-basis may either be Whole-arm-weight, or Forearm-weight, or Forearm down-force along with free upper arm; or lastly (and to be avoided as much as possible!) Upper-arm forced forward along with the down-forced Forearm.

Moreover, our poised arm (a more or less fully supported arm) is required *in between* the sounding of *all* notes whether in *legato* or *staccato;* and, finally:

The Forearm-rotation Element is universally required in all forms of Touch, always has been and ever will be.

Meanwhile remember, in learning these necessary things, that the purpose must ever be: *the making of Music.*

Additional Note No. X

THE "PURE FINGER-WORK" MYTH

Some lamentations heard in the London Press, etc. (even recently) over the absence of "Pure Finger-touch" in "our modern playing" would be amusing, were it not so tragic — for it shows such complacent and abysmal ignorance of the most elementary fundamentals of all technique, past and present. This superstition as to "Pure Finger-Work" is caused by the persistence of the old notion that in MOVEMENT one could find the *explanation* of our touch-effects. The finger or the hand was seen to move and it was straightaway assumed that the *cause* of touch had thus fully manifested itself. Whereas, as I have proved all along, *Movement* is no evidence whatever that the touch-processes are right or wrong. This obsession is caused by lack of apprehension that Finger-*movements* may nevertheless entail the *invisible* use of the full weight of the arm, etc., forearm-rotation and hand-exertion, although all supplied *quite invisibly.*

There never has been any such thing as "pure finger-touch," as thus ignorantly alleged. No passage can *ever* have been played on any keyboard without the intervention at least of the Forearm-rotational element along with the finger. "First species" (with its light finger-force only, in conjunction with Rotational stresses) may possibly have served well enough on the Clavichord; but, since the arrival of the "Hammerklavier," to try to play a *cantabile* with "First species" would be just as foolish, and worse, than trying to play a Double-bass with a Violin bow! When you really use finger-exertion (*by its "small" muscles only*) for each note *without individualized actions of the hand*, that indeed forms a true "First Species" of touch—rarely however applicable. Yet, even this demands the help of Forearm-rotation, like every other touch-form, and it needs, besides, the arm in its continuously poised condition. In no form of touch, therefore, can the hand and arm be said to be "absent." Thus, with "First Species," along with the Forearm-rotational-element and poised arm, you have *individualized* actions *solely of the finger* — with loose-lying hand; while in "Second Species" *individualized* (reiterated) exertions of the hand are added for each note; and for "Third Species" *individualized* down-stresses from the Whole-arm or Forearm.

"Pure-finger-touch" is therefore a Pure Myth.[1]

[1] *See* also the previous Note, "On the Visible and Invisible in Piano-playing."

Additional Note No. XI

USEFUL *VERSUS* USELESS ANATOMY TEACHING

The Futility of Anatomically-directed Pedagogics

A reiterated warning is perhaps here necessary, since anatomical teaching can be useful and is indeed necessary in some directions, whereas in others it is not only useless, but can be positively harmful to the student. In fact, the demon of Nomenclature has once again tried to raise its head.

To comprehend the playing-actions (his physical equipment) the student certainly needs some (but quite elementary) knowledge of the mechanics of his own limbs — some "skeletal" knowledge; he needs some understanding of the actions, reactions and interactions of the set of levers which form his playing outfit — the upper-arm, forearm, hand and finger levers. Also, he must have some common-sense understanding of their muscular endowment; he must understand that to produce a movement, or, what is more important, an exertion of one of these "living levers," he must call into activity the attached muscles. It is well also to understand that for every direction in which he can thus *actuate* any of these levers, they are also endowed with muscles that have the opposite, or "antagonistic," effect, and that if he allows *both* of these to act simultaneously, then the resulting *invisible* tug-of-war will necessarily create stiffness, with all its disabling effects. Also, it is helpful to know that we have a *dual* muscular equipment for most actions, *i.e.*, strong muscles and weak muscles for the same action. It is also well to recognize the fact that the actuating muscles of a limb (or portion of a limb) are mostly located on the next portion — since by his being able to notice the sensation of tension *across a joint*, he can learn both to avoid the unrequired stresses, and to provide the right ones.

But beyond this, Anatomy cannot help the student, but may indeed hamper him, since any attempt to "think" the required actions *in terms of individual muscles* will only lead to confusion of mind, and will distract his attention from where it is urgently needed — and that is: on *limb*-action, purposed to move the key *for the sake of an intended Musical Effect.* Excepting then the broad and general principles enunciated, any further detailed anatomical knowledge can be of little service to the student, even *were it attainable.* As a matter of fact, however, accuracy in this respect is *unattainable*, owing to the practical difficulties in the way. True, by dissection we can discover which are the main muscles attached to the various portions of our playing-limb, but dissection cannot tell us exactly *how* and where we must use them in playing. Experiments, on the other hand, made on the living body, are not only unreliable and misleading, but are often even impossible to attempt. Mechanical tests of the tension or laxity of muscles and tendons *during the actual performance* of a sufficiently competent artist suffer from the grave disadvantage and uncertainty that the player is quite unlikely to "be himself" under such ordeal, and is instead likely to become more or less self-conscious and tense, and to do quite unusual things muscularly at the critical moment. Moreover, it is manifestly impossible to test the more deep-seated muscles in the living subject by calipers or other machines. And again, most of the apparently quite simple actions are in reality quite complex in the muscular co-ordinations required, and therefore far too brain-reelingly complex to calculate, or to direct as separate muscular impulses, even if we could know exactly what they are, and could directly influence muscles into action — neither of which is possible to us!

Thus, in the end, the anatomical method can only offer us vague *conjecture* (instead of the supposed certainty) as to what really does happen in many of the actions of actual playing.

Finally, even were such analysis not impossible, it would yet be useless and quite futile for the simple (but quite final) reason that it is physiologically and psychologically *impossible* for us *directly* to prompt, influence, or stimulate any muscle into action by *any exertion of our will*, however concentrated our attention.

Muscles will only consent to spring into action in response to our desire *for a particular limb-exertion* or *limb-movement*. All we can do is earnestly to *will* and time the exertion or movement of the *limb*, or portion of it, by recalling the accompanying *sensations*, and the suitable muscles may then spring into responsive activity. To think of the particular muscle is futile![1]

In a recently published book, however, great stress is laid on the utility of knowledge of the precise locality and anatomical names of the muscles concerned, and it is copiously illustrated with more or less accurate diagrams and pictures of the dissected arm, hand and finger — reproduced from Anatomy-primers. It is mistakenly assumed that the pupil will thus be able at will to call up any required muscle. We see, however, that all this is based on fallacy, for, as already stated, it is physically impossible to call any muscle directly into action; and let me repeat it, the only way to call any muscle into action, the only way to obtain its help, is to *will* the required action of the *limb* to which it is attached — and at the Piano to *time* this wish accurately with the Key.

For instance, we may be inclined to smile at what seems to be this author's impossible proposition, but we cannot summon up the faintest smile by trying to influence our facial muscles directly; the only way to call up that smile is either to think of the required facial expression, or, better still, to try to see the humorous side of the proposition before us — and the needed muscles will obediently line-up!

Or, as another instance, supposing I wish to sound a note at the Piano with my middle finger, it is folly to say to the bits of

[1] This holds good even in the case of our being startled, when *all* our muscles may become more or less tense. This tenseness occurs in response to our S.O.S., our call for preparedness, for self-defence; we instinctively then call upon *all* our limbs to be ready for attack, and all the muscles again respond to the *indirect* stimulus.

flesh on my forearm and inside my hand, "Here, John and Jane (and other helpers), look alive and be busy and give that middle finger a pull inwards"! Try it, yourself, by calling upon them by their pet anatomical names, yet nothing will happen! Or, if the foolish attempt to influence them in this way is persisted in, probably "Thomas and Emily, and James and Kitty" and all the rest of the family may indirectly be roused up and called into undesirable activity, and you will find your whole arm, and whole body perhaps, become stiff and set, including perhaps your jaw and your toes! No, to obtain definite muscular response, the only way is vividly to recall the precise *sensation* of the particular *limb*-activity needed — of the required *invisible* stress, or exertion, or the required *visible* movement, and unconsciously our automatic centres will then call up the right muscles to act — if we have been good *limb*-teachers! It is only by *experiment* that we can acquire such automatic response, and thus acquire *remembrance* of the right or wrong limb-sensations. Moreover, pedagogically, the point is to guide these experiments *into the right channels* by knowledge of what is required not of our individual muscles (which we cannot guide) but of our *limbs*, so that our efforts may not be wasted in wrong directions.

It is also claimed that this (misplaced) reliance on anatomical names and places is more "scientific" than my own "Act of Touch"! This, however, is again a delusion; my work should have been read a little more attentively!

To be "scientific" signifies to be in accord with attainable Truth. Whereas, to try to bring the student's mind upon the names and addresses of muscles is a totally wrong road by which to achieve Limb-control — and therefore *un*-scientific! Moreover, the attempt is again made to analyse the touch-actions *from outside*, as so often done before. Therefore, any work thus based on such pedagogic fallacies, so far from having achieved any hoped-for "scientific" status, must be pronounced to be sadly lacking in this respect!

It has lately been suggested that candidates for professional

Diplomas should be expected to possess this useless and misleading knowledge of muscular Names and Places!

Anything more retrograde could not well be imagined. It would only be a case of "Eye-wash." Even when a medical practitioner is inclined to dally with anatomical language, we generally begin to suspect his ability.

Coming now to a more recent book, that of Hugo Ortmann, which has appeared while this one was preparing for Press, this is on a different plane altogether. Here we have honest research by means of patient and painstaking experiments — laboratory experiments — and it is delightful to find so many corroborations of what was already said in "The Act of Touch." But here again, far too much reliance seems to have been placed on Touch-analysis *from without*, analysis based on the visible *movements*, instead of analysis *from inside* — through the sensations experienced during *right doing*. Far too much importance is also again attached to knowledge of the precise locality of the muscles employed, which, while thoroughly interesting, is, as we see, of little avail to teacher and learner. No one would claim that such unpractical knowledge would benefit the Golfer, Cricketer, Tennis or Billiard player. Whence then this obsession that it can help the Pianist? It is with regret that one cannot at all agree with some of the deductions he makes from these admirable experiments. Finally, granted, that such anatomical knowledge may be quite interesting (although useless in practical application) — and that *all* knowledge is certainly entrancing and mind-awakening, and we have also seen that some broad facts of anatomy may be helpful — yet to imagine that a glib knowledge of the *precise* locality of his muscles can help the Piano-student to use his muscles and keys rightly, is just as hopeless as to suppose that he could be helped therein by an intimate knowledge, say, of the habits and names of Flowers, or a knowledge (very far-off knowledge indeed!) of the stars in the vastness of the night skies.

During the years I was engaged upon my "Act of Touch," being of German descent, I was therefore naturally bent on being "recht gründlich" as to my facts; I, also, for a time was misled into the anatomical field. Consequently I misspent (?) a good deal of time trying to master, anyway, *our* part of Anatomy; and was well abetted therein by my late brother-in-law, Dr. CHARLES KENNEDY, of Edinburgh, an excellent anatomist. When, however, it dawned upon me that it was impossible to obtain any muscular response by directing one's attention upon the concerned muscle, I had the common-sense to throw all this overboard, and to delete unnecessary encumbrances from my pages, voluminous though my work had to be in those dark ages of Pianistic ignorance! I therefore restricted myself on this point to about *one single page* (p. 148 of "The Act of Touch") devoted to rudimentary facts, and that single page is ample for the aspiring Pianist!

Additional Note No. XII

ON KEY-BEDDING

The following, which appeared in the London *Musical Times* of Feb. 1, 1931, explains itself:—

SIR, — May I, in the public interest, correct a misstatement in your last issue?

Your correspondent, ..., asserts there are *two kinds* of "key-bedding." There are not. As I invented the term twenty-eight years ago for my "Act of Touch" I suppose I have the best right to its definition! It was invented to denote that most pernicious of all faults — which has killed so much music-making and so many pianists — the fault of applying the muscular impulse intended to produce a tone *too late during key-descent* to effect its purpose. It denotes misapplication upon the key-beds *of the force intended to produce key-movement* — obviously a purely mechanical fact. Whether the muscular co-ordinations employed at the moment would serve to produce a tone pleasant to the ear, or a tone of that extreme stridency apparently enjoyed by some modern writers and players, has nothing to do with the matter. If the tone-making impulse, good or bad, is misplaced on the key-beds the tonal result is bound to be *less* in amount than that *intended*, and therefore cannot accurately represent the performer's musical intention.

If .... chooses to direct her pupils to "press deeply into the key-beds," "past them," or "down to the floor," that is her lookout; it does not alter the meaning of the term "Key-bedding."

Additional Note No. XIII

BENT AND FLAT FINGER

—An amplification

In the old days "Position" was the All-god of every Piano "Method." It was the only thing that seemed to matter, and nothing else was ever thought of, except the mandate "Never, oh, never, move the arm!" Hence full reliance was placed on pictures of the "well-arched" hand, with "well-curved fingers," and all was thought to be well and safe if left "to instinct and inspiration." Later on, *Movement* became the idol. Nevertheless, as we have seen, reliance on either of these fetishes forms no guarantee whatever that those invisible changes of limb-*condition* will be fulfilled which form the Cause of right-doing, muscularly.

The terms "bent" and "flat" finger, used in the past, prove however that there was, even then, some vague notion of the distinction between the "thrusting" and "clinging" actions of the finger.[1]

Perhaps it would have been better to adopt instead of these terms the more embracing one: the *Unfolding* and *Infolding* finger-action, since the finger must *either* "unfold" or "infold" during the act of touch. But it seems difficult to dislodge a term once it has come to be accepted.

Moreover, as insisted upon earlier, the *Position* of the finger on the keyboard with key down, gives no indication as to which of the two has been applied. Thus the *bent* (incurved) position of the finger can be reached both during thrusting and clinging touches.

Conversely, we may reach a quite "flat" position with key *down*, and yet may have been applying that nasty, vicious upper-arm forward-thrust or dig (with forearm down-exertion) which we should strictly avoid, except in rare cases.

The difference is, that with "bent" finger, we *must start* with a fully-bent position, the finger opening out towards and with the key; whereas with "flat" finger we may *start* with the finger more or less fully straightened out, and may then curve it inwards — more or less — during the subsequent journey towards and with the key. The final *Position* may therefore be precisely the same in both cases. *See* photos on page 35 of the *Epitome*.

Thus it is again proved that reliance on the outside trappings of touch (Movement and Position) must be relegated to oblivion as one of those primitive superstitions which have done so much in the past to impede progress pianistically. As I have shown before (Chapter XIII), the position of the finger and hand must necessarily adapt itself to the actual size and conformation of one's hand, since the keyboard is an inflexible quantity. The large hand is therefore compelled to be more arched than a small hand hardly able to stretch an octave.

"Piano-Tutors," in the past, were apparently always written

[1] As we know, *Chopin* is reported often to have mystified his pupils by using a "flat finger."

by large men! And it is amusing to find a more recent one, evidently written by the possessor of a medium-sized hand, therefore recommending a far more flat position of the knuckles as being "more modern"!

Additional Note No. XIV

THE THREE "LIVING LEVERS"

The following appeared in the *Musical Times* of July 1, 1924: —

Sir, Dr. R. asserts that my *Act of Touch* is criticizable, and then proceeds to fill a page of your valuable space with quibbles supposed to prove that in two instances my Terminology is wrong!

The Act of Touch was published just a quarter of a century ago. It may be a satisfaction to Dr. R. to know that I, myself, have adversely criticized its Terminology ever since — but the facts have remained unshaken! — "The laws of nature never apologize."

Dr. R. contends that I have no right to speak of the finger, hand and arm as *levers*, and his ground of objection is that their fulcrums "*are movable.*" He cites as an instance of the true lever the bar of a pair of scales. Does Dr. R. then seriously contend that if I use a pair of scales on board of a moving train this acknowledged lever will then no longer be a true lever — since its fulcrum will then be moving, say, at sixty miles per hour; and that the scales are no longer scales, but should be called, say, a Mangle or Garden-roller? My motor car has many levers, but when I start the car many of these fulcrums are on the move, hence (according to Dr. R.'s contention) these levers all instantly cease to be levers, and perhaps the car should then be called — say, a Boat? The sheer muddle he makes of the Rotational-element is a natural consequence of such perverseness of outlook.

Seriously, however, I must protest that I have nowhere in my writings ever made the idiotic statement that the fulcrum of the finger is "at its tip," nor have I ever said that the knuckle of the hand or the wrist-joint must "*move upwards*" during or "after" the "act of touch"!

Such misstatements show the true spirit of Dr. R.'s attempted criticisms, and I leave it to your readers to apply the *correct* Terminology!

Additional Note No. XV

AN IMPOSSIBLE RECONCILIATION

Recently, it has been claimed that a "Reconciliation" can be effected between the old exploded technical teachings and our present-day knowledge of the facts. Such obviously puerile proposition hardly needs serious refutation; but let us examine the facts.

We have read of the attempts to reconcile Science and Religion — and Art. That is a possible task, seeing that all three are but various ways of becoming conscious of the *Something* beyond Material Things. But one cannot reconcile Truth and Untruth as to the facts of Pianistic physics and physiology! Either these facts are understood or they are not! Refer to *Note* to ¶45 of Chapter V.

The "old" notion was that tone-production could be and should be effected by a *blow* upon the Key, whereas we now know that hitting a key down is not permissible if the playing is to be musical; nor is the old notion of squeezing the tone out of the key-beds ("like ripe-fruit") compatible with our knowledge that tone is fully-produced even before the key fully reaches its bottom level. How can such opposite ideas be "reconciled"? How can there be any reconciliation between the fallacious ideas of Touch-Cause precariously founded on the observed *Movements* — the trappings of touch, and those based upon analysis of the constantly changing (but invisible) Condition or State of the limbs concerned? You cannot realize that each and every tone in a *musical* passage must have a *separate* musical and technical entity, and at the same time believe in the "full weight of the arm" (Breithaupt's "Schwere Tastenbelastung") carried from key-*bed* to key-*bed* — to the utter destruction of Music-sense, and risk to limb and Piano! The claimant to this proposed wizardry complains of having suffered from "cramp"; and is not "cramp" (or Neuritis) so often induced precisely by such fallacious and clumsy *full-weight-carrying* process?

How can one reconcile the old primitive ideas of visible Forearm Rotation, or "Rollung," which dealt solely with tremolos, etc. (tremolos played by actual rolling *movements*) with our understanding of the immanence of the Forearm rotational *invisible* stresses and relaxations, repetitions and alternations from note to note in *every passage* that ever is, or has been played easily, or ever will be? Is our present knowledge that the Arm participates largely as weight or force in many forms of touch compatible with the old insistence on "the penny on the back of the hand," intended to *prevent* at all costs any participation of the Arm? How can there possibly be any "reconciliation" between ideas so diametrically contradictory?

It would be like trying to "reconcile" the pre-Galileo and post-Galileo ideas of Astronomy — the ancient idea that the Sun rotates around the earth, and recognition of the fact that it is the earth that rotates around the sun. You cannot subscribe to both notions! You cannot subscribe both to the pre-Darwinian and post-Darwinian ideas of Evolution! The discovery of Oxygen entirely revolutionized our ideas of combustion, and you cannot "reconcile" the old chemistry, with its belief in the supposed substance, "Phlogiston" (as resident in things which made them burn!), with our knowledge that it is the Oxygen, etc., outside that is the cause of the effect.

Either you do recognize the fact that in Finger-passage work (both *f* and *p*) the "individualized finger" implies the co-ordination, co-operation and coincidence *for each individual note* of finger-exertion *plus* an invisible hand-exertion and forearm rotational stress, or you do not, and are still under the delusion that there is such a thing as "Pure Finger Touch" without help from hand and arm — but which last would imply a true "First Species," produced solely by the *small* muscles of the finger — and producing but a feeble tickling of our modern keyboard![1]

Incidentally, it does not constitute a world-shattering discovery to substitute a new term for "Finger-individualization," for it does not in the least affect the facts as shown in my various books! Either the facts of Technique are as I have stated them in *The Act of Touch* or they are not. You can accept them or reject them, but you cannot "reconcile" them with the false tenets of the Past! Right and wrong are ever opposite, and any attempted reconciliation between them is therefore not only untenable, but is in fact fatuous.

Yet, the facts of Technique are in the main as demonstrated in *The Act of Touch.* No doubt these facts may yet be stated more clearly, and new knowledge may be added. That is precisely what I have attempted in the present volume.

[1] See Additional Note, No. X, *The "Pure Finger-Work" Myth.*

Additional Note No. XVI

THE NATURE OF RHYTHM

As there may still be many who have not grasped the true nature of the sensation of Rhythm in Music, I feel that a reprint of the annexed letter to the *R.A.M. Magazine* may prove helpful. It explains itself:—

In your last issue the following, from a recent book, is sponsored by a contributor of yours as being "the most complete and satisfying definition [of Rhythm] which I have as yet read." This definition runs thus:

"Rhythm is that property of a succession (sequence) of events in time which produces on the mind of the observer the sense of proportion between the duration of the several events or groups of events of which the succession is composed."

May one venture a gentle protest against this recommendation of a definition which again exemplifies that vague outlook as to the nature of musical Rhythm (and lack of rhythmical sense) which is at the root of so much failure musically? It avoids the real issue, and is like the play of *Hamlet* without the Prince!

Some thirty years ago I defined Rhythm as musical MOTION; that is, "The sensing of a succession of sounds as *Movement, Progression* or *Growth*" — Movement in its four main aspects: 1), the progression of a series of sounds *towards* the Phrase-climax; 2), the movement of a group of quick notes *towards* the next beat; 3), the growth of the successive phrases into those larger Shapes constituting a piece (or Movement) of music as a palpable Whole; and at the Pianoforte, 4), the precisely-directed movement of the Piano-key itself.

This elucidation of Rhythm has since become axiomatic.

Accentuation certainly is not Rhythm, it is but a *means* of expressing the rhythmical sense of Growth or Movement.

Indeed, as the years roll on, I feel more and more convinced that the main distinction between the only half-musical and really musical person lies just in the degree of this perception of Rhythm as a sense of *Movement*. All vitality implies Growth — a striving onwards, and musical vitality forms no exception. Without this sense of Onwardness or Towardsness rhythmically, successions of notes mean nothing.

Whatever other (perhaps admirable) excellencies there may be in one's teaching or performing or composing, if there be weakness or vagueness with regard to this sense of musical Progression, then all remains fundamentally unconvincing, flabby, drab — and dead! [1]

Additional Note No. XVII

ON STRONG *VERSUS* WEAK FINGERS

As to the question of "strong finger passages" the fact is here quite overlooked that there are differences in *Piano voices* just as much as there are in larynxeal voices, as already pointed out in "The Act of Touch," pp. 42 and 262.

We, teachers, can only teach a performer successfully to obtain the full benefit of such voice (and such modicum of musical imagination) as he may happen to have inherited. A powerful man should therefore indeed be expected to play his finger-passages far more powerfully in *fortes* than can a girl of fragile build.

In the end, however, it is not at all mere volume that counts; a Clara Butt may astonish and ravish the public with the wonderful resonance of her beautiful organ, but we also have singers with "a mere thread of a voice" who, nevertheless, can move us to tears by the sheer perfection of their art. It is the same at the Pianoforte. The really great artists are indeed found to

[1] *See* Additional Note, No. XIX, "On Rhythmical Attention" — a reprint from 1893.

produce their most striking technical effects, not at all by lion-like roaring, but by exemplifying tones at their softest. It was the perfect *pp* of the great giants of the past that struck one most — LISZT, ANTON RUBINSTEIN and PADEREWSKI, — but happily Paderewski is still with us! The three greatest living Piano writers of the day — MEDTNER, RACHMANINOFF and our own ARNOLD BAX, show the same predilection in their own playing; and the greatest living Pianists of today all excel in their real *pianissimos* — to mention only one, our MYRA HESS, generally accepted as "The Empress of Pianists," as America has well said!

PABLO CASALS (perhaps the greatest living instrumentalist of all) also does not strive to make the greatest possible noise, but instead always relies on the least possible tone appropriate for the occasion in hand. *Forte*, after all, is only a contrast to *piano!*

Certainly, if you wish to produce nasty, harsh, strident effects (and in showing you *how to avoid them* I have also shown you how to produce them), nothing is easier. *See* Chapter V on the *fourth* of the four optional Arm-conditions.

Certain of our present-day composers apparently revel in this! Unable to invent new things beautiful, and thereby achieve acclamation, they have tried (and succeeded too!) in gaining notoriety by writing things ugly, and they like these played as aggressively as possible — a brilliant idea that never occurred to the great Masters, who only tried to evolve the Beautiful, and did not write for advertisement purposes. Happily, there are some few composers of today, ahead of their times, who use all the newest harmonic, melodic and rhythmic contrivances, and yet who try to evolve the beautiful, the romantic and classical, and who still advocate the use of Music as the most direct language of the emotions.

Personally, I confess preference for the Tone-range from *pppp* to *ff* — with an occasional *fff*. Yet I am no purist, for I enjoy the "kitchen utensils" of the orchestra when the musical occasion is propitious. Indeed, I revel in that beating-out of Rhythm by close reiterations of the cymbals in that marvellous climax in DVOŘÁK's "Husitzka" Overture. It is an effect here justified, musically, and not a flamboyant advertisement-device. But I intensely dislike the tone-range apparently advocated by some of my would-be critics, that is, starting no lower than a bare *piano*, and then constantly going up to sheer cacophonous clatter. I loathe it, just as one loathes people who insist on always talking with full use of the larynx, and Pianists who try to approximate to a pneumatic stone-drill.

Indeed, I prefer (and I believe the public also is learning to prefer) the "still, small voice" — musical sensitiveness in place of the most overwhelming raukishness.

However much it may seem like *Sport* to some to witness a Pianist *v.* Piano contest, it has no relationship to the Art of Music.

Additional Note No. XVIII

AN ALTERNATIVE *ppp* METHOD

Instead of the method of producing *ppp* shown on page 8 of this *Digest*, and on page 5 of the *Epitome*, an alternate way is optional. Here, instead of beginning the tone-producing action "half-way down" (or strictly speaking two thirds down), i.e., FROM that "hump" which we can feel during key-descent (on every Piano more or less markedly), we must in this alternate *ppp* touch-form begin our tone-producing action from key-surface (as in all other touches), but we must here swing the key down only TO that "hump." That is, we must aim our action *to it*, and must promptly cease it there, and not, as usual, play *through* it so as to take the key right down.[1]

Owing to the little knock or jerk delivered *at* this "hump," the hammer in this case flies off the hopper at this point, and is therefore here *not* helped on beyond it to the point where the hopper-escapement acts, as in ordinary touch.

In this way the Key-lever is again deprived of half its efficacy, just as by the previously explained *ppp* method, and thus renders very soft playing easier. The difference between the two methods is, that when we play FROM "half-way down" we *use* the *lower* half of key-descent; whereas, in the alternative way we *use* only the *first* half. A very thin, thread-like tone is the result, which can be whittled down almost to inaudibility. The action required is in the nature of a gentle little *staccato* blow delivered *at* that hump-obstruction. Beware, however, not instead to knock *at* the key itself — at surface-level! As the action must be so delicate and subtle, needless to add that the arm must be in its *perfectly* poised or floating condition; a good-sized hand, lying loosely on the keyboard, may prove to be an ample basis without any exertion of it whatever; and the forearm, rotationally, just holds the hand level by its "small" muscles only.

This alternative *ppp* method serves well where swift passages are required at their softest, and *non-legato*. Obviously, as the key is only taken down half-way, and allowed to rebound from there, there can be no real *legato*, although the ear may be deceived at the speed. For artistic playing *both* methods should be mastered, but when and where to apply them is largely a matter of Taste. I, personally, for instance, like to play the

[1] As explained before, the "hump" or obstruction felt during key-descent arises from the repetition-lever being pressed-up against its regulating screw, thus compressing the little spring which actuates both it and the hopper. It is the compression of this spring which we feel as an obstruction during the course of key-descent. The exercise given on page 9 can be of great help towards the acquisition of *both* forms of *ppp*-playing — taking a chord down repeatedly only *so far as* this obstruction, and without sounding the notes at all.

swift delicate accompaniment of the Chopin A Flat study (quoted on page 96) by "passing-on" touch, and therefore for this accompaniment use the "second half" of key-descent only, so as to attain the required *ppp*; whereas in the F minor study (quoted on page 78) for the "echo" effects I prefer the alternate method, with its "first half" of the key only used, and its rebounding *staccato* touch; and with fingers fully bent and more — on their tips, close to the nail!

Evidently, some artists have succeeded in instinctively acquiring one or even both of these two methods of obtaining the softest sounds; but now that the explanations are at hand, every player who strives for artistic finish should make a point of mastering both, since it ensures a greater colour-range.

Additional Note No. XIX

RHYTHMICAL ATTENTION

Individualism v. Mechanism

In this connection, and in view of the extreme importance of Rhythmical Attention (and certain discussions lately) the following verbatim reprint of an article of mine which appeared in *The Keyboard* as long ago as November, *1893*, may prove helpful: —

All musicians of course admit and preach, and are agreed, that *rhythm* is the most important of all in music. Yet it is just this very point which is not sufficiently insisted upon, not sufficiently clearly seen, and most often failed in! It would therefore seem profitable to investigate this a little.

Undoubtedly, it is impossible to conceive anything existing in the entire absence of the element Time. Nevertheless, looking at a painting, for instance, we are not at all particularly conscious of time-space. But when we come to music, its very foundation is *Duration*. Hence the importance of Rhythm — Rhythm not only with regard to contrasts of tone, accentuation, etc., but Rhythm in the sense of contrast of note-lengths.

Now here comes the particular point the importance of which I would impress as vividly as possible upon all — myself included! — whether young students or full-fledged artists. And this point is: that the "rhythm" must be a NEW THING every time a piece is played. It must be done — made — at that very instant, and must not merely "occur" automatically. The notes can be, and should be, found automatically by the fingers, it is true; but not so with regard to rhythm. A sheer automatic performance is the result as soon as the rhythm is allowed to "do" itself. In it will be found to lie the greatest difference between the performances of a barrel-organ and of a sentient being. In the machine, the rhythm is not remade, originated, not at the moment produced for each note; in the human performance it *may be*. And when it is, then we hear a real performance. Notes may be wrong by the hundred, the phrasing and conception may be totally against our notions of what they should be, but when the rhythm is turned out a new thing by the player at the moment of playing, then we all are compelled to concede that we are anyway witnessing a real "reading" of the piece — a performance which, though it may or may not meet with our approval, we all the same feel to be a real *living thing*. In a word, it is an intended thing, and not an article turned out by the dozen.

Very well then, what is the moral of all this? . . . How often has it not been preached — "Concentration," "Attention" — and yet how little living fruit does this preaching seem to bear after all! The failure results from people not seeing how to insure this necessary concentration. Here we learn why intimately close attention on the rhythm is so immeasurably important.

With the very best will in the world we may say to ourselves: "Now then, 'attention'!" "Now then, concentration on the piece I am playing" — and yet the desired "grip" will not come!

The reason is that such phrases are too indefinite to help us. To bring our attention to bear, we must have some definite point. One may look on a page of music with complete attention, and yet truly see nothing of the text! It is only when the vision is brought to bear on a particular passage, or single note, that one really *sees!* In other words, attention only succeeds when there is for the moment a definite point.

"Nervousness," too, is of course merely incapacity of solely arresting the attention upon the matter in hand. How important then is it, indeed, to gain this power of giving one's mind fully at will. And the point I am endeavouring to lead up to is THE WAY, and the only way, to succeed in this.

It is simplicity itself! Every note in every piece most certainly has a spot in time *at* which it should occur. Now just here we do have the something definite required, which the mind may grip:

"Will," intend, determine, then, that the first note of the piece, and every subsequent one, does sound just when your own rhythmical sense of the moment demands it shall sound, "and the trick is done." Play each note at the beginning of a beat rhythmically on purpose. Wilfully put, place, spot, each intervening note and rest, and at once you feel (and everyone who listens feels it too) that you "have" the piece. It is felt that you have *grip* of it. Determining the occurrence of each note just like this is playing the piece on purpose. Concentrated attention is necessarily at once fully given. For to think of the place in Time at which the sounds shall occur, involves that the place on the keyboard, and the particular finger for that moment belonging to it, is also mentally realized. Hence accuracy is promoted all round. And as it is impossible to determine the rhythmical details of a piece without also considering the musical sense of it, the aim of all playing is fulfilled more adequately.

Let it be clearly understood, it is not merely "playing in time" that is required — a barrel-piano can do that quite excellently! — no, it is the making the time on purpose at the very moment of performance, that is the point. The executant's idea may be quite different from a metronome's diction; yet, if he really intends the time-spot for each note, his version will sound infinitely more satisfying than the un-living metronome's! That, in fact, precisely is the difference: in "making the rhythm" he makes the music live — putting some of his own Life into it. And undoubtedly that is just the difference between all Art and mere Mechanism, however finished and perfect the latter may be as such. "The artist lives in his work" — i.e., those who listen, or see, or read, feel a fellow-human's individuality asserting itself. They are conscious of being in the presence of living thought — whether expressed in picture, novel or a musical creation or performance, it is all the same — and that is something ever incalculably higher than the most perfect resultant of a penny-in-the-slot system!

FOREWORD TO EPITOME

This Epitome forms the Summary of "The Visible and Invisible in Piano-playing" — a complete Revise and Digest of my teachings up to date. The Epitome is complete in itself, being designed for separate publication as a School Text-book. I have been urged to issue this at once, without awaiting the publication of its parent work, the demand for such Epitome appearing to be imperative. The Daily Maxims and Final Precepts appended form a concise survey of the most vital points of the subject. When more detailed information is required, refer to the same Section in the Digest itself, and to my earlier works.

Tobias Matthay

Section I

THE MEANING OF TECHNIQUE

1. The sole purpose of Technique should be to express Music. It is useless therefore to practise Technique as such.

2. While trying to gain this technical equipment to express music you must unremittingly give close attention to Music itself. Not to do this is self-defeating and harmful.

3. To try to acquire Technique (as in the past) without constant reference to Music itself is just as stupid as trying to learn the use of the cricket-bat, tennis-racket or golf-club without reference to the ball!

4. Definitely to give musical-attention, you must successfully *imagine* the precise Time-place and Tone-place needed for every note you play, and you must also choose the *kind* of Tone, and precise Duration required for every note.

5. Likewise, to enable you definitely and purposefully to *sound* (and use) the Piano-key you must give to it the *same* definite attention (as to Time and Tone) for every note you play.

6. Musical attention and Technical attention therefore equally demand Time-attention and Tonal attention. Here they meet and become *one*. It is the only way you can bring them into close association and co-operation. There is no other way.

Note. — It is the only way to avoid strumming, and the only way to make your hearer listen to you with pleasure.

7. Therefore you must never dissociate these things, not even in your first attempts at the keyboard.

8. In short: during Practice and Performance never allow your Time-attention to flag for a moment.

9. The four main aspects of Rhythmical Attention in playing are: —

(*a*) You must *time* the movement of the key itself towards Sound.

(*b*) You must feel the swing of each group of quick notes towards the pulse ahead.

(*c*) You must feel the *growth* of each phrase-unit to its climax near the end of each phrase; and

(*d*) You must realize the Growth of a Movement into a Whole.[1]

NOTE. — To enable you to "think" Music and Technique, you must thus feel the sense of Progression or Movement all the while you are playing.

Section II

THE PHYSICAL ASPECT

— *How you must use the Piano-key*

1. The "hopper" action of the key-mechanism allows the hammer to fall back at the moment you have struck the string with it — otherwise it would jam against the string and stop the sound.[2]

2. Consequently, once the key is down you cannot do anything further to make the sound.

NOTE. — In fact, when you *feel* the key's motion *stopped* by the keybed the hammer has *already* struck the string and made the sound. All you can do after this is to keep the damper up, and thus allow the string to continue sounding — but you are not then *making* any sound, you are only allowing it to continue.

[1] See Chapter II, *Musical Interpretation* — Joseph Williams.

[2] See *The Act of Touch*, Chapter VIII — "*The Instrument.*" (Longmans, Green and Co.) You will there find an illustration of the Piano-action, and full explanation of it.

3. You can only produce sound by *making the key move.*

4. The louder you wish the sound to be, the quicker must you move the key down.

5. To obtain the best result from this tone-producing motion you must never hit or jerk a key down.

6. Instead, you must always produce the down-speed *gradually* — by acceleration.

7. This acceleration during descent must be not only "gradual," it must be at an *increasing* rate of increase as the finger goes down with the key — it must be at "increasing ratio."[1]

8. It does not matter whether you call the result a better *quality* of tone, or merely a better *controlled* tone. Unless you form this habit of *acceleration* during key-depression you cannot control the tone with nicety, and your playing will always be unmusical to the extent that you are careless in this respect.

9. For *ppp* you must exaggerate this solely correct form of key-attack. Here you must bring the key down some two-thirds of the way before you give it the final little tone-producing swing.

10. You can only stop the sound by allowing the key to rise, when the damper at once returns to the string and stops its motion.

11. For a true Staccato you must allow the key actually to rebound — with your finger-tip on it.

12. Tone, in the making, can never take longer than it does for the most absolute *staccatissimo.*

13. It takes no more force to hold a key down for Tenuto or Legato, than it does to sound it at its softest. In fact, it takes rather less.

[1] The principle applies *in a measure* even for the sharpest percussion touch.

Section III

ACCURACY OF TONE, AND THE *LINK* BETWEEN MUSIC AND TECHNIQUE

1. Your playing cannot sound musical unless you *mean* every note of it rightly.

2. You can only *produce* your musical intentions tonally by using your "key-sense" for each and every note.

3. "Key-sense" means *physically feeling* how much force is needed before and *during* each key-descent, and applying this force in due acceleration for each note.

4. Your feeling the key's *resistance to motion* in this way is mainly a muscular-sense — a sense of work being done during key-descent — it is a *Work-sense,* in fact.

5. You cannot purposefully produce any note nor can your playing sound intentional and musically intelligent unless you use this *work-sense* for every note.

6. You can only tell *how short-lived* is the force needed to produce the tone by *listening alertly.*

7. By thus listening, and also feeling the key, your musical and technical attention become *one* and indivisible.

8. Your playing cannot mean anything musically unless you do thus both *listen* and *feel* for every note.

9. **To Sum Up:** (1) You must feel the key *before* and *while* you move it down; (2) You must feel it *while* you are holding it down; and (3) You must feel *its coming up* — you must feel the *cessation* of the holding-down action; and unless you do this last you cannot be sure of your Duration effects — i.e., the precise length of your *tenuti.*

Section IV

THE PHYSIOLOGY OF TECHNIQUE

1. The acquisition of any muscular habit, good or bad, is always a *mental* act.

2. You cannot teach your muscles to act rightly, you can only teach your brain to *direct* your muscles rightly.

3. "Stiffness" arises when you *exert a limb* (or portion of it), not only in the required direction, but also in the opposite and contrary direction.

4. Thus you create a tug-of-war between the two opposite limb-exertions.

To remedy this, teach your mind to distinguish between these conflicting and antagonistic limb-*states* — or conditions.

5. Two opposite exertions nullify each other completely if they are equal, but the slightest contrariness is sufficient to spoil your playing. You cannot *see* this fault, but you can *feel* it, if you are sufficiently alert.

6. Indeed, there are *three* distinct ways of "stiffening":

(1) You may use the antagonistic muscles as well as the required ones.

(2) You may jam your limb against the keybeds by playing "too late,"[1] and

(3) You may allow the psychological effect of Fear to cause you to contract more or less every muscle in your body!

7. By no possible effort of mind can you *directly* actuate any muscle. You can only actuate a muscle by vividly imagining and *wanting* the required action or exertion OF YOUR LIMB.

And you can only achieve free action of the limb by *wishing* its action to be free.[2]

[1] That is, by continuing the effort *intended* to produce tone after the tone is made!

[2] This applies both when you need an actual movement and when you need a stress *without movement*.

8. Therefore do *not* try to think of the actual muscles used, or their locality. This will only lead to self-consciousness and stiffness, and will inevitably hamper you in the acquisition of easy technique and sure musicality of expression. Remember, you can only "think" or prompt LIMB-action, not muscular action!

9. You cannot sound any note without *actuating* (i.e. exerting) the finger concerned.

NOTE. — Unless you use your fist sideways, as you should do in the first steps of learning. Here refer to my "Nine Steps," "First Solo Book," "Child's First Steps," "First Music Making," "Playthings," etc., Oxford University Press.

10. This *exertion* of the finger may be accompanied by a *movement* of the finger (relatively to the hand), but *not necessarily so.*

11. Realize, in applying Power, that action and re-action *are always equal.* Therefore, in order effectively to apply power (or Force, or Energy) at the business end of a limb, or portion of it (such as the finger) you must supply a sufficiently stable *basis* as required at the *other* end of that limb (or portion of it) else the force you use will be there misspent, and you will fail to attain the intended tone.[1]

12. *Hence you cannot* actuate or exert your finger efficiently, unless you help it by the Hand-and-Arm element in some form or other.

Without such efficient *Basis* or Foundation, your finger-action will certainly fail in its purpose to move the key accurately.

13. When you apply force with the tip of your finger against the key to move it, the reaction is felt at the *knuckle;* consequently you must supply a stable *basis* there at that moment — the knuckle must not give way, else you will lose your intended

[1] The necessity of a stable foundation for each action was vaguely felt in the past, hence those fallacious ideas of "Fixation," unhappily copied by some recent authors.

effect. This required steady Basis at the knuckle is obtained by *exerting* (or actuating) your Hand during the moment you use your finger for key-depression.

14. This exertion of the hand does *not* necessarily imply a *movement* of it.

NOTE. — You can exert the hand without moving it. Try it on the top of a table. Press quite forcibly — you can feel it, but cannot see it.

15. Again, when you thus help the finger by a down-exertion of the *hand* at the knuckle, the re-action is then felt at the Wrist-joint — up towards the arm there. Clearly then, you must there also supply a stable Basis *when the tone requires it*, else the wrist will be driven up.

But this *Basis* for the down-exertion of the hand upon the finger is provided by the Arm-element, in one of its *six* forms, considered later.

16. Roughly speaking, therefore, the physiological elements available are three: —

(1) Finger exertion
(2) Hand-exertion and
(3) The Arm-element.

17. You can optionally apply any or all of these three elements at the moment of key-descent, while depressing the key by the *Movement* of only one of these; i.e., there need be only a movement of one of these, the other two elements showing no movement whatever.

18. Be sure not to confuse the *exertion* or *relaxation* of a limb with the *movement* of it.

19. Also, do not confuse the application of Weight with *movement* of the weight.

NOTE. — When you drop your arm at your side, you have an example of Movement *without exertion*. Whereas, when your arm lies passively on a table, you can feel the Weight of it there, but there is no movement. In the same way, you can *exert* your arm, or hand or finger without showing any Movement. *See* Note to ¶14.

20. Indeed, most of the muscular changes-in-state which you have to apply in playing are quite hidden from the eye.

21. The particular movement is a relatively unimportant matter, but the particular *Condition* (or state of limb) is all-important. And this last is almost always *invisible.*

Section V

THE PHYSIOLOGICAL DETAILS OF TOUCH

—*How to use your finger, hand, and arm:*

The Finger:

1. Never try to hit the key down. Instead bring the finger gently upon the surface of the Key, and when you reach this surface exert the finger (maybe quite vigorously) during key-descent, to the extent you feel the key needs for each particular Tone.

2. There are two possible modes of finger-use:—

(*a*) You can use a folding-inwards or gripping exertion, or—

(*b*) You can use an opening-out or unfolding exertion and you can supply both without any corresponding *movement* whatever. *See* Section IX, "Bent *v.* Flat Finger-use."

3. The CONDITION of the Upper-arm and Elbow is compelled to be in sympathy with these two opposite forms of finger action.[1]

[1] For quite soft running passages the *inertia* of the perfectly poised arm will serve sufficiently as basis both for "clinging" and "thrusting" finger; but for larger tones played by "clinging" finger the upper arm and elbow must tend to fall backwards, whereas with "bent-finger" the upper arm tends to be exerted forwards. *See* Section IX, "Flat and Bent Finger."

The Hand:

1. To enable the finger to do its work effectively, you must *exert* the hand downwards upon it at the knuckle during each momentary act of tone-production, as pointed out in ¶¶11 and 12 of this Section. This, however, does not necessarily imply any *movement* whatever of the hand itself.

2. As you cannot *exert the finger* vigorously against the key without this corresponding exertion of the hand, you also cannot *exert your hand* upon the key without the corresponding exertion of the intervening finger.

3. When you exert both finger and hand you may *move* either the finger only, or the hand only, during key-descent. Therefore, one of these exertions will then be entirely *hidden from view.*

4. Thus, in all normal playing by finger-*movement* (or so-called "finger-touch") you must always back-up your finger exertion by a hand-exertion, delivered for each note *individually*, although this hand-exertion may remain quite invisible.

The Arm:

1. This matter is bound to seem complex at first sight, but is perfectly simple once it is grasped.

Without mastery of it, there cannot be any real understanding of the rationale of Technique.

2. To enable finger and hand to have their proper *basis*, you must (as shown) back-up the hand exertion by some form of Arm-use — some particular condition or state of the arm.

3. There are SIX WAYS you can thus apply the Arm: —

4. *Four* of these are OPTIONAL, being determined by the desired tone. These four are applied *only during the moment of key-descent* — to enable the finger and hand to do their work effectively.

5. Whereas *two* are COMPULSORY, and constantly needed, whatever the nature of the passage.

6. **The Four Optional and Momentary Forms of Arm-Use:**

I. THE WEIGHT OF THE WHOLE ARM, relaxed only during key-descent.

II. THE WEIGHT OF THE FORE-ARM ONLY in place of whole-arm weight.

III. A DOWN-EXERTION OF THE FOREARM; but in conjunction with the loosened upper-arm and lastly

IV. THIS SAME DOWN-EXERTION OF THE FOREARM, but here in conjunction with a FORWARD-DRIVEN UPPER-ARM.

NOTE. — This No. IV is a type of technique carefully to be shunned in *forte!*

7. *Singing-tone*, chords, etc., demand the use of No. I — here you must *momentarily* release the whole arm (either fully or less fully) as felt necessary for the particular tone.[1]

This triple combination of arm-weight, finger and hand exertion needed for singing tone, lends itself to the distinction between "Weight-initiated" and "Muscularly-initiated" touch, and is one you must also learn to recognize. If you *think* of Weight-release the musical result will be rounder and fuller than when you *think* of the implied Finger-and-hand exertions.

NOTE. — This is more a psychological than a physical distinction, but none the less real, musically, for all that. *See* "Act of Touch," Chapter XX, etc.

8. *Lighter effects* need only No. II — here release only Fore-arm Weight.

9. *For greater tone* than can be provided by the full Weight-basis (No. I alone), No. III is needed — here you must *exert*

[1] The key-resistance encountered during the moment of key-descent tells you *how* much, if you attend alertly. This gives you *pp* up to *mf*, and possibly *f* — but do not forget also the required *momentary* exertions of finger and hand! — so as to render the weight of the arm effective behind the exerted finger and hand during the moment of key-descent, or when continuously so needed (slightly) for "Passing-on" touch or legato "Resting," etc. (Sections VIII and XII).

This weight-release, however, does NOT necessarily imply any *movement* whatever of the arm itself.

the Forearm downwards *in addition* to the full release of the Upper-arm, with its *free elbow.*

10. *Never use No. IV instead for loud tones* — i.e., never, for *fortes*, *exert* the Upperarm *forwards* while you exert the Forearm downwards.

NOTE. — This Forward-drive of the Upper-arm, given *very gently indeed*, may however occasionally be appropriate for light "dry" effects. But in *fortes* this forward-driven Upper-arm and down-forced Forearm (with its rigid Elbow) is responsible for all those harsh, noisy, dull, thuddy effects one so often hears, even from otherwise quite good artists. It is not only destructive of all natural beauty and control of utterance, but is also most injurious to the instrument itself. Avoid it!

11. **The Two Compulsory Forms of Arm-use are:**

{ (*A*) THE POISED ARM, and —
{ (*B*) THE ROTATIVE FOREARM.

12. (*A*) THE POISED ARM is used for *all* passages, but is applied either *Continuously*, or *Intermittently.*

(*B*) THE FOREARM ROTATIVE CONDITIONS must be applied correctly to *every note*, whatever the Touch-form used.

13. **The Poised Condition of the Whole Arm:**

This is a freely-balanced, self-supported, floating or buoyant state (or condition) of the whole arm. It is used in the *two ways:* —

{ (*a*) Intermittently, and —
{ (*b*) Continuously. Thus: —

14. (*a*) INTERMITTENTLY, the poised arm is applied *in-between the sounding of all* the notes in passages which require the arm *during* key-descent in one of the *four* ways mentioned in ¶6.

In this case the arm *reverts* to its poised condition *instantly* on the completion of each separate act of tone-production, both in loud and soft passages, and both in Legato and Staccato.

15. (*b*) CONTINUOUSLY, the poised arm is needed, without break, for the duration of each phrase in most *Agility* passages.

It forms the Basis of *Arm-vibration* touch, and also "The

Act of Resting," both in Staccato and in "*Artificial* Legato." *See* Sections VIII, XI, and XII.

16. This *continuously* poised arm may, moreover, be either used in its FULLY-POISED or in a SLIGHTLY LESS poised condition. Thus: —

(*a*) When *fully-poised* (or self-supported) *none* of its weight reaches the keybeds — and you "rest" at the surface-level of the keyboard.

(*b*) When *slightly less* than fully-poised, enough weight may be allowed to rest on the keybeds (and there *passed on* from keybed to keybed) to form "Natural" Legato-resting, and also for "Passing-on" or "Weight-transfer Touch." (*See* Sections VIII and XI, for Legato and Staccato, and Section XII for Weight-transfer Touch.)

NOTE. — In playing the louder swirls of "Passing-on" touch, the arm may be released a *little* more to provoke *crescendi;* and even with "Arm-vibration" touch it may be a little less than fully-poised in rapid *forte* passages, without such weight reaching the keybeds after all. Anything beyond this (still light) degree of continuously passed-on Weight will ruin your possibility of accurately choosing your tones, will seriously impede all Agility and may even injure your arms, hands and fingers — unless you have exceptionally strong arms and fingers, when possibly you may go unscathed in spite of much wrong-doing! *See* Section XII.

17. All these matters will become clearer when more fully dealt with under their respective headings. *See* Section XI, "How to play Staccato and Legato," page 38, and Section XII, on "Arm-vibration and Weight-transfer Touches," page 41.

18. **The Rotative Forearm:**

Reversals or Repetitions in the condition (or state) of the Forearm, rotatively, are needed for *every note* played, either as alternate changes of state, or as repetitions.

They are mostly quite *invisible*, but so important that the next Section (VI) is entirely devoted to their consideration.

19. These different forms of Arm-help can be applied during the act of touch either *without* any accompanying visible *movements* of the arm itself, *or* while exhibiting such visible movements. In the last case, these may be either vertical movements

of the whole arm or forearm only, or they may be rotational movements of the forearm.

NOTE. — Distinction in MOVEMENT is however quite an unimportant matter. It merely signifies that *one* particular component of touch here outbalances the remaining components, hence this one becomes visible, while the rest remain *invisible*.

Thus, we call it "Arm-touch" when the whole arm or forearm is moved vertically; whereas we call it "Rotation-touch" when the Forearm is rocked rotationally. *See* Section VII, "The Movements of Touch," and Section XIV, "The Names of Touch."

20. To sum up these facts as to the arm: —

(*a*) To enable you to help the necessary (but momentary) Finger-exertion required for each note, a momentary exertion of *the HAND is also required,* together with the right *Arm-conditions.*

(*b*) You must learn to apply the arm in *six distinct ways:*

(*c*) *Four* of these are *optional,* and only applied during key-descent; whereas *two* are *compulsory* in all passages.

(*d*) The *four optional and momentary applications of Arm-energy* are: —

1. The *whole arm* more or less than fully released during the act of tone-production — for singing and chord effects.

2. The *forearm weight* alone released — for light effects.

3. *Forearm down-exertion* added to *upper*-Arm Weight-release for loudest tone effects.

4. *Upper-arm forward-drive* along with the Forearm *down*-exertion — to be strictly avoided — unless for special effects.

(*e*) Whereas the *two compulsory forms of arm-condition* are: —

The *Poised* Arm, and
The *Rotative* Arm,

— these two forms apply to all Technique.

(*f*) The POISED Arm is used CONTINUOUSLY for all true Agility passages needing tonal *selectivity* for each note.

It can be used either *fully*-poised as in Staccato Resting and Agility-work, or *slightly less* fully-poised as for Legato Resting, and for Weight-transfer Touch.

(*g*) The Poised Arm is nevertheless applied INTERMITTENTLY when one of the above *optional* ways of Arm-use is applied *during key-descent.*

That is, the Arm must always resume its *poised* condition *in-between* the sounding of the notes in all passages, even when it is "lapsed" during the Act of Tone-production.

(*h*) The *Forearm rotational exertions and relaxations* (reversed or repeated) must in the meantime be correctly applied to *every note* you play, without exception — unless you play with your fist sideways, as required in my "First Steps"!

SOME ADDITIONAL ADVICE ON ARM-USE

21. If a *singing* or *chord* passage sounds too *thin* in tone, probably the error is that you are *not* using arm-weight properly during key-descent; either you are but imperfectly relaxing it, or not relaxing the whole mass from the shoulder, or are doing so *too late* during key-descent.

22. Remember, if you relax (or lapse) your whole arm *properly* (with or *without* movement) your Elbow will feel free and elastic, and will tend to fall away from the keys, and the whole arm will *tend* to collapse or fold up at the Elbow — like a book allowed to slip down.

23. Beauty of tone and Control of tone directly depend on the elision of any stiffness or rigidity at the Elbow-joint.

24. For *louder* passages you must add (as noted) an *exertion* of the Forearm downwards to this relaxation of the up-holding muscles of the *Whole* arm — both those of the forearm and upper-arm.

NOTE. — When you help yourself upstairs by the bannisters you are employing a similar leverage action as this one for *forte* tone.

25. *Whenever* your *forte* tone sounds harsh or dead, you are using the objectionable poke-forward of the Upper-arm along with the required down-exertion of the Forearm.

However long-standing your bad habits are in this respect, you can instantly cure this Music and Piano killing muscular gesture by realizing *the cause* of the fault, as here shown.

26. For light effects the *weight* of the *Forearm* by itself suffices; but remember here to keep the *Upper*-arm in its nicely poised or balanced condition.

27. Moreover, for the gentlest lightest effects you *may* use the Upper-arm forwards — provided you carefully *avoid* using any down-exertion of the Forearm at that moment.

28. For so-called "Finger-passages" at quick Tempo, it is best to use "Arm-vibration touch" if you desire to retain selectivity of tone. This demands that you must keep the Arm throughout in its fully *poised* condition. The whole arm must here be so accurately poised or balanced that it can be set into *sympathetic* vibration by reaction from the momentary finger AND HAND impulses delivered against the keys. This use of the inertia of the poised arm gives "body" to your finger-passages. (*See* Section XII, on "*Arm-vibration* and *Weight-transfer* Touches"; also Note to ¶16.)

29. "Arm-*off*" is therefore the slogan and secret of Agility. Realize also that "arm-off" applies when you are *holding* notes! (*See* Section VIII.)

30. Thus you must first learn to *use* Arm-weight, etc., when necessary, and then you must carefully learn to *avoid* it — when it is not required.

31. If your running passages are clumsy, colourless or sticky, you are either allowing your arm continuously to rest *too heavily* on the keyboard, or you are not *timing* your action accurately enough for each individual note, or — and most probably of all — you are applying rotatory stresses of the Forearm where they should be omitted.

32. Realize, then, that you must "actuate" (or exert) your

finger and hand, separately for every note, whether showing an actual movement or not; and also at the same moment provide the requisite Forearm rotatory conditions.

33. The determining factor in Tone and Agility always lies in the correct application of these *four optional* and the *two ever-present* distinct arm-elements, which help the finger and hand, *visibly* or *invisibly* as the case may be.

34. The most important of all to insist upon are the two "ever-present" arm-elements described under *A* and *B* of ¶11, page 15 — the Forearm Rotational element and the Poised arm-element, since without mastery of these all true Technique remains unattainable.

The Forearm rotational stresses and relaxations, although mostly *invisible*, are indeed so vital to one's well-being pianistically that they now receive the following Section VI to themselves.

Section VI

FOREARM ROTATION

— Its visible movements and its invisible stresses. When to apply them and when not.

1. No playing is possible without the intervention of Forearm-rotation, and never has been. Mostly, however, the Forearm Rotative Element remains QUITE INVISIBLE.

2. It is used both in its visible *and invisible* forms in almost everything you do, as, for instance, when trying to turn a stiff door handle — you can feel the stress before the handle gives way.

3. In its *visible* form it implies a partial rotation of the forearm at the wrist, and when thus shown as *movement* is called "Ro-

tation-touch." The effect is caused by your twisting the *two* forearm-bones (socketed at the elbow) one upon the other, and then allowing these to untwist again.

4. These rotatory exertions you can disclose by actual movements, or you can apply them WITHOUT ANY MOVEMENT WHATSOEVER.

5. At the Piano they have been totally overlooked in the past when not exhibited as *Movement.*[1]

6. To practise scales and exercises with the object of "equalizing the fingers," or to "strengthen the fourth and fifth fingers" is therefore the height of folly, and thoroughly harmful, unless you see to it that these rotatory impulses of the forearm are correctly delivered.

7. Learn to apply this twisting and untwisting action properly, and your fingers will at once all be equally "strong" and responsive.

8. To render this clear, try the following experiments:—

Drop your arm at your side, really fully relaxed. You will find that your hand now hangs flat with the side of your body — because you have really relaxed the rotatory effort *towards the thumb.*

Or: — Drop your arm on your knees, equally relaxed, and you find that your hand tends to roll over almost onto its back. Now with this completely relaxed and inactive state of the forearm, rotationally, bring your hand onto the surface of the keyboard — with the hand sideways therefore, and with the thumb turned up.

9. Clearly, now, if you wish to turn your hand into its usual level playing position, you are compelled to *exert* and turn the forearm rotationally towards the thumb-side of the hand.

[1] Even today there are still writers who fail to grasp this simple fact, that rotational stress does NOT necessarily signify *Movement;* and their attempted Touch-explanations lamentably and completely founder in consequence of this misapprehension.

In the old days this was excusable, but not Now!

It is indeed a very slight exertion towards the thumb, but is an exertion for all that.

10. Now note particularly, that *if you wish to retain your hand* in that level position, you must also *continue* this slight but *invisible* exertion towards the thumb, otherwise the hand will again roll back onto its side, with thumb up.

NOTE. — Evidently, we possess both "weak" and "strong" forearm-rotative muscles, both for twisting the forearm *inwards* and *outwards* — "pronation" and "supination." Now we have to use *both* to turn our hand over into its level playing position; but the "small" muscles suffice to *retain* the hand in this position.

The *dual* nature of our muscular equipment is here again likely to mislead us. We may imagine, because we have quite correctly ceased the activity of the "strong" muscles, that there is *no* exertion continued towards the thumb, in spite of the fact that the "weak" muscles are retaining the hand in its level position.

Yet, unless we *cease* even this slight residue of rotational exertion towards the thumb (thus provided by these "weak" muscles) we shall inevitably gravely impair the action of the *next* finger in sounding its note, and it will seem "weak," because deprived of its natural rotational help — to the little finger side. *See* Sect. VIII, "On Holding Notes," p. 31.

11. Next realize, that when you wish to sound that thumb note strongly, you must increase that slight forearm rotatory exertion towards the thumb — precisely to the extent you wish to exert the thumb during the moment of key-depression.

That is where all the mischief arises and has arisen!

12. No one ever yet has been able *to retain the hand in its playing position*, nor to sound the thumb strongly, *without* this usually INVISIBLE rotatory help. But as this help is mostly applied *without any visible movement* of the forearm, it is likely to escape attention as in the past, hence this Rotative Exertion is then unwittingly *continued beyond the moment of tone-production*, instead of being ceased instantly. And if this invisible exertion towards the thumb is thus unwittingly continued, and not accurately ceased, this will inevitably prevent your attaining any ease or fluency technically.

13. Therefore, the first thing to learn, is, completely to CEASE *this rotative exertion* towards the thumb the very moment it has fulfilled its purpose.

14. When you cease it thus completely and promptly, your hand will tend to roll over onto its side — outwards — *unless caught up* by one of the other fingers.

NOTE. — As already noted under ¶10, evidently we possess "weak" as well as "strong" rotative muscles, just as in the case of the fingers. Now be sure that you cease *all residue* of rotatory exertion (*even of these "weak" rotation-muscles*) in the *wrong* direction when you play the next finger. Else you will inevitably impair the rotative-help due to that finger.

15. When playing softly, this pure *relaxation* of the forearm rotationally will here serve amply as basis for any of the other fingers used after the thumb. But to sound these other notes at all forcibly, you must also *add* an actual rotative *exertion* of the forearm in their direction — towards the little finger side.

16. Apply this process to the sounding of either fourth or fifth fingers after the thumb, and you will at once find those fingers perfectly "strong" — and not needing thousands of futile and music-killing exercises!

17. The simple law is, if you wish to give rotatory help in one direction be sure to *omit the opposite exertion.*

18. As with any other muscular exertion required at the Piano (or anywhere else) freedom and ease are the most essential factors — without any tug-of-war between opposite or antagonistic sets of muscles.

19. Moreover, in rapid finger passages, be careful to give the rapid, but here invisible, rotative *reversals* or *reiterations* always in the right DIRECTION.

NOTE. — In referring to the necessary rotatory help of the forearm for each individual note of a rapid "finger" passage, remember I am speaking of INVISIBLE actions, alternate reversals or reiterations muscularly, and undisplayed by any rotatory or rocking *movements*. This warning is repeatedly necessary, as I find that some have foolishly imagined that in speaking of Rotation in this connection I mean *movement* — actual visibility. I do *not*, whatever mistake others have made in this respect! Certainly, in slower passages, actual movements may optionally be displayed. In the learning stage actual movements are in fact an advantage, but the *Tempo* must then be slow enough to admit of such movements.

20. The *direction* of Rotation is always FROM the finger last used, and TOWARDS the finger next used. Thus, for instance: —

When you use the middle-finger *after the thumb,* your forearm must rotationally help in the direction of the little finger; whereas, when you use this same middle-finger *after the little finger,* then your forearm must rotationally help in the opposite direction — towards the thumb.

21. When a passage moves with notes melodically alternately rising and falling, then you must supply ALTERNATE conditions rotatively; but when the fingers succeed each other *in their natural order* then you must REPEAT the same rotatory impulse for each note.

NOTE. — Either accompanied by a visible rolling movement, or *none whatever.*

22. Thus, in a straight-on five-finger succession (or five-finger exercise) if you begin with the thumb, you must give rotatory help towards the thumb, but must follow this by four repeated rotatory impulses towards the *little finger.* Whereas, in returning, you must give four repeated rotatory impulses towards the *thumb.* Thus: —

Ex. No. 1.

23. This law of *Direction* applies equally when you turn a finger *over the thumb.* Thus in a Scale or Arpeggio, when you turn your finger over, the direction of rotation is not (as you might suppose) in the direction of the passage, but instead, the rotatory help must be given in the direction of the *little finger.*

NOTE. — Try a shake or tremolo *with the thumb under the fingers.* Try it first with reiterated rotations towards the thumb (visible or *invisible*), and then with alternate rotations, and the matter will be clear to you forever afterwards.

24. Next realize, when you play a passage with the two hands moving melodically in the *same* direction, that the rotatory changes required are in the *opposite direction* in the two hands.

Unless you recognize this fact, you are likely to make such passage in similar motion a difficulty, where none really exists.

It even applies when the hands are not playing together but are playing the passage alternately.

NOTE. — Hence, for the beginner, it is always best when he first plays his hands together, to have the notes moving by contrary motion melodically, so far as possible. This principle has been carried out in "Pianist's First Music Making" and in my "First Solo Book," and "Playthings," Book I — Oxford University Press.

25. Octave playing usually fails simply owing to rotational stiffening. In all octave and double-notes passages the required slight (but invisible) rotatory exertions towards the thumb must be *repeated* freely each time, individually, for each octave, and likewise for any other passage in double-notes, sixths, etc.[1]

26. The quickest and most certain way to acquire this required harmony between finger and forearm, rotatively, is to work through the logically successive steps indicated in my little pamphlet "*The Nine Steps towards Finger Individualization*" — a Summary of "The Child's First Steps" — to which refer.[2]

27. Whenever any finger-passage seems sticky or otherwise technically deficient, again and again recur to THE FIRST FOUR of these Steps; also rotationally *re-analyze the passage* in question. This can be done in a few minutes, and the passage is at once bettered.

[1] No, they are *not* movements rotationally — the help is *invisible!* The old idea of "forming the hand" for the octave passage was sheer folly, with its stiff arm, wrist, and forearm rotationally set; in fact it was criminally bad teaching!

[2] "The Nine Steps towards Finger Individualization" (The Oxford Press). "The Child's First Steps" (Joseph Williams). These steps are the ONLY POSSIBLE ones, and they are given in the only possible logical order. One step only is taken at a time, and they naturally lead up to the straight-on five-finger exercise. *See* also "On Method in Teaching" — Oxford University Press.

28. Remember, these first *four* steps are:—

I. With the hand closed as a *fist*, and vertical,—with the thumb up—sound two adjacent black keys, *pp*.

Ex. No. 2.

II. Do the same, but with the fist now horizontal—in playing position.

III. Now rhythmically rock on the same two notes, still with fist horizontal and still *pp*—and the slightest weight only.

IV. Now *add* to this last (the soft passing on of light weight from note to note) and still with your fist, a stronger impulse (rotationally) during each key-descent, from *pp* to *f*, thus:—

Ex. No. 3.

Notice, that no finger at all has so far been used in this, but you will nevertheless have SET RIGHT the *basis* for your finger-action!

Then follow this by the five remaining steps, adding finger-action to the preceding, and thus leading up to the five-finger exercise, as shown in "The Nine Steps"—which see.

29. Or, for an advanced player or artist, instead substitute the two following test-exercises only, or the last one only, as this covers the ground. After that, transmit the right sensations thus learnt to the passage that has given trouble, and you will find the difficulty has vanished.

Ex. No. 4.

Hands separately at first, then together, and lastly by similar motion.

The in-between notes quite light, but the accents well pronounced. The hands separate at first, then together, and lastly by similar motion. Each bar might be repeated several times before proceeding to the next.

30. Finally, realize that you can only attain successful "finger" passage-work (or any other form of technique) by your insisting on attuning perfect harmony between finger and forearm in this respect. The forearm rotational-help must be correctly forthcoming for each note, and the finger itself (and hand) must be sufficiently exerted to *make use* of this help; and the *movement* may either be that of the Finger, or Hand, or Forearm-Rotation itself!

31. In short, the finger and the forearm elements must be

accurately *balanced* and timed for every note you play. Without such balancing and timing it is impossible to succeed.

32. Finally, always *play freely*.

The word "RELAXATION" is however sometimes turned into a Fetish. It has even been stupidly (and lately *maliciously*) perverted and twisted into signifying a general flabbiness, feebleness and Ineptitude! It means nothing of the kind! Without Relaxation you cannot play at all, and noone ever has or ever will.

33. Realize and master the *three* distinct rôles of Relaxation in Technique. Thus:

(1) To obtain the use of the free weight of your Arm, you must learn to relax its upholding muscles.

(2) To enable you to play freely you must learn to relax the antagonistic (or contrary) muscles.

(3) To enable you to ensure tonal accuracy you must learn to relax all stresses used during and for tone-production the moment their mission is complete.

NOTE. — This last does *not* preclude a light "after-pressure" upon the key-beds for Legato, which helps to apprise you *how long* you are holding those notes down; and this does *not* constitute what I meant when I invented the term "key-bedding." Key-bedding signifies a *mis-timing* of the tone-intended force, *too late* in key-descent — a *burying* of the tone therefore!

34. Remember, THAT THE SOLE PURPOSE OF RELAXATION is to *enable* you to exert your Finger and hand adequately and easily in playing. Never forget that!

35. In past days only geniuses stumbled upon the correct processes of Technique or Touch. Nowadays you and everyone else who can or will use his brains sufficiently to understand the facts herein made plain, and will work on these lines, can and assuredly *will* succeed — technically!

36. But remember, "successful technique" only signifies the power to express that which you can *see* or *feel* musically.

Therefore, *do try* all the while to *perceive* musical sense, for only in this way can you also improve your Musical Sight — and your Technique!

Section VII

THE MOVEMENTS OF TOUCH

— Before the key is reached, and with it.

The Movements of Touch:

1. Most of the harmful attempts to teach Touch have arisen from the delusion that the CAUSE of Touch lies in the exhibited accompanying *visible movements;* whereas, obviously, the true causes of Touch can only be found in the actuating but *quite invisible* muscular changes in *state* of the Arm, Hand, and Finger.

2. While *all* Touch demands reversals or repetitions in the visible or mostly *invisible* state of the *Forearm rotatively* for every note, and *all touch* also needs the "*poised*" (or self-supported) state of the Arm in its several ways — either *continuous* during each phrase, or instantly *resumed* during each interval *between* the sounding of the notes — you may accompany these actuating *conditions* either by Finger, Hand, or Arm *movements*. Thus:

3. I. **Finger-Movement,** caused either: —

(*a*) Solely by exertion of the "small" muscles of the finger (situated inside the hand) but really too weak for certainty in tone-production, but most suitable for holding notes down after they have been sounded.

NOTE. — A touch-form only suitable for certain quite light effects, grace-notes, etc., and no doubt available in the old Clavichord days. It has indeed been said of Bach that he sometimes used only the Nail-phalanges!

(*b*) By the exertion of the "strong" muscles of the finger (situated on the Forearm); but this implies also an exertion *via* the Hand, as these tendons run through the wrist-joint: the Arm in the meantime remains *continuously* either in its fully or slightly less-fully "*poised*" condition. Or optionally: The finger may be helped in its work of tone-production (*via* an *invisible* exertion of the hand) by a *momentary* but again invisible application of *down-arm* energy in one of the *four* ways noted below under Arm-movement, and already fully discussed (as *actuating* causes) in Section V — "The Arm," which see.

II. **Hand-Movement** caused by an exertion of the Hand itself, along with an *invisible* exertion of the Finger, and either with:

(*a*) The *Poised* condition of the Arm, or

(*b*) Helped again by *momentary* but *invisible* Down-arm impulses, provided in either of the before-mentioned *four* ways.

III. **Arm-Movement** (either Whole-arm or Forearm vertically, or Forearm rotationally) along with *invisible* exertions of both Finger and Hand; an arm-movement caused either: —

(*a*) by a momentary *relaxation of the whole arm* from its poised condition, or —

(*b*) by *Forearm weight* only; or —

(*c*) by a momentary *down-exertion of the Forearm* in conjunction with the relaxation of the Upper-arm — for full *fortes;* or —

(*d*) by a momentary *forward-drive of the Upper-arm* along with the down-exertion of the Forearm.

NOTE. — But, as already said, a form of touch imperatively *to be avoided* except for special effects, if you wish your *fortes* to sound pleasant to the ear!

4. The determining factor as to which of these *movements* shall arise, lies in the respective *balance of power* between the three main factors — Finger, Hand, and Arm —

For instance, when you use the complete muscular combination of Finger-Hand-and-Arm, you will have *Finger-movement* when the finger-exertion is slightly in excess of the other two components of Touch; whereas you will have *Hand-movement* when the hand-exertion is slightly in excess; whereas *Arm-movement* itself will supervene, when finger and hand exertions are slightly in the minority.

NOTE. — *Rotatory movements* of the Forearm are available whatever the Touch-form.

5. Touch-movements, moreover, also tend to *merge* one into the other, just as do the various causal Touch-*actuations* themselves.

6. *No* laws can be laid down as to which movement *should* be used for any particular passage, as this depends largely on Taste, and thus the artistic impulse or caprice of the moment often determines choice of Movement as well as Touch-*kind*.

7. The only certain point is, that for quicker passages the *shorter levers* are more convenient to move. Thus for slow passages, you can conveniently move the whole arm or forearm only for each note, whereas for quicker passages, Hand or Rotation movements are more comfortable; while for the quickest successions of notes there is no time except for Finger-movement. Small oscillatory (rotational) movements of the Forearm, however, are quite serviceable even in quick tremolos and shakes, since the forearm, rotationally, is very agile!

8. The PRELIMINARY gentle movements of the finger, hand, arm *towards* the key (preliminary to the true act of touch, which is *with* the key) may and should be quite ample, if the speed of the passage admits of it.

9. Plenty of movement helps freedom and is healthy for the muscles, since it promotes circulation.

Such preliminary movements, however, should always occur naturally, and neither finger nor hand should ever be strained back. Moreover, the force needed to depress the key must not be supplied until and after the key is reached.[1]

10. In the case of actual movements of the arm, it is mechanically helpful, however, to get the arm *under way* before reaching the key, since this enables you to overcome the sluggishness (or Inertia) of the mass of the arm before you actually *begin*

[1] Hence also the mis-teaching that "the louder the note the higher must be the fall" of your arm — another fallacy which a recent author and his subsequent imitator have had the impudence to ascribe to myself (of all people!) in books replete with similar total misrepresentations of my teachings. How could one judge Key-resistance if the arm were really thus "dropped down"!

the act of tone-production — from the surface-level of the keyboard.

11. Moreover, be careful never actually to *hit* the key down; for you cannot feel *how* much the key needs for each sound if you do, and your playing must then suffer musically.

NOTE. — In the old days finger and hand "lifting" were made into a craze under the foolish notion that the higher one "lifted" one's fingers and hand the harder could one "Hit" or "Strike" the key down! But that is now a long exploded notion, since we realize, as here shown, that if one hits a note down one cannot possibly *feel how much* the key needs, and cannot choose one's tone-colour with any certainty.

12. Do not quit the surface of the key, when you have to repeat a note quickly.

13. For comparatively soft notes, on a Grand, you do not even need to let the key rise fully before sounding it afresh, since the "Repetition-lever" is designed with this very purpose.

On an Upright Piano, however, you must let the key rise fully.

14. For Octave passages, which necessarily imply muscular *repetitions*, also as a rule do not quit the keyboard, but slide your way along from note to note — unless you play by arm-movement. *See* Section X, ¶¶5–7. This sliding is done by the thumb when moving outwards, and by the fifth or fourth fingers when moving towards you.

15. Finally, remember always, that such *visible* manifestations of Movement do not in the least indicate what is happening "behind the scenes" — what is happening *invisibly* in the way of Limb-exertion or relaxation during the processes of touch. These causal actions you must acquire through experiment and sensation, and your eye cannot help you.[1]

[1] *See* Additional Note in "Digest" — "The pure Finger-work fallacy."

Section VIII

ON HOLDING NOTES

— The right way and the wrong way.

1. You must almost invariably use the "strong" muscles of the finger to *sound* the notes at the Pianoforte. These "strong" muscles are situated on the Forearm.

2. Therefore, during key-descent you may be able to notice a slight *tension* across the under-side of the wrist-joint during the moment of key-depression.

3. Promptly *cease working* with these "strong" muscles the very moment you hear the sound begin.

4. In the meantime you have also used the "*small*" muscles of the fingers during the moment of key-depression. These "small" muscles lie inside the hand itself.

5. Now, you must always *hold* the key down in tenuto and legato (or at surface-level during Staccato) *solely* by continuing the gentle exertion of these *small* muscles of the finger. To know their names or the precise locality of these muscles will not help you in the least, but when you do the right thing, remember it *feels as if* the exertion were solely on the underside of the finger itself — the gentlest tension on their underside, and *seemingly* located between finger-tip and knuckle.

6. That is, you may use *all* the muscles connected with the finger *during* the sounding-action, but you must hold the notes afterwards *solely* by these "small" muscles.[1]

7. Constantly *test* yourself for such *light holding of notes*, by insisting on freedom (or mobility) at the knuckles while holding notes; or even while depressing the Keys.[2]

[1] Or, translated into the impressive *quasi*-scientific jargon affected by some recent writers: "Use both the *lumbricalis* and the *flexor sublimis digitorum* during key-descent." This, however, does not seem materially to help things forward?

[2] *See* "Relaxation Studies" for these three and other test-exercises.

8. To teach you this correct way of holding notes down, and the distinction between the action of sounding notes and the action of holding them, the simplest test is as follows: —

(*a*) Clench your fingers firmly into the palm of your hand, and notice that while you continue this stress it provokes a certain rigidity of the wrist at its under-side. (*b*) Suddenly *let go* this strain, while still keeping the finger-tips touching the palm of your hand — but now quite lightly. You will find that you can now freely move your hand in every direction — *so long as* you thus use only the "small" muscles of the fingers — and this without the slightest sensation of strain across the wrist. This is the only right way to hold notes.

9. Also practise the traditional "Holding-notes exercise" at the keyboard. But always be careful to do so accurately in accordance with this knowledge — that the "holding" must be done perfectly lightly. You can easily ensure this, provided you insist on employing only these "small" muscles of the fingers — with free and *mobile* knuckles.

NOTE. — This "holding-notes exercise" is one of the oldest and best known of all exercises. Practised correctly it is extremely helpful as a *test* for correct technique, whereas, practised wrongly (as mostly done!) nothing can be more harmful. It forms Section XVI of my "Relaxation Studies" (Bosworth). Many others of the *Test-exercises* there given, also help towards the same purpose, such as Sets I, III, and XIII.

10. By testing yourself in the way here indicated, you can learn to realize the nature of the correct muscular habits required, and can learn to avoid one of the worst of all the wrong ones — the sustaining of notes stiffly and clumsily!

11. **In short, hold down your notes (in legato and tenuto) quite comfortably firmly, by pressure solely of the "small" muscles of the finger — with loose knuckles. This slight "after-pressure" is not "key-bedding"!**

Don't do so with the "strong" finger muscles, which you have to use in sounding the notes. That *is* "key-bedding," because

you are then mis-timing the forces intended to produce the tones, and are technically and musically spoiling all your playing.[1]

Section IX

BENT AND FLAT FINGER-ACTION

— *Thrusting* v. *Clinging, or* Un*folding* v. In-*folding actions.*

Thrusting *v.* Clinging.

1. As already pointed out in Section V, ¶2, you can use the finger itself in two quite distinct and opposite ways while moving towards the key and *with* it. Thus: —

A): THE "THRUSTING" OR "BENT" FINGER ACTION

2. In this mode of action, the raised finger is considerably curved (bent or folded-in) and you then open it out somewhat during its descent to the key, and *with* the key during key-descent, the nail-phalange (the end "joint" of the finger) remaining almost vertical throughout — both with finger up and with finger down.

3. This thrusting, shoving, "bent" or *unfolding* action of the finger needs for its *invisible* basis a more or less forwardly supported (or even forwardly exerted) Upper-arm and Elbow. *See* 4th form of Arm-use, *Section V.*

4. This thrusting or shoving action of the finger (a downward and *outward* action) is, however, really quite a complex process — while the middle joint descends, the nail-phalange has to remain vertical.

Carefully compare the "up" and "down" positions of the "bent" finger in the photos annexed.

[1] *See* Note to ¶14, of Section XI, "Staccato and Legato."

NOTE. — With the "thrusting" finger the tone can neither be sympathetic, full, nor carrying in melodic passages. Nicety of tone-*control* is also greatly stultified. For "dry" effects it may be appropriate, but the unavoidable elision of *upper*-arm weight with this form of finger-action precludes all true volume or resonance *in fortes* — as a musical ear would describe the result.

B): THE "CLINGING" OR "FLAT" FINGER ACTION

5. In complete contrast to this "thrusting" form of finger-action, the finger here starts more or less *opened-out;* and will then be more or less folded *inwards* while moving towards the key and with it. In this case, *if* you raise the finger considerably before playing, the nail-phalange (or end "joint") may actually become visible to you for the moment.

6. This "*clinging*" or "flat" action of the finger needs as its *invisible* Basis a more or less relaxed (and therefore backward-*tending*) Upper-arm, and with it a likewise backward-tending Elbow. *See* 1st and 3rd forms of Arm-use, *Section V.*

NOTE. — Applied to the key, the whole limb here remains far more *elastic* than in the opposite forward or thrusting touch previously described. Thus it renders proper key-acceleration more easy for you, and thus also an easier attainment of full, sympathetic, carrying tone, and of nicety of tonal gradation and control.

7. This *folding-in* action of the finger is by far the most natural form of finger-use at the Piano. It is the same action you naturally use all day when gripping hold of objects. It thus enables you also to "take hold of" (and "cling") to the key.

8. Actually, with the "flat" or clinging (or in-folding) action, the finger MAY fold in so much that *when the key is down* it is as much bent-in as with "bent" finger-touch.

But notice, that although *the position*, with finger down, of both modes of finger-action may be identical, that with "clinging" finger it is most bent *when down*, whereas with "thrusting" finger it is most bent *when up*. (*See* annexed photos.)

NOTE. — With the key down, the eye cannot distinguish which has been used — although your ear apprises you of the difference in sound.

9. Alternatively, with this "clinging" action you may also leave the finger almost straight (or "flat") during the whole of

FIG. 1

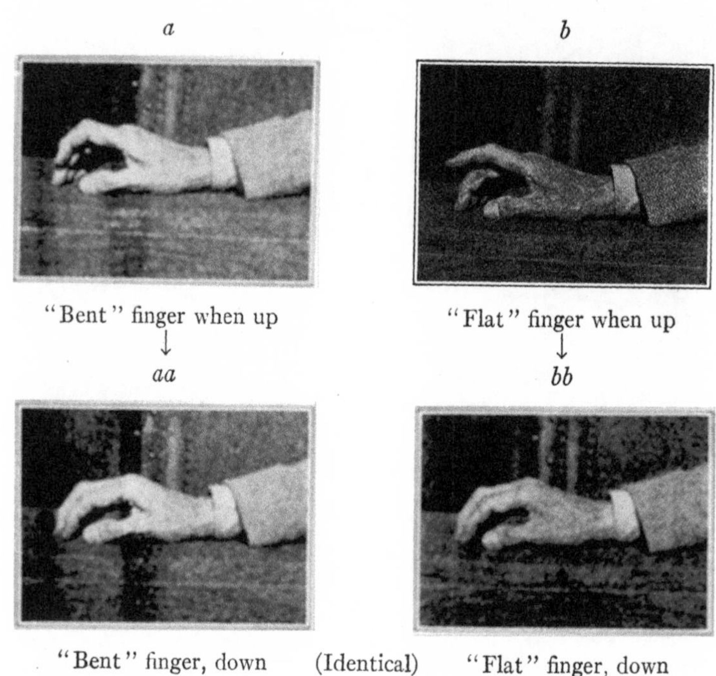

a — "Bent" finger when up ↓ *aa* — "Bent" finger, down

b — "Flat" finger when up ↓ *bb* — "Flat" finger, down

(Identical)

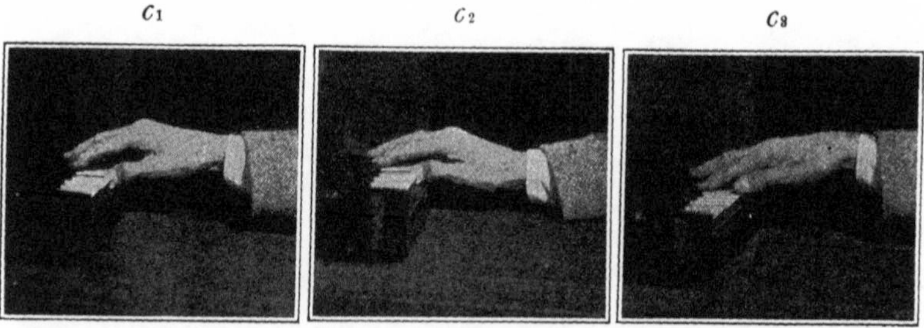

c_1 c_2 c_3

"Flat" finger left unbent when down — shown in three varying positions

its action, and it may remain thus flat with the key down. Thus has arisen, in the past, its name "flat finger."

10. The annexed photographs show you these *visible* differences, (*a*) is the finger well raised before its *thrusting* (unfolding) action, (*aa*) is the same when down; whereas (*b*) is the finger well raised before its *clinging* (or in-folding) action, and (*bb*) the same down with the key — and therefore folded-in during descent; (*c*) on the other hand, shows you the "clinging" finger left "flat" (or more or less straight) when down with the key — with several optional positions of the wrist.

11. Realize also that with the *Upper-arm relaxed* during the moment of key-descent you are compelled to use the *in-folding* ("flat") action of the finger, whereas with the upper-arm (or Elbow) in the least pushing forward you are compelled to use the *unfolding* (bent or thrusting) action of the finger.

But with the upper-arm nicely *poised*, you have the option of using *either* of the two finger-actions, in softer passages.

NOTE. — Moreover, with the "poised" arm, you may, for quite light passages, even play on tip-toe as it were — on the very tips of the fingers — provided you have flat, paddy finger tips, and your nails are not too long!

Section X

HOW TO FIND THE RIGHT NOTES

1. To reach the right places on the keyboard (the right notes) is obviously an important matter. To attain Certainty in this respect, you must always physically *feel* your way along *from* the last note played.

2. You must spiritually *want* to hear the needed melodic succession of *intervals*, and you must also physically *feel* the corresponding set of physical *intervals* on the keyboard.

3. This "feeling-your-way" is mostly done by the true touch-sense — sense of contact or tactile faculty; it is done, for the most part, by your not quitting the last note until you have found the next one.[1]

4. The law applies equally in skips — you must still feel your way along the key-surface from note to note.

5. It consequently also applies in octave passages. You must *feel* your way from one octave to the next. Thus becomes possible the trick of so-called "lightning octave passages."

6. Both in octave passages and larger skips you must feel your way along with your thumb, *when the passage travels outwards* — away from you; whereas, you must feel your way along with your fifth or fourth fingers, etc., when the passage moves *inwards* — towards you. *See* Section VII, ¶14.

7. In the meantime do not forget, that each octave you play demands the *repetition* each time of the necessary forearm rotatory exertion towards the thumb, besides the exertion each time of the two fingers concerned, and also that of the hand.

8. This law of *physical continuity* on the keyboard-surface is equally imperative when you play passages distributed between the two hands. Here *do not quit the keyboard* with one hand until you have found the place of the next-following note with a finger of the other hand. In the meantime also *think* such passage in Rhythmical Continuity.

The "secret" of such passages lies in your insisting upon Rhythmical *Continuity* as well as Physical *Continuity*. Such passages thus become quite easy of attainment. Whereas, if you do *not* give this double form of attention (by touch-sense *and* rhythmic sense) then they are impossible.

[1] Supplemented no doubt by our muscular and "kinesthetic" sensations and memories generally.

But "a bird in hand is worth more than two in the bush," therefore depend as much as possible on the actual touch-sensation of the last-used note until you find the next. It is safest!

9. In short, while always thus feeling your way along the Keyboard-intervals FROM the last-played note to the next, you must, nevertheless, in the meantime, also think and play TOWARDS the rhythmical landmarks ahead.

NOTE. — That is: you must think *towards* tone in key-descent; *towards* each next Pulse (or beat) ahead in groups of quick notes; *towards* the rhythmical climax point of each Phrase or Section, and *towards* the point of consummation of the Whole piece. *See* "Child's First Steps," "First Principles," and "Musical Interpretation," p. 28, etc. (Joseph Williams).

10. To enable you to travel from one note to another, you must, where necessary, supply *sideway* movements of the fingers, of the hand, and of the arm — both of the whole upper-arm and the forearm. As these lateral or horizontal movements are visible, they are obvious and need little explanation.

11. There are however three points to notice: —

I. In taking skips *within* the compass of two octaves it is best to leave the Elbow stationary. To succeed in this, you must, before beginning the skip, turn the elbow out sufficiently to enable you to reach the note furthest out.

II. When you turn your finger over your thumb (or *vice versa*) this requires a movement of the hand — with the thumb stationary; whereas, when you move the thumb under a stationary finger, this requires a movement (sideways) both of the wrist and of the forearm — though not of the Elbow.

III. When playing scales, etc., it is best to have the wrist (and consequently the forearm also) turned rather "outwards" (away from you), as this allows of your turning the fingers over the thumb without disturbing the relative position of wrist and forearm during the passage.[1]

12. This necessity to feel your way along physically finally resolves itself into *an* "ACT OF RESTING *on the keyboard*," either at its *surface*, or *depressed* level; and this leads us naturally into the consideration of the problems of Staccato and Legato.

[1] The Forearm therefore here travels with the wrist *in advance*, when the passage moves outwards. *See* also: ¶¶14, 15, etc. of Section XII, "On Position."

Section XI

STACCATO AND LEGATO

1. The term *staccato* should properly signify "staccatissimo," practically *without duration*, as short as possible. The term "Staccato," as used colloquially and loosely, is however unfortunately applied to *all* notes *not* played Tenuto or Legato. Hence, when playing passages marked *staccato*, remember that the sounds, in spite of their notation, may probably, nevertheless, need more or less slight *durations*. Therefore, be most careful to choose the *precise degree* of Duration musically needed for every note marked "staccato."

2. Now, in true Staccato (or *Staccatissimo*) the key must be free to *rebound*, so that the damper may instantaneously stop the sound, almost at its birth.

3. To obtain such true Staccato you must accurately *time* your tone-making impulse to cease completely the moment you reach sound in key depression. Thus the key will be free to rebound even with your finger-tip still upon it, and the damper will consequently reach the strings instantly.

NOTE. — The following Diagram may here prove suggestive:

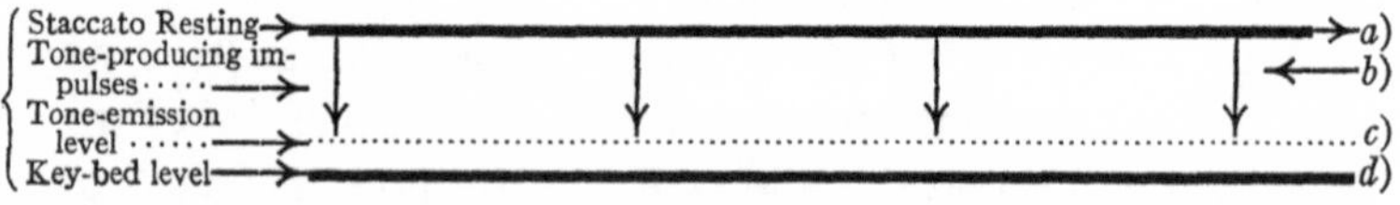

(*a*) *Staccato resting* — at *surface-level* of keyboard — continuous.
(*b*) *Tone-producing impulses*, directed and aimed to:
(*c*) The *tone-emission* level.
(*d*) The *key-bed level* — momentarily touched but rebounded from, for each note.

4. Realize particularly, that you cannot "make" staccato by trying to *pull* the key or your fingers up! All you can do is accurately to stop both the down-impulse of your finger, as well as the help given by hand and arm during key-descent.

5. To enable your finger, etc., in Staccato thus to stop its action accurately and completely, you must *rest* very lightly indeed on the keyboard-*surface* — not more heavily than the keys will bear at their surface-level, without becoming depressed.

Thus, in Staccato, *in between* the sounding of the notes, your arm must be more or less completely "poised" (supported by its own muscles) and with the hand, alone, lying loosely upon the keyboard-surface for the sake of the sense of continuity. See "*The Poised Arm,*" Section V.

6. Agility passages as a rule demand a precisely similar *light* Resting on the keyboard, — arm "off" with hand lying loosely on the keys; and with similar accuracy in the aiming and cessation of your finger-action, etc.

The arm thus comes into sympathetic *vibration* in consequence of the reiterated impulses of the finger and hand against the Keys, and thus forms true "Arm-vibration" touch. *See* Section XII for this.

7. To obtain TENUTO, do *not*, as in Staccato, thus fully and completely cease your finger-exertion, etc., but allow this exertion to continue in a slight measure on the *key-beds* — just sufficient exertion to keep the keys depressed.

This Tenuto will last just so long as you continue this slight action upon the key-beds with your finger-tips.

NOTE. — This sustaining action must be provided solely by the "small muscles" of the fingers. *See* Section VIII, ¶¶4 and 5, also Note to ¶6 — "The Holding of Notes."

8. Moreover, to obtain a true *legato* you must continue this light holding action *until* the next sound; and if you continue it beyond that moment you obtain *legatissimo*.

9. It is in this way that you produce the ARTIFICIAL form of legato. Notice, however, that you do not here employ sufficient weight continuously resting on the keyboard to *compel* the fingers to hold their notes down. The keys are only held down so long as you choose, thus quite lightly but sufficiently to exert your fingers and hand upon the key-beds. The moment,

however, that you stop this slight exertion, that moment the key jumps up, and the sound stops. This "artificial" form of legato is therefore *un-compelled* by the resting-weight.

10. There is also another form of Legato — the NATURAL-legato.

Here you very slightly relax the arm, so that it is *not* so fully poised or balanced as for staccato, or for "artificial" legato. A very little of the weight of the forearm or whole arm is here allowed to lie *continuously* on the key-beds during each phrase. This extra weight *compels* some finger or other to continue its slight exertion in support of the weight, until relieved of its duty by another finger. Realize that one finger or other is consequently here *compelled* to support this carried weight, until relieved by another taking its duty.

You thus have a legato *automatically* induced by the weight you allow to rest on the keys at bottom-level. This "natural" legato you might also term "Compelled legato"; for it is *compelled* by this slightly heavier Resting-weight.

11. It is easiest to learn this "compelled" form of legato first. But the *un-compelled* (or "artificial") form of legato is the one you will have to use most often in playing. You may even use it along with the "compelled" form at times.

12. **To sum this up:** You can produce Legato, or Tenuto, in either of two quite distinct ways: —

(*a*) You can *compel* your fingers to hold notes down by a continuous and sufficient Resting-weight — "Natural legato"; or

(*b*) You can hold notes down by your fingers *without* such compelling weight — "Artificial legato."

NOTE. — In the meantime, as already insisted upon, never hold notes down except by the "small" muscles of the fingers — with *loose* knuckles. Never hold them by the "strong" *playing* muscles (situated on the forearm) with immobile knuckles and wrist, and consequent fatal pressure-inducing effects. *See* Section VIII, "On Holding Notes," ¶5, etc.

13. Obviously, it does not take more force to hold a note down than is required to sound it at its softest — in fact rather less.

14. There is, however, no harm in occasionally using a little *more pressure* on the key-beds than thus necessary, provided you do so purposely, and so long as you keep clear in your mind the distinction between the sounding and the holding of notes.
You should apply such "after-pressure" only for the sake of comfortably knowing that you *are* holding those particular notes down, and so as to warn you, muscularly, when to let them go.

NOTE. — As already pointed out, this *slight* extra pressure on the keybeds, thus purposely used to remind you that you are holding certain notes down, does *not* constitute "key-bedding" as you might imagine.

"Key-bedding," as a fault, arises when you *mis-time* the action *intended* to produce a tone, and mis-apply *this force* to the pads under the Keys instead of carefully timing its culmination and completion *during* key-descent and with the tone, and its cessation forthwith.

See the next Section — "On Weight-transfer" or Passing-on Touch, also Section VIII, "On Holding Notes." This reiteration is emphatically necessary.

Section XII

WEIGHT-TRANSFER AND ARM-VIBRATION TOUCHES

1. Weight passed-on from note to note — much as in the case of the heavier form of "Resting" used for "natural legato" — may itself form a cause of tone-production, and thus constitutes "Weight-transfer" or "*passing-on*" touch.

2. Such *continuously* passed-on Weight (though light) also entails a CONTINUOUS (but quite *invisible*) exertion of the Hand — in place of the *individual* hand-impulses used in all other touches.

3. The essential difference between "Passing-on" and "Arm-vibration" touches lies in this difference in the (invisible) application of this *continuous Hand-force:* —

In Passing-on touch the Hand-exertion is *continuous* (to the extent of the weight carried); whereas with Arm-vibration touch it is *separately* applied for each finger.

NOTE. — This continuous action of the hand may also entail *intermittently*-continuous Rotatory conditions. *See* ¶¶21 and 22.

4. The use of Passing-on touch however seriously handicaps musicality, since it almost entirely precludes *tonal selectivity from note to note* — the very life and soul of playing, and also precludes Duration-contrasts shorter than Legato.

5. All rapid *musical* passage-work, such as you find in BACH, BEETHOVEN, and CHOPIN for instance, imperatively demands such tonal and durational individualization, or musical choice from note to note by Arm-vibration touch. This forms the difference between musical playing and mere rattling through!

6. Moreover, however advanced a player you may be, there is a very definite *speed-limit* beyond which you cannot give these separate (*but invisible*) hand exertions for each note, and beyond which speed they are bound to merge into a continuous though light hand pressure behind the racing-along fingers (Passing-on touch therefore) to the destruction of Music.

7. The moral is, *never play musical passage-work faster* than you can give these *separate* hand-stresses for each note.

NOTE. — The composer surely meant them to be played *musically*, but he himself could not play them musically beyond a definite speed. Always remember this fact — unless you do not mind giving up everything to mere Agility-virtuosity and Display, and have no sense of Musical Morality!

8. Passing-on (or Weight-transfer) touch is only appropriate for certain light Arabesques and harmonic swirls of notes needing no more than "mass-production" effects of Crescendo and Diminuendo, and for accompanying passages *not* needing Note-

individualization. Spread chords, and the soft end-notes of the ordinary "slur" also call for it.[1]

9. As already indicated (*see* Section V, ¶18) all musically melodic passage-work demands the use of Arm-vibration touch, since the fully *poised* arm alone allows you to apply the hand *separately* (but invisibly) for each finger used, and thus enables you really to *choose* your tones.

10. The advantage of the fully poised arm is, that by reaction from the reiterated shocks it receives from the momentary impulses you deliver against the keys with your finger and hand, it is here *actually brought into vibration* as before explained; and it thus serves as an ample Basis for their exertion — and hence its name. — *See* Section V, ¶¶14, 15, and 28.

11. This sympathetic, trembling effect of the arm should however always arise by reaction from these short-lived and tonally accurately-aimed impulses of finger and hand. Never, instead, try to produce the effect by *shaking your arm* — as supposed by some misguided ones. It will certainly ruin your playing!

12. Above all things remember that the hand must (invisibly) *act separately* for each note!

13. The seemingly absurd reminder is here called for, that you have *only one hand* for each set of *five* fingers!

Much passage-work, however, founders just because this simple fact is overlooked!

Ponder well on this, and realize its truth the next time you touch the Piano!

Note. — It is so easy to *see* the movement of the five fingers in succession, but not so easy to realize that you must give *five* successive (although *invisible*) exertions of that *one* Hand to render those five fingers effective!

14. Remember, the arm condition *is precisely identical* for Arm-vibration touch and for the *Staccato* Resting; for you must

[1] *See* "The Slur or Couplet of Notes — in all its Variety, its Interpretation and Execution." Oxford University Press.

rest at the *surface-level* of the keyboard in both — with the hand lying loosely on it *in-between the sounding* of the notes. — (*See* Section XI, on "Staccato and Legato.") In fact all *light* Agility passages must be played with this lighter, or Staccato-Resting, although the aural impression may be Legato!

NOTE. — Do not forget that the difference between "lightness" and "heaviness" in musical effect depends mostly on *difference in Duration* — on the presence or absence of *holes* in the continuity of the sound.

15. But while all rapid *Staccato* passages necessarily take the form of "Arm-vibration," it does *not* follow that all Arm-vibration passages are necessarily Staccato! Arm-vibration touch *can* be turned into a Legato, by applying the "artificial legato" process to it. (*See* Section XI, ¶9.) Remember, that you here hold the notes down — on their beds — by the fingers "working on their own," and not here compelled into holding-action by a light superimposed Weight resting on the key-beds — as in "Natural-legato" Resting. *See* Section XI.

16. Here once again the urgent reiteration, that you must *not* hold notes down by the "strong" muscles of the fingers (situated on the Fore-arm) through which you *sound* the notes, but instead you must hold them down solely by their "small" muscles.[1]

17. Always realize, if you (wrongly) *continue* on the key-beds the exertion of the "strong" finger-muscles you use *during Tone-making*, that you hereby again lapse into "Passing-on" (or Weight-transfer) touch, with all its disadvantages musically and physically.

NOTE. — Moreover, if, in addition to this fault, you continue to lapse the "FULL WEIGHT" of the arm on the key-beds, you are doing your best to wreck your playing and your Piano, and besides, seriously risk contracting Cramp and Neuritis, and all the physical ills associated with bad Technique — an evil teaching-inheritance of the Past, and which some of our present-day writers are foolishly trying to revive or perpetuate!

18. Much of the musically arid passage playing, and "*too fast*" playing (rattling and strumming) so often heard even

[1] Or "lumbricalis," to use the anatomical jargon affected by certain writers of today. *See* Section VIII, ¶¶4 and 5.

from the Concert-platform must be laid to the door of the mis-use of Passing-on (or Weight-transfer) touch in place of the needed Arm-vibration touch, — unless it is the outcome of sheer laziness, in which case no Touch-form can help the *un*-maker of music!

19. Anyway, avoid the folly of trying to run at the Piano with a heavily-resting Arm. In ordinary life, when you wish to run, you rid yourself of all unnecessary baggage!

20. Reversals or reiterations of the Forearm-rotatory Element are obviously needed for Arm-vibration touch (as everywhere else) for each note *individually* — although usually quite hidden from the eye in a rapid passage.

21. But with Weight-transfer touch the rotative changes may occur sometimes in conjunction with whole *groups* of notes.

That is, with the *continuously* applied hand-and-arm stresses of Passing-on touch you have the option also of Forearm-rotatory *continuity* (in a measure) in place of the usual individually applied rotative reversals or repetitions from finger to finger; whereas, in other touches there cannot be such option. If, however, such optional *continuous* rotation-stress is used, it will then naturally alternate in direction according to the various succession of fingering *groups*.

22. Lastly, with such exceptional touch-form, you may allow actual rotatory group-*movements* to accompany such optional *continuous* rotatory impulses. For instance, a scale moving outwards would be in *two* groups, with a rolling *movement* from thumb to middle finger, then a momentary reversal to the thumb, followed again by another continuous roll till the ring or little finger is reached.

NOTE. — No doubt such optional rolling *movements* (or rotational grouping of notes), feasible with Passing-on touch, have suggested those childish "*Undulatory Theories* of Touch" which certain recent authors (and some more ancient ones) have propounded. Such fancies, however, can never be accepted as the *explanation* of Touch, since we know that mere *movements* cannot be the *actuating* Cause of Touch. Some artists may have adopted such particular fads of Movement, as they also adopt others; but they do not owe their success to such "undulatory" movements, or to any other fancy of the moment; but because they nevertheless happen (invisibly) to *exemplify the right things muscularly* in the meantime — along with a sufficiency of Musical Sight. And given *that*, any amiable little fads are quite forgivable!

23. This chapter is earnestly commended to very searching study. Perhaps it is the most important of all, since so many otherwise fine players often fail owing to lack of understanding of the facts herein made plain.

Section XIII

ON POSITION

— *And Movement.*

1. Good Position is the *resultant*—but not an assurance — of correct *balance* in the forces you use. Position, on the whole, will take care of itself if you apply the actuating forces correctly — but these are mostly *invisible.*[1]

2. While neither good nor bad Position can ensure good or bad playing, yet there are some points where ill-chosen Position may make things that matter more difficult. Hence study the following warnings and advice.[2]

3. Avoid sitting too close to the instrument, with your upper-arm straight down from the shoulder, since you then lose the option and advantage of Upper-arm weight when you need it for singing tones, etc. Sit sufficiently far away, so that your upper-arm slopes forward with the Elbow, and does not hang straight down or even slope backwards. *See* Photo annexed.

NOTE. — *See* also page 305, "The Act of Touch,"— the outlined figure of ANTON RUBINSTEIN.

[1] Study also this same Section in the "Digest" itself, and the Chapter on "Position" in "The Act of Touch" — Longmans, Green & Co.

[2] You may hold your fingers, hands and arms in perfectly orthodox positions and yet your (invisible) playing-*actions* may be perfectly wrong and ineffective.

Photo by kind permission of The Press Bureau

General Position of Arm, etc.

4. Sit neither too high nor too low. It is best that the Elbow should be about level with the keys or slightly lower.

If you sit higher than this, you are likely to *drive* forward when you should be using Upper-arm Weight; and if you sit lower you are likely to allow the upper-arm to hang on to the keyboard, when its Weight should be "off."

5. If you have a long *Upper*-arm you are compelled to sit *higher* than those born with a shorter *upper*-arm, else your Elbow will be too low to be comfortable.

6. Do not sit all hunched and bunched up — do not relax all your Body-muscles because you have to relax your arms at times! It is distinctly unhealthy, of no profit technically, and ugly. Besides, to see an ugly thing before him, is apt to make the listener imagine that the sounds also are ugly.

Freely and *easily* therefore keep your body erect.

7. Do not sway and move about unnecessarily — neither with your body nor with your arms.

If you make the listener watch your body, to that extent he listens less to your soul — which one hopes you may be trying to express!

NOTE. — If you play freely as you should, it is easy to move about — but *don't!* Whereas you dare not move about if you play stiffly and badly. But *don't* play stiffly and badly for the sake of sitting immobile!

8. Avoid using UPPER-arm rotatory *movements* — and exertions — in place of the much neater, easier, and effective *forearm* rotatory movements, when playing tremolos, etc.

Again, this is waste of energy and also distinctly ugly. Liszt used to deride such Elbow-circling — he called it "making Omelette!"

NOTE. — In any case it is abominably bad Technique to substitute *upper*-arm rotatory *stresses* (actions and relaxations) in place of the necessary ones of the Forearm.

9. Always keep distinct the process of *moving towards a note* from the process of actually *sounding* a note, when found.

10. Avoid jabbing at the notes with sideway (horizontal)

actions of your arm. First arrive on each key, or over it, and *then* proceed purposefully to play that note. This does not mean that you should pause between the two operations!

11. As already pointed out in Section X, ¶11, to enable you to turn your fingers over the thumb easily, allow the Wrist to turn slightly *outwards* — with the hand therefore pointing slightly *inwards*.

During *Scale playing* retain that position permanently. It avoids unnecessary to-and-fro movements of Wrist, Hand, and Forearm.

12. Reverse this when turning a long finger over a shorter one, as in double-notes passages — turn the wrist inwards then.

13. In arpeggio playing you cannot permanently keep your hand thus turned inwards. To-and-fro (sideway) movements of the hand, wrist, and forearm cannot here be avoided, but let their range be as small as need be.

NOTE. — Slight rolling movements, even, may also be permissible, although *not* in the least essential.

14. When taking *skips* within a two-octave range, turn the elbow outwards sufficiently, before beginning the skip. To move the elbow *during* such skips is cumbrous and unsafe. *See* Section X, ¶11.

15. For larger skips you cannot avoid moving the whole arm. A composer who knows how to write well for his instrument usually bears this in mind, unless it is done for "sport"!

16. With regard to Hand-position, the main point is, avoid *kinking* the knuckles in. It is a very bad method of playing, and is almost sure to render hand and fingers stiff and weak.

17. If you allow your knuckles thus to drop in, or to be forced in, you are either (*a*), applying too much energy from the hand and arm, or (*b*), you are insufficiently exerting the fingers themselves at the moment of depressing the key — or after that!

18. The same thing applies at the wrist-joint. If your wrist drops down too much, you are either exerting your hand insufficiently, or are giving too much Arm-energy in proportion

to the finger and hand exertions, — since action and reaction should always nicely balance.

19. The actual *shape* assumed by the hand and fingers, however, varies with each individual, and *even with each passage* — whereas the keyboard never varies! Hence the folly of laying down any inflexible rule on this point, although it is well to realize that the arch is *mechanically* more effective than any other position.

In short, the Position of your hand and fingers which enables you to play at your easiest (and therefore best) is also *the best possible position!*

NOTE. — I, personally, vary the position of my wrist, hand and fingers to suit each particular passage. Position is not a thing to worry over, it effects itself, if you correctly supply the *invisible* actions.

20. *Finger-position* and *movement* have been fully discussed in Section IX, "Flat and Bent Finger," and in Section VII, and illustrations are there given.

21. Finally then, if you learn to provide the correct *balance* between the exertions and relaxations of your finger, hand and arm which we have discussed, well-poised Position will ensue naturally.

Section XIV

ON NOMENCLATURE — THE NAMING OF THINGS

1. Nomenclature is of little consequence. It is only a matter of convenience.

2. "Touch" is a generic term, including everything relating to Tone-production and Technique.

3. In past days it included: —

(*a*) Tone contrasts — "Forte and Piano touch."
(*b*) Duration — "Legato and Staccato touch."
(*c*) Movement — "Finger, Hand, and Arm touch."

4. Nomenclature in the past thus referred only to the aural and *visual* effects noticed, and not at all to the invisible *causal processes* of Touch — those far more important but *invisible stresses* of Touch which you have to provide, so to create the differences in Tone, Duration and Time-inflection.

5. Thus you can help your finger exertion by: —

(1) a *loose-lying hand* (and rotation), ("First Species"), or

(2) a *down-exerted hand* (along with these), ("Second Species"), or

(3) some form of *arm-stress* (along with these), "Third Species") — and the arm can give you four *sub*-species!

6. For rapid finger-passages you may use either Weight-transfer or Arm-vibration touch, preferably the last, or else a cross between the two.

NOTE. — Remember: *Weight-transfer touch* is a modification of the heavier form of Resting needed for "Natural Legato"; whereas *Arm-vibration* touch mainly consists of "second species," with a well-poised arm, but may waver towards first and third "species" as occasion demands.

7. It does not help things much whether you remember or not that I adopted the term "Species of Touch" to denote these three basic differences in DOING, so long as you vividly remember the facts concerned in actual performance.[1]

8. Likewise, it does not matter whether you call the differences between horrid-sounding and well-sounding tone a difference in *quality* of Tone, or "XYZ and VWQ-tone," or call it a difference of "Quantity." But unless you have mastered and can exemplify *such differences* in playing, you cannot fully express yourself musically.[2]

[1] *See* "The Act of Touch," Chapter XII (Longmans); also an additional Chapter on this point in "Relaxation Studies" (Bosworth); and "Commentaries" on the merging of the three species, p. 14.

[2] *See* Additional Note in the *Digest:* "On the Ugly and Beautiful in Piano Touch."

9. Nomenclature suggestive of *wrong* Doing may however prove harmful — the term "Fixation" is such a term. It is obnoxious as it suggests "stiffening."[1]

10. "Fixation" was invented to express the fact that there must be an immobile, stable, or resisting Basis for all the actions we use in playing. Unfortunately, as shown in previous pages, it suggests quite the wrong way of attaining such required Basis.

11. Remember, the proper way to *counter* the upward reactions is by supplying a down-stress (in some form or other) from the next adjacent part of the limb.[2]

12. Avoid, therefore, this ill-gotten term "Fixation," and at all cost learn to avoid *all* "stiffening."

13. Finally: all such cataloguing, or naming of things is very arid, and does not matter musically — unless suggestive of ill-doing! What does matter, is to acquire and remember the *sensations* of *Right Doing* — expertness in *sensation*-ally recalling and thus re-creating the necessary tonal effects, so that your musical Self-expression shall be unfettered, and shall fully convey to others what you are able to perceive musically.

14. Unless you have mastered *Technique* in this practical and spiritual way you will ever remain an inefficient Pianist, instead of being a true Music-maker, or even a Prophet of Music!

[1] It was invented in the recent past by those who could still see no further than the observed *Movements*, hence their wrong diagnosis of Touch.

[2] Thus to recapitulate once again; to use your finger effectively against the Key you must indeed do something to *counter* its reaction upwards against the knuckle during Key-descent. But it was wrongly supposed that the knuckle must therefore be *stiffened* — hence this term "Fixation." Whereas you now know, that although the knuckles must be made to *resist* during the finger's action against the Key, there should be no "stiffening" whatever, but instead you must give a nicely-timed down-exertion *of the hand* to counter the recoil at the knuckle; moreover, remember, that this down-exertion of the hand must *cease* instantly it has served its purpose, and that the knuckle must therefore be quite mobile and loose *in-between* the sounding of the notes; while the "small" muscles of the finger alone continue the holding of the key either at surface or key-bed level.

FIFTY-FIVE DAILY MAXIMS

— *For all players.*

1. Without Rhythm there is but Emptiness.

2. The day for Piano-typewriting is past. But it is never past for Music!

3. What you have to learn is to *intend every note* you play — an *intentional sound* and an intentional *time* — and an **intentional Duration.**

Note. — To succeed in this, Limb-Knowledge is needed — not Muscle-Knowledge!

4. That is the long and short of "Technique." Therefore you cannot learn Technique without learning to attend just like that — *to* Music.

5. The worst crime in the Past was to try to teach Technique apart from exercise in Music.

6. *Musically*, always sound each note *as late as you dare*, yet *technically* always make each note *early enough* — in key-descent!

7. First learn to use Arm-weight so that you can sing.[1]

After that, learn to keep the arm "off" — so that you can run. Feel and hear it is "off" — you cannot see it!

8. Don't *put* your arm down, but instead allow it to "give," when you need its weight.

9. The arm is never "dropped" upon the keys, "the louder the note, the greater the height," *except by fools!* [2]

[1] That is: the whole arm momentarily free from the shoulder (to the tone-required extent) — either visibly or invisibly — with *elbow* always free.

[2] To ascribe such mis-teaching to myself is indeed folly at its height!

10. *If* you really hit the key down by a "drop" of the arm, you can neither "feel" the key nor make Music!

11. You need the *Poised Arm* (the self-supported, floating "arm-off" condition) *in every passage* — either fully poised, or sometimes a little less so. But in some passages (for Agility, Staccato, etc.) this poised condition is *continuous*, whereas elsewhere (for chords, cantabile, etc.), it is *momentarily relaxed during key-descent*, but afterwards instantly resumed.

12. To kill Music — and your Piano, drive well forward and downward with rigid Elbow! But don't be so foolish!

Even when you momentarily use Forearm Down-force in addition to Upper-arm weight, always keep the Elbow *still free!*

13. In the meantime don't forget to "use" your key — and to *exert* your finger — and hand-exertion behind it — for each note, every time.

14. If you want to *run* you throw all baggage away! At the Piano do the same — keep the "arm-off" when you want to play a run! With the arm "off," choose every note's tonal and durational inflection when playing real music at speed.

Never play faster than you *can* thus choose.

15. *In-between* the sounding of the notes (however heavily you sound them) again "Arm-off," with nicely loose knuckles — if you wish to play musically.

16. The teaching of "Weight" without insistence on its due *cessation* is just as pernicious and mischievous as the old teaching of key-hitting "solely by finger-*stroke!*"

Note. — In very quick passages you *may* carry along *slightly* more weight with impunity, as the so quickly succeeding keys here keep the burden off the key-beds.

17. Always hold notes solely by the "small" muscles of the finger — with free, mobile knuckles, however forcibly your

finger may "grip" the key during its descent. Else you can neither choose your tone, nor move along freely.

18. Don't make *cantabile* passages *sting*, make them *sing* instead!

19. For singing tone, keep the *elbow* elastic, keep it free, easy — *always* easy at the Elbow.

20. While the Elbow feels free to fall, catch and grip well at the keys with your finger *and your hand each time* — just as naturally as when gripping hold of anything else.

21. Let the grip be an *increasing* grip as you swing the key into movement. Don't do it *too late* — always remember Maxim 6!

22. Never use Poke-touch or Shove-touch, with Elbow and Forearm digging into the keyboard.

23. Nor *jab* the key down — instead always *feel* your way *with* it.

24. To help the finger, there are *six* ways of using the arm. Don't *mis*-use them!

You *must always use:* the POISED-ARM and the ROTATIVE-FOREARM.

You *may use* during Key-descent:

Forearm weight only, or
Whole-arm weight, or
Forearm Down-exertion with the last, or finally
Upper-arm forward-exertion with the last.

Avoid the last in all *forte*-playing!

25. The most popular Mis-use of the arm is in its Forearm-rotational aspect. It has thus been misused — invisibly — ever since the invention of the Keyboard!

26. The mischief at the root of most bad Passage-work is in the wrong rotatory exertions of the Forearm — invisibly applied.

27. Be sure, therefore, to cease *all* rotatory exertion in the

wrong direction — even of the "weak" rotatory muscles — when you have to reverse the rotatory help required from finger to finger.

28. Freedom, rotationally, is a *sine qua non* in all playing.

29. Rotational Freedom, in its direction, must always be *away from* the finger last used.

This applies also when a finger is turned over the thumb.

30. When in doubt about a passage, always *re-analyse* it rotationally.

31. The very first time you use your fingers on any keyboard learn at once what is *meant* by rotational-help. Learn it first as Movement, but afterwards learn to give the required stresses *without any such rocking movement* whatsoever.

32. When in doubt, no matter how advanced a player you may be, refer to the first four of the "*Nine Steps towards Finger-individualization*" — played by your fist, just as a child should do.

33. Learn correct Doing at the age of four. It is easiest then! Don't wait until you are perhaps forty, and then have to un-learn all the acquired "*Wrongth,*" rotationally, and in many another way!

34. Avoid "Passing-on" (Weight-transfer) touch for quick passages that demand musical and muscular individualization of the successive notes. Use Arm-vibration touch instead.

Passed-on Weight means passed-on Tone — musical aridness and barrenness.

35. Never play really *musical* passages quicker than you *can* thus select, time and *mean* each note.

36. Only use Weight-transfer touch for spread chords, arabesques, slur-end notes, and for certain quick passages which do *not* need musical individualization from note to note.

37. Remember, to the extent you *pass-on* continuous Weight, to the same extent you are compelled to pass-on and transfer continuous Hand-stress.

NOTE. — This last may sometimes be accompanied by actual *rolling* (rotatory) *movements* over groups of notes. This quite exceptional touch-form has however given rise to absurd "Undulatory Theories of Touch." Avoid them!

38. Correct POSITION is the resultant of good Balance between the invisible and visible playing elements.

39. CHOPIN said "if your playing *looks* well it probably also sounds well." One might add: "If you *do* well it will also probably *look* well!"

40. Don't sit at the Piano as at a Dinner-table! Give arm-weight a chance, by your sitting reasonably far away.

41. Sit with elbow about level with the keys, and better too low than too high.

42. Avoid pressing your knuckles "*in*." You cannot run nor walk comfortably with your legs bent double!

43. Don't try to express yourself by *wild movements* of your body and arms; — "Don't *leak*," as MYRA HESS has well said!

44. Don't force the listener to use his eyes upon you, instead of his ears upon your music.

45. Don't sit all huddled up; it is unhealthy and looks ugly. You want your playing to sound well, therefore avoid distracting the hearer by making it *look ugly*.

46. The *Naming* of things does not explain things!

47. Always substitute a softer note for a louder one, whenever you can. People only BEGIN *to listen* to you when you play softly.

48. This does not imply flabbiness in your singing passages, nor anywhere else.

On the contrary, make every melody note *carry*. Play "inside" the key, even in *ppp*.

49. Nor does *this* mean that you should not use the fullest tone in your climaxes.

50. But *quality* in performance is everything — in spite of the Foolishness that has been talked, and whatever the explanation. Mere noise never convinces anyone!

51. Never rattle along. Instead, always try to *see* Music.

52. Always try to see the Beautiful — through Key and Time.

53. Look for the Beautiful, which is always there *if it be music* — look for the physical, emotional, and spiritual beauty.

54. Always use both your *physical* and your *spiritual* Ear.

55. If it is NOT Music, then it is not worth worrying over. A typewriter will serve as well!

FINAL PRECEPTS

I. Never touch the keyboard without meaning to make Music.

II. Even in your first exercises —

- mean the *Moment* of each sound, and see that you get it.
- mean the *Kind of sound for each note,* and see that you get it.

III. *Feel* what the musical effect should be — and *feel* the Key — and *how* you move it.

IV. "*Elbow elastic*" for all singing and big tone — during Key-descent — not rigid and pushed into the key.

V. "Arm-off" *in between* the sounding of all notes, and *during* all light running passages.

VI. You have ten fingers! So do not forget that you usually need ten separate hands to help them, and often also ten separate arms!

VII. The *Duration* of each note is as important as the *kind* of tone.

VIII. In the quickest passages *mean* every note.

IX. Be a sentient human being, not a contemptible automaton musically.

X. Cleanliness is said to be next to godliness. Sense of the Beautiful IS sense of God.

CPSIA information can be obtained
at www.ICGtesting.com
Printed in the USA
BVHW070042011019
559817BV00001B/69/P

9 781473 331006